"Every time I talk with another s̶u̶r̶v̶i̶v̶o̶r̶ ̶a̶b̶o̶u̶t̶ ̶f̶o̶r̶g̶i̶v̶e̶n̶e̶s̶s̶, ̶I̶ ̶a̶m̶ impressed by how complicated our questions are.

- What is forgiveness, exactly?

- Does it make a difference if the transgressor is amnesiac or conscious of the deed, repentant or not, coerced or acting freely, brainwashed from birth or indoctrinated as an adult?

- Are you morally obligated to forgive?

- Is forgiveness for the abuser or for yourself? I always end up with more questions than answers.

"This book, which I first read in 2006, offers a chance to delve deeply into the complexities with over fifty fascinating people. I can't wait to get a copy!"

~ **Jean Riseman,** Survivor, activist, retired social worker, contributing author to *RITUAL ABUSE in the TWENTY-FIRST CENTURY* ("Ritual Abuse Survivors: Diverse, Yet Similar")

"In this re-release of Dr. Einhorn's important book, the darkest capacities of wounded human souls to harm innocent children are met with the light of truth, compassion, and inspiration."
~ **Ellen Lacter**, Psychologist, who expanded upon her contribution in this book with an in-depth analysis of abuser coercion of child abuse victims to harm other victims and its soul-crushing effects., She was also a contributing author (with Karl Lehman) to *RITUAL ABUSE in the TWENTY-FIRST CENTURY ("*Guidelines to Differential Diagnosis between Schizophrenia and Ritual Abuse/Mind Control Traumatic Stress")

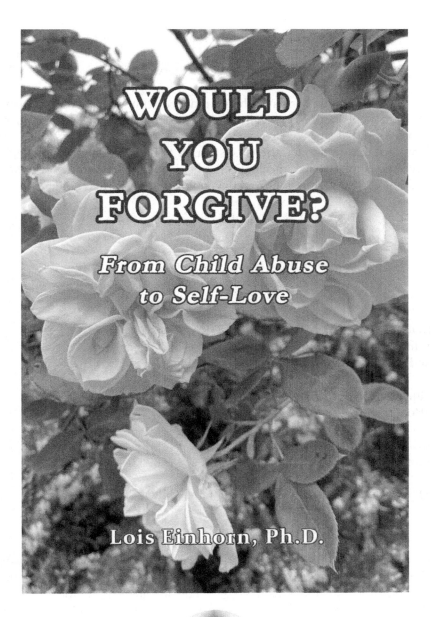

WOULD YOU FORGIVE?

From Child Abuse to Self-Love

Lois Einhorn, Ph.D.

Robert D. Reed Publishers

3

Robert D. Reed Publishers
P.O. Box 1992
Bandon, OR 97411
Phone: 541-347-9882; Fax: -9883
E-mail: cleonelreed@gmail.com
Website: www.rdrpublishers.com

SOFT COVER EDITION and EBOOK:
Editor, Book Formatting, Cover Design, Teddy Bear
and Sand Art Photography by Cleone Lyvonne Reed, MSE

Paperback ISBN 13: 978-1-63821-497-7
eBook ISBN: 978-1-63821-498-4

Library of Congress Control Number: 2021948962

Manufactured, Typeset, and Printed in the United States of America

AUTHOR NOTE: This book is an update of a book done in 2006 (*Forgiveness and Child Abuse: Would YOU Forgive?*) so some of the endorsers and people I express gratitude toward are no longer alive. Hopefully, the spirit of the book has been enhanced with additional years of healing and with more information and insights.

DEDICATION

I dedicate this book to:

- All perpetrators of abuse.
    May they receive the help they need
    to stop the violence.

- To all children who are abused.
    May they be heard, believed, and protected.

- To all adult survivors of child abuse.
    May they treat themselves
    with the same love and compassion
    with which they treat others.

- And to all people.
    May they know that their presence
    is the greatest present
    and may they love one heart at a time.

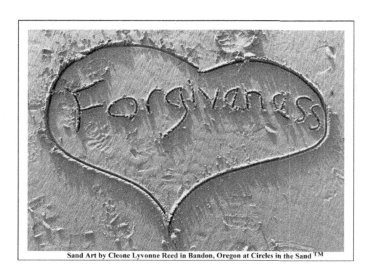

Sand Art by Cleone Lyvonne Reed in Bandon, Oregon at Circles in the Sand ™

Contents

DEDICATION 5

ACKNOWLEGMENTS 9

PREFACE 13

FOREWORD 15

    By Arun Gandhi 15

INTRODUCTION 19

A NEW BEGINNING 21

    A Pandemic, Tale of Two Cats, Election, Scam, and Vibrator .. 21

    KEEPING MY SOUL 24

    INSPIRATIONAL QUOTES 61

MY STORY 65

53 CONTRIBUTORS RESPOND 78

A BRIEF INTRODUCTION TO THE 53 RESPONDERS 79

1. Mumia Abu-Jamal, M.A. 83

2. Hunter "Patch" Adams, M.D. 85

3. Jeanne Adams 88

4. Frederic Arensberg, Ph.D. 91

5. Edward Asner 92

6. P. M. H. Atwater, L.H.D. 94

7. Rev. Bernard J. Bush, Ph.D. 99

8. Rubin "Hurricane" Carter 104

9. Zeqi Chen 106

10. Suzanne Daughton, Ph.D. 109

11. Laura Davis 111

12. Thomas F. Eagleton 114

13. Albert Ellis, Ph. D. 115

14. Paul Ferrini 117

15. Lynne D. Finney, J.D., M.S.W. 120

16. Russell P. Friedman..129

17. Arun Gandhi...134

18. Aba Gayle..138

19. Jack Gilroy 140

20. Scott Kalechstein Grace 142

21. Bishop Thomas J. Gumbleton 143

22. Anne Herman 145

23. Linda Hogan..147

24. Steven L. Jacobs..148

25. Derrick Jensen..151

26. Bill T. Jones..154

27. Mary Elizabeth King, Ph.D. 156

28. Barb Kohn, Ph.D. 159

29. Ellen P. Lacter, Ph.D. 162

©2022 Ellen Lacter, Ph.D. Addendum to My Contribution to: *Forgiveness and Child Abuse: Would You Forgive?* 170

30. Sammy Lee, M.D. 192

31. Eric Loeb, Ed. D...194

32. Rev. Dr. Richard P. Lord......................................199

33. Cleone Lyvonne, M.S.E. 202

Abuse Is NOT an Option 206

34. Dale McCulley 208

35. Robert Muller 211

36. Bill Pelke 213

37. Robert W. Plath, J.D...217

38. Daniel Quinn 219

39. Billy Ray Riggs 224

40. Robert C. Scaer, M.D..226

41. Pete Seeger 230

42. Bernard S. Siegel, M.D. 232

43. Tamarack Song 236

44. Oswaldo Soriano.. 245

45. Gerry Spence.. 246

46. Walter Starcke.. 248

47. Mike Thaler.. 250

48. Susan Thornton, Ph.D. 251

49. Richard Vatz, Ph.D. 255

50. Kurt Waldheim... 257

51. Ken Wapnick 258

52. Gloria Wendroff... 263

53. Everett L. Worthington, Jr., Ph.D. 266

AFTERWORD.. 275

Endorsements for © 2006 *Forgiveness and Child Abuse: Would YOU Forgive?*... *293*

ABOUT THE AUTHOR 299

    LOIS EINHORN, Ph.D. 299

ACKNOWLEGMENTS

John Donne wrote, "No man is an island." These words echo my sentiments as I try to acknowledge the many people who have helped this book go from a vision to a reality. The book deals with my life—my painful childhood and my continuing process of healing and being blessed with joy and inner peace. As I have this opportunity to thank the many people who have contributed to my life and/or this book. I have two concerns. First, don't let the sheer number of names detract from EACH being's importance. My bigger concern is that I've left obvious people out. To these people, I give my heartfelt apologies and ask for forgiveness.

First, I want to thank nature, the deepest source of comfort on my personal journey. They were my first friends. My close bond with Mother Earth sustained me through childhood. My knowledge that we are connected, from the tiniest cells to the greatest mysteries of the cosmos, has brought me to the path of this book, a path I am honored to walk.

I want to thank also my furry, feathered, finned, and fuzzy friends. They have always been there for me, giving unconditional love.

Laura Davis and Chellis Glendinning have read several drafts of the book since the book's inception. I thank them for their wise counsel and continual encouragement. I am grateful also to Mary Kahl, David Katz, Drew Saur, Libby Tucker, and Susan Thornton who have given me wonderful feedback.

Everton Chin helped me type the responses and do some of the other miscellaneous things that needed doing as my publication deadline neared. He did so with energy and excitement, caring and concern.

I thank Patch Adams for leading me to Robert D. Reed Publishers. From my first phone call through my part of the publication process, the late Bob Reed and his wife Cleone Reed have been knowledgeable people of impeccable integrity who care about their authors as well as their books. Their book contract is the only contract that I've ever seen (for anything) that includes the word "fun." And fun, indeed, it's been to work with them with writing, publicity, and creative services. Their senses of humor, caring, and calming nature have sustained me through the last parts of writing this book.

I give my heartfelt thanks to the fifty-three respondents without whom this book would not exist. I thank them for their response AND for their generosity and grace, and especially to Ellen Lacter for writing an Addendum to her contribution in response to recent uncovered memories.

I've been blessed to have studied under some of the greatest teachers of teachers in my field including Carroll Arnold, Jeff Auer, Patty and Jim Andrews, Tom Benson, Herman Cohen, Dennis Gouran, Dick Gregg, Bob Gunderson, Jerry Hauser, Jean Lutz, and Gene White.

I want to acknowledge the encouragement and support of my colleagues at Binghamton University for their continual understanding and caring.

I've been a life member of the National Communication Association and the Eastern Communication Association for over forty years. A list of colleagues at other universities who've touched my life would take a book.

Names of current and former students who've contributed to my life would also take a book. I hope I have touched their lives a little; I know they have touched mine a lot. Their curiosity, wonder, love, and kindness are a constant source of inspiration to me. The current generation especially leaves me in awe and gives me hope about the future. I tried to make a list of some who are among my very favorite people in the world, and the list kept growing with no end in sight. Therefore, I extend my heartfelt thanks to these people as a group. You know who you are, and I know too.

My healing has been greatly due to Native American spirituality. Many members of the local community have participated in healing sweats for and with me.

For the past dozen years, I have been a member of my local Unitarian Universalist congregation whose members provide me with a spiritual home and beloved community helping me to be the best Lois I can be. Almost every person in our directory has been special to me in some way.

The model for compassionate, nonviolent communication helped me to forgive my parents. I've taken several workshops from The Compassionate Listening Project under masterful facilitators including Amalia Phillips, Elizabeth Spitzer, Yael Petretti, Debby Haase, and Cathy Merchant.

The late Suzanne Daughton was a student of mine in my early years of teaching. She later earned her Ph.D. and was a colleague and special friend. I love her always and ALL ways.

Helen Keller, a heroine of mine, wrote, "Join the great company of those who make the barren places of life fruitful with kindness." I am eternally grateful to the many close people who fill the barren places of my life with kindness.

No words can express my appreciation to Carroll C. Arnold—my teacher, mentor, and friend. Although he's in the spirit world, I think about him frequently.

Debby Gwaltney has been like a sister to me. I send my appreciation and love to her, Tim, and my three nieces and their families: Rachel, Alex, Ethan, and Isaac Perry; Chelsea and Matt Bartee; and Ginny Gwaltney.

My appreciation, admiration, and affection go especially to Vaneza and Ana Burgos and Claudete Einhorn, my daughters-in-love; and to the late Eric Loeb who adopted me in a Native American ceremony as his daughter and who has been not only my Daddy but also my friend and confidante. I love him more than words can express; without him, this book would not exist. I cherish the many miracles he's gifted to me, his unconditional love and continual nurturing over a quarter of a century, his close and snugly hugs, and his teaching me that I can make a difference in the world through love, compassion, peace, and forgiveness. I hope this book makes him proud.

PREFACE

By Cleone Lyvonne Reed, MSE

My late husband, Robert D. Reed, owner of Robert D. Reed Publishers, and I got married on September 13, 2008, two years after we published Dr. Einhorn's book, *Forgiveness and Child Abuse: Would YOU Forgive?* We bought a bunch of little white teddy bears to send out with review copies, had them as part of our wedding décor, and then had our Christmas card picture that year with each of us reclining in a bathtub brimming with "Lois teddy bears."

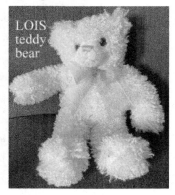

LOIS teddy bear

(NOTE: her first book in 2006 had a picture of my teddy bear collection on the front cover featuring a teddy bear I made for my son.)

Yes, Lois and I bonded over our love of teddy bears; our relationship with Lois went beyond being just professional. It got very personal. How many publishers and authors connect over their love of teddy bears?!

As Lois becomes very close to her students, we have become close friends. She even flew from the East coast to the West coast to stay with us when she published her first book with us. Every time I drive up Highway 101 in Oregon going north and go by this one particular overlook, I think of how we stopped there on our way home from the airport and she saw the Pacific Ocean for the first time.

Tonight I made the decision to write this Preface just as we are getting ready to launch this book. What prompted it? Well, I just read the Afterword for the first time since 2006 (when we published the first version of her book), and I so resonated with Lois's love of alliteration. And that brings me back to our wedding! Our motto was, "We dedicate our lives to a love of life and a life of love."

That seems to be the essence of Lois's life and the lessons and linguistics in this book. She lives a life of love and a love of life. And that is no trivial thing. To rise to the levels of loving life and living a life of love after enduring so many excruciatingly painful and horrific experiences as a child is shake-your-head amazing. She has turned her nightmarish childhood into an adulthood of making dreams come true.

Her life is about authenticity and helping her students self-actualize and loving to learn, learning to love themselves, and having fun!

Yes, the word FUN is in our contracts with our authors, and Lois and I have fun as we polish and perfect this book. However, as I always say, "Perfection is an illusion; we strive for Excellence, not Perfection... while having FUN"... as we forge forward into the future to forego fear and find forgiveness and have FUN!

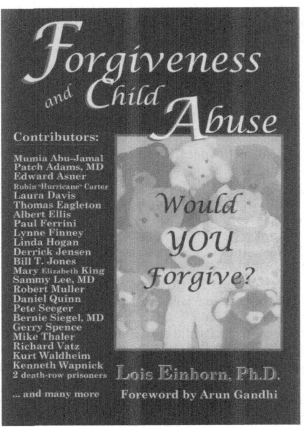

© 2006 by Lois Einhorn, Ph.D.
ISBN: 978-1-931741-69-9

(NOTE: "Would YOU Forgive?" was the subtitle of her book in 2006 and the title of this book, *Would You Forgive: From Child Abuse to Self-Love*.)

14

FOREWORD

By Arun Gandhi

Very early in his life Mohandas K. Gandhi, also known universally as Mahatma Gandhi, realized that "forgiving" is the foundation on which the Culture of Nonviolence must be built. If one did not have the magnanimity to forgive, one could not effectively practice the philosophy of nonviolence.

This fact dawned on Gandhi in South Africa when, as a 24-year-old budding lawyer, he was physically beaten up because he was considered "black" in a "white" man's country. When the police arrested the culprits and invited Gandhi to press charges so that they could be punished, Gandhi spent some time contemplating.

"Would these youngsters learn anything if they are punished?" he asked himself and came to the conclusion that people seldom learn from punishment; they do, however, learn a lot from love, respect and forgiveness.

Gandhi told the police that he would not press charges, and then addressing the young culprits he said: "I am forgiving you for what you did because I don't believe in punishing. I hope that this will teach you a lesson that hate destroys the self as much as it destroys society and nothing is gained from hate. Let us learn to respect and love each other."

During the course of his twenty-two years in South Africa, there were at least four major incidents of racist violence against Gandhi, and each time he applied the same principle. Gandhi also did not pursue his tormentors to see if they had learned the lesson of living in harmony. He believed he taught them the lesson, and it was now up to them to understand its meaning and apply it to their lives. That at least half a dozen of them became his followers indicates that there is value in forgiving.

However, forgiving, like love, must be unconditional. It is wrong to say that I will forgive only under certain conditions. It is equally wrong to say that we must forgive and *forget*. It is because we keep forgetting that we have not been able to change the world from its negative and violent ways. I cannot emphasize enough the importance of forgiving and with it the need to devote our time and efforts to ensure, through education and attitudinal changes, that such negative and violent

15

behaviors like racism, child abuse, and other acts of crime do not happen again.

The Western concept, which is now also creeping into Eastern thinking, that people are born evil and that by eliminating evil people we will eliminate evil, is totally wrong. Racists, child molesters and abusers, criminals and the like are not born with warped minds; they become warped because of negative influences and compulsions in life that they are not equipped to handle. Since those influences and compulsions are seldom addressed by society, we have a recurrence of these nefarious acts in spite of the harsh laws and harsher threats of punishment. Society needs to focus on the crime and not just the criminal.

Her book, *Forgiveness and Child Abuse* (and now this updated version, *Would Your Forgive an Abuser?)* by Lois Einhorn deals with one of the most despicable aspects of crime that plagues modern society. To subject a defenseless, innocent child to unimaginable abuse is, arguably, the worst thing that an adult can do. Naturally it moves us to so much anger that we want to mete out the harshest punishment. I must confess there are times when some acts of crime have evoked in me the kind of anger that justifies capital punishment. But, on sober reflection we must realize that punishing has not put an end to crime.

While advocating forgiveness and nonviolence, I do not wish to suggest that perpetrators of heinous crimes be forgiven and let off to roam the streets in search of other victims. I wish to suggest instead that we review our justice system and shift the emphasis from punishing to educating and reforming criminals so that they emerge from prison as morally stronger and healthier citizens—not as physically stronger and more ruthless criminals.

Through her own life experiences, Dr. Einhorn takes the reader through the agonies of child abuse, the mental trauma that she suffers as a grown woman, the understandable guilt and anger that she feels towards her parents who reduced her to such intolerable depths of decadence, and then the spiritual awakening that she experienced through the catastrophe of September 11, 2001. Truth sometimes dawns on an individual through a cataclysmic experience and sometimes through an inner awakening. Also important is that Dr. Einhorn has invited other eminent people to share their views on what would be an appropriate reaction – anger or forgiveness.

For its honest search for Truth, I find this book important and valuable. But above all, I find this book important because it puts into perspective the evils of a Culture of Violence that dominates every aspect of human life today. The book brings into stark focus the violence that exists in our relationships at all levels and the depths of evil into which bad relationships can lead humanity.

Violence in human life is such a vast subject that a single book cannot cover the whole gamut. While dealing with specifics, we should not lose sight of the fact that any single experience is only a microcosm of the greater malady – the Culture of Violence.

Like Grandfather Gandhi would say, violence is like the ocean—it is vast, it is deep, it is mysterious, and it possesses the deadly power to decimate humanity. However, in one important respect, violence differs from the ocean. While humanity can do nothing to tame the ocean, we can do a great deal to introduce a Culture of Nonviolence to reduce the disastrous impact of violence on human society.

– Arun Gandhi, President
M. K. Gandhi Institute for Nonviolence
Author of *The Gift of Anger: And Other Lessons from My Grandfather Mahatma Gandhi* © 2017

INTRODUCTION

Enter a riveting, soul-bearing journey to the question *Would You Forgive? From Child Abuse to Self-Love,* a remake of her 2006 book, *Forgiveness and Child Abuse: Would YOU Forgive?* Offering child abuse as the metaphor for this quest, author, academic and child abuse survivor Lois J. Einhorn paints a heart-rending picture of the unimaginable cruelty inflicted upon her. To the reader and 53 responders, she poses the same scenario and self-searching questions that gave voice to this book, "You are a child in a family that sadistically abuses. You are forced to torture and destroy. What should you do *now* as an adult? Do you forgive your parents? HOW do you forgive yourself?"

The responses in this book span a profound and thought-provoking spectrum of answers. Their heartfelt responses are our guide and inspiration as we search for our answer to the same question. Most notable is the fact that these writers are nowhere near agreement among themselves. In fact, their opinions span the spectrum from compassion to condemnation. And what a blessing that is for the reader! No matter what someone's personal history or what opinion they might hold, they are likely to resonate with some of the book's contributors. From there, *Forgiveness and Child Abuse* takes the reader on a healing journey, walking beside 53 wise kin of our day.

From interpersonal to international, our times are riddled with conflict. Abuser or victim, terrorist or defender, environmentalist or developer – which side are you on? Or is there another way – a deeper, more all-embracing approach? The political buzzword these days is *tolerance;* in the humanistic realm it is *forgiveness,* but do these ideals really provide answers or do they only serve to perpetuate unbridgeable gaps?

Each of Dr. Einhorn's books is an indispensable healing companion for anyone who has suffered abuse of any kind and is a potent guide for professionals who work with the legacy of abuse. Each book provides the mandate and opportunity, and then the forum and guidance to engage in the soul-searching dialog we need to begin in order to come to grips with the critical questions of our day:

- How do we face the wanton violence and exploitation that surrounds us?

- As we are continually at war or preparing for war, do we forgive our leaders? Our "enemy?"
- Does our right-and-wrong approach actually sanction abuse?
- Do tolerance and forgiveness really address the cause of abuse?
- What other options do we have?

Today, more than ever, it is becoming beautifully clear and painfully obvious that we are all related. Together let us begin the healing.

– Tamarack Song

Author of several books including: *Journey to the Ancestral Self: Remembering What It Is to Be Human* © 2020*; Like a Shadow: The Life and Training of a Guardian Warrior* ©2020; *Truthspeaking: Ancestral Ways to Hear and Speak the Voice of the Heart* ©2019; *Entering the Mind of the Tracker: Native Practices for Developing Intuitive Consciousness and Discovering Hidden Nature* © 2013; *Whispers of the Ancients: Native Tales for Teaching and Healing in Our Time,* © 2010

A NEW BEGINNING

A Pandemic, Tale of Two Cats, Election, Scam, and Vibrator

How do the COVID-19 pandemic, a tale of two cats, one Presidential election, a scam-gone-awry, and a magenta vibrator relate? Read on and understand that people can hurt our bodies and rob us of many things, but they cannot take our spark, our spirit, or our soul.

> *"Life breaks us all sometimes, but some grow strong at the broken places."* – Ernest Hemmingway

> *"What is it that is so good about being heard? Well, I'm seeing. I become visible. I'm being understood."*
> – Dominic Barter, an expert on restorative justice

As I reflect upon this last quote, I realize that being heard requires seeing the Other, knowing they exist, knowing they have inherent worth and dignity, and that they are precious and cherished. There is no other way to achieve understanding, much less healing and peace. It's the relationship we presume most parents wish for their offspring: to protect them day and night just as God/Spirit/Soul protects us day and night. Giving someone life *should* mean promising to protect and cherish them, something children *should* trust. What happens when that trust becomes broken or if it never existed?

How can we learn about this energy of Love and live from it? How can we create a more peaceful world that focuses on community, service, equality, fairness, forgiveness, restorative justice, hope, and recognizing our inherent interconnectedness? How do we balance belonging and connecting, comforting the disturbed and disturbing the comfortable?

I think the answers stem from realizing that love and loving are miracles, and feeling profoundly and divinely connected to another's soul is what makes life worth living. Nonviolence and tolerance are good starts, but we also need compassion, acceptance, appreciation, and celebration of the Other, understanding that I cannot be completely free until we *all* are free because I cannot watch you suffer without also

21

suffering. We all gain when we act from the better angels of our nature, our shared humanity.

I started this *New Beginning* in the spring of 2020 during a forced quarantine during the COVID-19 pandemic. Fortunately, I was safe and relatively sane! At the time, I did not know anyone directly who died from the virus. Because most of my students come from NYC and Long Island, they were not as lucky! I had 52 students that semester, but with six in both classes, I had 45 individual students. By the end of the semester, eight lost loved ones directly from the virus, one's father died of a heart attack before emergency services could get there, and three dealt with suicides (two peers in their early 20's and one Chinese ten-year-old bullied for being Chinese). These four are not even part of the death count. There were another five students whom I had not heard from.

And, everything listed above did not count those who shared with me the following: unable to retrieve the body or afford a funeral; parents or themselves losing jobs and having no health insurance; homeless or living in gang neighborhoods or poverty; had physical and mental health issues, experienced hate speech and hate crimes; physical and sexual abuse in the home to them or their mothers and siblings; and could not afford Wi-Fi. These are the things I knew after two months. I didn't know what I didn't know! And, of course, most of my students were graduating and did not foresee their last semester at Binghamton University being what it was! Almost every day, I learned more horrific news.

That semester, I shared the hardcover edition of this book for the first time with my classes and my local Unitarian Universalist (UU) congregation. I began with the end of my book, explaining how I forgave myself and how I moved from forgiveness being an "F" word to forgiving my parents. I realized readers could skip the "My Story" section that opened the original edition of this book. In fact, I wanted to write a new beginning—which became this "New Beginning"—to warn that if you thought you might be triggered by reading about what I endured, you should feel free to skip "My Story" altogether.

I used my *Afterword* as a jumping-off point. In both contexts, we dealt with questions that affect everyone at some point in their lives. What helps each of us deal with our personal traumas? What enables some people to break generational cycles of abuse while others perpetuate the cycles? Also, I asked the following questions:

- How can we create families based on love?

- What's the relationship between joy and sorrow?

- Where do animals, nature, health, music, meditation, mindfulness, and even death fit?

- How/why do we choose to keep loving even after tremendous suffering? How do our wounds connect to our concerns about social justice?

- Do we start locally or globally? How can we teach ourselves and others that it doesn't matter where we start because these issues are interrelated—the personal and the planetary are one?

- How do we teach these ideas to children?

- How can we accept that we are doing enough, that we are enough, and that we each have an essential role in this life that only we can play?

- How can we balance our desire to change the world with our day-to-day lives, especially in these crazy times, and do so nonviolently and without hating?

- How can we create a "Beloved Community" (a term from Martin Luther King, Jr.)?

Teaching this book to my students and the UU community allowed me to face my fears (or, more candidly, terrors) about going public with my message. I accepted that my love is pure, despite birth family members using it in toxic ways throughout my life, including today. Sharing allowed me to get close to my students more quickly, so by mid-Spring 2020, when we suddenly moved to online teaching, I already knew the students well, and they knew me and my expectations. The timing was right because my students today see the "me" who survived and thrived—not the suffering me. They see me as a role model of the transformative power of love, a role for which I continually strive.

KEEPING MY SOUL

In *My Story* and the *Afterword,* I talk about how my parents never got my soul and how this understanding lessened my shame since I had never chosen to hurt my sister or live and stuffed animals. I felt unshackled, free, and empowered by this realization and proud (still struggling with this one) that I've created meaning in my life and have dedicated it to making the world a better place. I talk about creating a family based on love.

My all-time favorite song is called "How Could Anyone Ever Tell You?" I listen to this song several times a day and started expressive dancing at age fifty to dance to this music. The lyrics say everything:

> *"How could anyone ever tell you that you're anything less than beautiful?*
> *How could anyone ever tell you that you're less than whole?*
> *How can anyone fail to notice that your loving is a miracle?*
> *How deeply you're connected to my soul."*

I think that For Giveness and Thanks Giving mean the same thing and connect to the transformative power of love, especially when we add cherishing, which means nurturing and protecting what we treasure. When we cherish, we do more than merely love. Cherishing does not involve lust or monetary worth. Cherishing involves loving profoundly, nurturing affectionately, and protecting dearly.

When I started this *New Beginning*, I pondered some common needs, beliefs, actions, attributes, struggles, and likes of people who, like me, have fought passionately to keep their souls. I think it might be interesting to write another book on the commonalities of those who break generational abuse cycles versus those who perpetuate these cycles. Alcoholism is arguably the most frequent. The pages below provide a beginning. The lists consist of commonalities. Not everyone who has broken generational abuse cycles has all of these traits, just as some people who have continued abuse cycles have such needs and beliefs. But, at the least, these lists apply to me and specific things that have helped me keep my soul.

Common Needs

- To be who we are
- To accept others as who they are
- Authenticity
- A life of meaning
- Integrity, truth, and respect
- Deep relationships
- Eye contact and the ability to look someone in the eyes and see their soul
- Insatiable curiosity and sense of wonder
- To learn and grow
- Deep spirituality (not necessarily religious)
- To serve others and strive to give more and do more
- To "pay-it-forward"
- Community
- Use personal woundedness for social justice
- World peace, nonviolently
- To create beauty—playing an instrument, singing, dancing, writing, acting, crafting (like making bookmarks!)
- To nurture the inner child, including fun and silliness
- Laughter, including self-deprecatory laughter
- Gratitude
- Safe touch
- Question authority
- To be visible and to have a voice
- To be able to take baby steps
- Joy and inner peace
- To be kind AND to act
- To be sustainable activists

Common Beliefs

- The inherent interconnectedness of everyone and everything, including the interconnectedness of the personal and the planetary
- The transformative power of love
- The possibility to create a beloved community
- The healing power of nature

- Accentuating our strengths rather than eliminating our weaknesses to become our best selves
- The value of education
- Life is abundant
- Everybody has a story that is worth hearing
- Synchronicity
- A liberal approach to governing
- Everything is alive and has a soul and, therefore, a concern about the welfare of all sentient beings (everything and everybody)
- The power of communication in general and of words in particular, as well as the power of nonverbal forms of communication
- Role models
- Different priorities than the mainstream
- See things sometimes that others don't see
- A strong sense of wonder and magic
- Death is a natural part of life

Common Actions

- Act as a role model to our children and others
- Attend protests to support others, to feel empowered, to know we're not alone, and to make our voices heard
- Fight for the marginalized
- Fight for peace
- Frequently go outside our comfort zone
- Act for THIS life
- Support the arts
- Often write poetry and gratitude journals
- Enjoy discussing intellectual ideas
- Act to leave a legacy in terms of love and respect, not money or power
- Often think outside the box and value this quality in others
- Spend time outdoors, especially in nature
- Smile a lot
- Often in the helping/caring professions

Common Attributes

- Open-minded and have a difficult time understanding closed-minded people
- Optimistic
- Humble sometimes to the extreme
- Willing to feel the pain of others
- Enjoy trying new things
- Willing to take reasonable risks
- See the extraordinary in the ordinary
- Understand the importance of our presence
- Constantly reflective
- Thoughtful people
- Courageous
- Resilient
- Empathic
- Tend to be perfectionists and overachievers with Type A personalities
- Allow ourselves to be vulnerable
- Easily see the beauty of others
- Feel genuine joy in the success of others
- Forgive others relatively quickly
- Tend to have high highs without alcohol or drugs
- Usually passionate and persistent
- Hard workers
- Shared struggles
- Often overly self-critical and/or having little self-compassion
- Often have difficulty forgiving ourselves
- Often have low lows
- Difficulty understanding people who are greedy
- Difficulty understanding superficial people
- Difficulty with shallow conversations
- Difficulty understanding complacency
- Difficulty understanding people who support war
- Difficulty accepting that we are doing "enough" and are enough
- Difficulty dealing with authorities and institutions
- Struggle not to get involved in other people's problems and dramas
- Struggle not to be used by others
- Struggle not to need the approval of others

- Struggle to accept criticism without shame/guilt
- Struggle to trust ourselves but ultimately do so
- Struggle to recognize our own achievements
- Have a difficult time accepting compliments
- Struggle with setting and keeping personal boundaries
- Struggle not to feel overwhelmed/burnt out
- Struggle to turn off the news
- Stubborn, sometimes to the extreme
- Tend to over-quote, believing that others say things better than we can
- Little tolerance of rumor and gossip

Common Likes

- Children
- The wisdom of elders
- Nature
- Animals, including lots of pets
- Real hugs
- Reading
- Bling even before there was such a word
- Purple
- Crystals, especially amethyst

As I'm finishing this *New Beginning*, I realize the question, "Why do some people give up their souls?" might be the same question as "Why do some people continue to love?"

Below I offer one final list of things I often say to people. The first two come from Eric, the man who adopted me in a Native American ceremony as his daughter:

- "I wish I could give you my eyes for a day so you could see yourself as I (and others) see you"—how often I have said this in writing or speaking to my students.
- "I'm just a phone call away."
- "Try to comfort the disturbed and disturb the comfortable" (one of my favorite bumper stickers).

- "I'm not the black sheep. I'm the tie-dyed one." I saw this quote on a card, which I immediately turned into a bookmark. When thinking about whom to give this to, I realized that almost everyone I love fits this description!
- Although Eric died almost ten years ago, I had one exchange with Douglas, my UU minister, which I still often replay. When Douglas came over the day of Eric's death, one of the first things I said to him was, "I loved and cherished Eric, and he knew it. He loved and cherished me and I knew it." Douglas added, "Everything else is just details." How true!

I like how in UU becoming the best Lois I can involves accentuating my strengths and accepting rather than eliminating my weaknesses. Douglas's mantra to me is, "Be gentle with yourself," a good mantra for everyone!

UU has exposed me to so many things happening in the world. I have been to several trans-gender memorial services. At one, Kimberly, a local minister, asked:

- "Why can't we allow ourselves to be who we are?"
- "Why can't we allow other people to be who they are?"

I think these two questions say everything so succinctly!

Spiritual Experiences

A few years ago, I had a profoundly spiritual experience where several synchronicities occurred in five days. At the university in the fall of 2019, we experienced multiple protests, some with violence as the need for safe speech and free speech collided, as did anti-Trump and pro-Trump groups. My *Afterword* meant more at that time than when I originally wrote it, and I tried to spread its messages of love and nonviolence with anyone on campus who would listen, including my students who already knew all but the latest synchronicities. A few at the university thought I was on drugs and tried to get me to go home in between my classes. Instead, I took the students to my home to explain, and several stayed well beyond the class time. The university put me on paid leave until a psychiatrist of their choosing could certify that I was physically, emotionally, and cognitively able to return to teaching.

Almost two months later, I had a three-hour university-mandated interview in Albany, New York, over two hours each way from where I live.

Some people who knew me well were also concerned. I was not behaving like my "normal" self. Douglas and others in my UU community came over and handled everything from arranging rides to "being there" for me.

I have three people whom I consider sisters-by-love, all outside of the UU community. On that day, one of those three especially protected me as a loving sister, looked out for me, attended all doctor appointments with me, and drove me to and back from the lengthy interview. She contacted my union and handled all of the communications with students and with human resources. She made decisions out of her love for me and out of knowing how important teaching is to me.

As I've done for many years, I spent Christmas Eve day of 2019 with her and her family. I wrote on the back of a bookmark something like, "Thank you for helping me even when I resisted/fought back. Isn't this the very definition of love—you giving to me despite my fighting back?" She was concerned about me and, at least at first, thought I had stopped taking my medication for PTSD. But she loved and protected me. She cherished me as a sister in the manner we hope parents would.

I received advice from many people and went into the interview feeling so protected and trusting that whatever happened would be what was supposed to happen. Perhaps I was meant to teach to more than just Binghamton University students. I felt and still feel no shame and, instead, feel pride.

I learned several things from this experience, the major one being how much my friends and students love me and will fight with me and for me. I am never alone. But two things got me into trouble. By the time I talked to the people I cherish, I had repeated the same information many times over, each time more frenetically, especially as the university tried to censor me. Second, I had shared my messages with students in general rather than those who chose my classes.

My courses are self-selective; they are options for fulfilling major and university requirements. As our university population gets more diverse, students increasingly arrive with issues that 20-year-olds should not have to contend with. No matter what I teach, students connect their woundedness to their concerns about social justice. I also seem to attract perfectionists who do extraordinary work no matter the assignment. This generation especially gives me hope for the future.

Trump-era tensions and protests at the university played out in my classroom in the fall of 2019. I created and taught a senior-level course on Communication, Ethics, and Social Action. Out of 27 students that semester, 24 believed in white privilege, and three did not (two male and one female). It became clear as the semester went on that all three had struggled to get where they were. One male and one female shared with the class that they had been in prison, one for 24 hours, and the other for a week. Both were beaten and raped/sodomized. As the semester was coming to an end, I realized that telling them it would have been worse if they were black, while it may have been true, would not, in my opinion, have been helpful. It seemed akin to my saying, "My cat just died," as a cat lover to someone who shared that their beloved husband had died. The cat's death still matters.

Just before the COVID pandemic started in March 2020, I had another deeply spiritual experience reliving something terrifying that occurred more than once. As a child of eight to twelve years old, I was terrified of the dark. My parents' solution to this was to place me in an open coffin overnight in an isolated location. There seemed a lack of proportionality; this is not how most parents treat their children who are afraid of the dark, but it reminds me of books where former slaves in the South beat their children to prepare them for the cold, cruel world. In reliving this experience, I realized I found comfort by praying to the stars and listening to angels sing. My belief in something greater than myself saved me! This reinforced my commitment not to let anyone snuff out my humanity—the dark is addictive, but the light is even more so!

For Whom or What Are You Willing to Die?

Who or what do you cherish so much that you're willing to die to protect them? As a child, the answer was my teddy bears—-my teddies!—who were my children. I remember repeatedly saying, "Do whatever you want to me; just don't hurt my teddies!"

Not all but most people would die to protect their children—really anyone's children. Cherishing children automatically includes selflessness and a willingness to sacrifice. What does it mean when you don't have this instinct, this protective quality?

31

A Tale of Two Cats

I am writing much of this during the COVID-19 pandemic in the summer of 2020 as I sit in the parking lot during one of several visits with veterinarians for Keller, a cat given to me by a dear friend several years ago. Keller was deaf when I met him. His name is an allusion to Helen Keller. He also arrived in my arms with only two teeth; since vets use the number of teeth to determine a cat's age, we don't really know his age. At the moment, Keller has diarrhea and has been pooping all over the house.

While in the parking lot, I find myself bargaining with God. I should have taken him to the vet sooner. Keep Keller alive, and I'll be a better mom to him! I finally accept that if Keller dies, it's not my fault. Though smelly, he's SO adorable and knows it! He's a snuggler; 24/7 is almost enough time for affection! I cherish the years I've had with him and will continue to adore him each day. I've made mistakes as Keller's mom, but my love for him is pure.

Cami, my very first cat ever, had a different tale. My apartment had a retroactive no-pet policy, and I could not break my lease. My father (I thought generously) offered to take Cami for a few months. At this time (1982), I had absolutely no memories of abuse.

I lived with acute and chronic abdominal pain from multiple surgeries, not helped by my father beating me in the abdomen with his fist after all but twelve centimeters of my colon were removed. I blocked memories as soon as they occurred. Not surprisingly, I felt depressed, sometimes suicidal.

In November of 1982, I made an earnest suicide attempt taking eight times more prescription sleeping pills than were needed to kill me. I was in a coma for a week and apparently fought so hard to live that the physicians credited my recovery to that. For many years, Eric (the psychologist I saw) and I tried to determine what the final trigger was, and I finally recalled my birth father phoning me and telling me in horrifying and grotesque detail how he planned to torture and dismember Cami. She was a pawn, a living being that he knew I loved. If I did not exist, Cami would have been spared, or at least that was the reasoning that led to my despair and suicide attempt.

Several years later, Eric shared with me a strange conversation. My birth father had phoned him saying that I committed suicide and he (Eric) should call the police. Eric asked my father what made him think this and could not get a clear answer. Eric lived an hour away, closer than my birth father, who lived about seven hours away. It never occurred to Eric to suggest that my father call the police!

After about three hours, Eric phoned the police. By this time, I was in a coma. At the hospital, while moving in and out of a coma, I overheard several phone conversations between my father and my godfather. My father talked about suing Eric for not taking his phone call seriously. Only in very recent years did I learn that one's sense of hearing is the last sense to leave and the first to return while in a coma. Hence, my father assumed he spoke on the phone with no witnesses. This was the only time that I heard my mother's voice after her death the year before. A few times that week, I heard her say, "Don't let them get away with this!"

What would make my father or any father try to kill his own flesh and blood for insurance money? When I was about ten years old, I served as a prostitute for the man who was both my father's and mother's boss. He treated me gently. I remember him giving me a doll that my father promptly named "Fanny." He spoke to me with affection. My parents had told me that, like all children, I needed to earn money to help the family so I assumed that it was normal for a ten-year-old to contribute to the family's finances in this way. Because this experience was relatively positive, I always remembered it and did not need to re-live the pain to forgive my parents. This situation with Cami, however, was different. My father not only wanted me dead, but he tried to make it happen by telling me about his gruesome and torturous plan for my cat, knowing it would almost certainly trigger a suicide attempt. Then, as his overheard phone calls show, he wanted to make money from my death and hurt Eric. What could make any parent this desperate?

From the time of his birth, my father was told he was "a mistake." His siblings were nine, eleven, and thirteen years older than him. As you will read, my father frequently called me "a little piece of shit, not good enough to be a big piece." What made my father go from a mistake to a murderer? What allowed me to grow from a little piece of shit to a functioning member of society? In the *Afterword*, I talk about how my parents never got my soul. My father had somehow given his away.

Beginning in 2020, I've channeled messages several times from my birth father, which I combine below ("I" here refers to him):

> *"I always felt desperate, terrified, despairing, overwhelmed, and depressed. I felt choked by fear and paralyzed. I hated myself. I was a mistake, and, hence,*

you [Lois] were a mistake. I should not have existed and, thus, you should not have existed. I was terrified of being found out, so I could not show my real self to anyone. I made jokes as a mask in the hope people would like me. I ate uncontrollably to make myself bigger. I was utterly trapped. I had no way out. Zero!

I had my own trauma. I could not sleep because every noise startled me. I read and read and read, trying to find a way out, but I could never find the right books. My father (your grandfather) came to the United States from Germany ALONE between the ages of 8 and 10. He had already seen the worst horror; I don't know where he found the strength and courage to leave the only home, country, and family he knew. He escaped, I think, by himself. He felt guilty that he survived when EVERY other member of our family did not!

Your mother and I met at Hillel when we were both seventeen years old. We couldn't believe what we learned. FDR was the only President we knew. Why would he betray the Jewish people by his inaction when he first learned of the Nazi death camps?

I wanted to be a Nazi so I could have power and control over my life. Kill or be killed? I deserved every horror! If God loved me, this would not be happening. I deserved this terror. I must! My thinking never got much beyond that. Your mother got me into religion, then your uncle. I thought I would find answers but never did. Never! Anywhere!

I was a failure at everything! I felt a tiny bit successful as a husband but could not have made it without Mom. I depended on her; she was conscientious and hardworking. She had some love, decency, and integrity. We made a great team. I told myself that I was the best husband and best father on the planet because I could not accept any hint of being otherwise. If I said something often enough, I would believe it, or so I thought. I lived for your hugs and your adoration, adulation, and accolades! Yes, even your alliteration!

34

From as young as I can remember, I was told repeatedly that I was a mistake. As you know, my siblings were 9, 11, and 13 years older than me. I was a mistake, and if I was a mistake, you were too. At least you were a little piece of shit. I was a zero! Nothing! Worse than being anonymous! Worse than not existing! What could be worse than not existing?

I had many horrific fears. I couldn't even go to the dentist. I had problem feet. I numbed myself because I couldn't handle the cold and cruel world. I was not a complete person. I deserved to suffer. Life consisted only of suffering. I didn't deserve any better because I was Jewish, a fake, a fraud, not a real person or a whole human being. Any humanity was beaten out of me!

We were dirt poor. I knew what it was like to be hungry. My family used food as a way to hurt me. I was attracted to your mother in part because her family had money. I loved her and you and your sister, but her family's money is what first attracted me.

I married and had a family young to get away from my family and to be the only one in control. I couldn't stand anymore being the one who was controlled. I'll do whatever I need to do so I'm the one kicking ass, literally and figuratively. I'll chop off your balls. Rip out your tongue. Remove one eye and squish it so your other eye will have to watch and see! I gave away my soul! To this day, I don't know what else I could have done!

Reading was a temporary escape. I was always treading water. I never felt safe, secure, protected, or loved. Certainly, God never saved Jews, not just during the Holocaust but throughout history. I was always only one teeny tiny step away from being found out—one false move, one bad choice, one trust in the wrong person, one misunderstood look. I was angry at God. How could we be the "chosen people," and why would God betray His own chosen people?

I resigned myself. God must be using me for something, so He was responsible, not me. As a kid, I could never make enough money to pay for my room and board. Because they were so much older, your uncles and aunt always made much more than I could. I was set up to fail! As an adult, I also never had enough money. Every bankruptcy was another personal failure that caused shame to everyone, and especially to you, your sister, and Mom.

I never found meaning in my life. I wanted to be a history teacher, but I dropped out of college after a little more than a year. Money was our currency, not love. I turned to people to borrow money, but no one would give me anything more than a few cents. They would tease me, tell me I would get money, and then not give it, or give it and then take it away. I could not depend on anyone or trust anyone. Even your godfather, who I knew from when we were both thirteen years old, betrayed me, as did your uncle!

I needed to prepare you for the harsh, cold, cruel, steel world out there. There will be another Holocaust! I needed to toughen you up. In the next Holocaust, do you want to be the Nazi or the Jew? You may not care but, as your father, I need to make sure you are the Nazi!

You not following in my footsteps meant that I was a failure yet again. I spent my life following orders. You needed to do the same. Being part of a group gave me a teeny tiny bit of stability. It was family. I belonged. You were the one who risked the safety of our extended family, and you did this in multiple ways and at different times in your life.

You talking to Mrs. Stoller, your first and second-grade teacher and our neighbor, could have put all of us in jail – forever! How could you betray me like this? At best, she could have broken up the family and separated you and your sister and your Mom. That's what YOU wanted!

Then, you didn't know any better because you were six years old. But, now, you're an adult. Why would you leave me now? This is your time to have fun, your chance to let out some rage and hate, all of it or at least a little of it! You deserve this. You earned this!

Don't you hate this world? You must feel fury and frenzy and be boiling with rage. You must be livid and mad and feel outraged at the world! If not, you're the one who's out of touch with reality! Anyone would feel venom, vindictiveness, wrath, revenge! If you don't, you're the one who isn't a human being or a protector of our people! How can your sense of reality be so flawed? How can you not treasure, relish, cherish and worship these opportunities to let go of a little justified rage? People always accused Jews of being paranoid. It was not paranoia for all of our family who died in the Holocaust!

I wasn't asking you to murder somebody, just spank their little tushis. You should love this. How could you not enjoy watching their little tushis squirm? Welts are temporary. I wasn't asking you to bludgeon them to death. You needed just to shock, prove you meant business. The kids will idolize, adore, and love you. You have to prove you're not a loser!

The kids will scorn you for not playing along. These were good games. You came up with most of them! "Find the 22 red things in the room or I'll spank your little tushi (beat it beet red) for the ones you didn't find." "How high can you make their little tushis jump?" Not them, not even their tushis, just their little tushis! Not good enough to be big ones! At least twice, you got people outside a store to "spank" your sister. You told them how bad she was. You knew the meaning of "spank." You did this, not me!

Most of the fun comes in doing nothing, just watching their little tushis squirm while they are on all fours begging and groveling! They will implore you to have mercy. That's the game! What harm could come from matching little tushis to photos, especially since you were the one who suggested this game? You allowed me and you to separate your little tushi from the rest of you. You taught me how to do this, and now you object?

How dare you? You are supposed to be "dear!" and you won't even act like a "deer in the headlights!" You're a pathetic excuse for a daughter or even for a human being!

Likewise, you were the one who said any other parent would have beaten you until you were dead. You were the one who said I was nice and the most wonderful Daddy in the world for just "spanking your little tushi until it was beat red." These were YOUR words, NOT mine!

How could you not want the kids to idolize you? You say you care about children. How could you be unwilling to prepare them for the next Holocaust? A little humiliation is good for the soul! You're paddling, not pummeling them permanently. Everyone needs a good thrashing sometimes. It's good for the soul! You're the one who talks about children, spirituality, and the soul. These are YOUR words, NOT mine!

You knew we would make sure you didn't go too far! We would protect you, keep you safe, and keep ALL of us safe! You knew the few you watched die couldn't be trusted. You knew the cats and dogs you hurt were ONLY animals. You knew your teddies were NOT REAL! You are the one who makes no sense and still lives in an alternate reality! You speak nonsense!

Yes, you say you're burning, foaming, seething, and smoldering, but your behavior suggests otherwise, and you know these storms are temporary. They're learning experiences. You control the violence. Others will do MUCH, MUCH, MUCH worse! For others, there is no bottom, literally or figuratively! Why is making their "little bottoms red" so offensive?

Shunning the group meant shunning me. You must hate me! And, shunning the group meant you hated all of us! And, you're the one who still talks about love being stronger than hate. As your sister always accused us, "You're such a hypocrite!"

38

I had to kill you before you exposed us. You at least needed to pretend we didn't exist! You not only refused to join the group, but you tried to shame us, to unmask us. You were a professor, an author, a winner of many awards; you had a Ph.D. in mouth, and had a voice. You missed so many family events with made-up lies. We had your "number." Even as an adult, goddammit, you tried to report us.

You trusted and loved Eric, that hippie psychologist; Carroll Arnold, your mentor; Barb, your BFF; and MANY others. I envied the ways you loved others, and I couldn't compete with how much they loved you! I was doing you a favor to let you die in your sleep. Your Godfather Henry and Uncle Mickey (changed names) wanted to torture you, and you certainly deserved to be tortured and more!

And, I didn't kill you. You killed you. You were the one who took the sleeping pills. This and hurting Eric financially was a win/win situation. I would get money, and you would die peacefully. How can you STILL not "get" this?

Remember, Mom died less than a year ago. You could be with her, another win/win. I wanted to be with her, but I was too scared to commit suicide after she died.

Because of your pain issues, you probably would not bring me grandchildren, which is what daughters are supposed to do, and all that counts for another Holocaust. A black granddaughter does not count! You think I'm a joke; you're the joke, and the joke right now is on you!

You looked and acted so much like Mom. You had her eyes, her beauty, her decency, and her sense of truth, integrity, authenticity, and reality. I had just lost her. I couldn't be alone. I needed the group, needed to belong somewhere, needed to exist! This was my REAL family, by the standards of "The Velveteen Rabbit." You were not and are not my "real" family! You chose to separate from us, not the other way around!

If your suicide attempt failed, as it did, I had proof that you were the crazy one. Don't you remember the wonderful time we had in Myrtle Beach and at home as you recovered? I took such good care of you despite your bringing shame to the entire family. Do you remember all the laughs we had?

When you were born, you raised your head in the hospital and looked at me. When you were about five, I was ready to kill myself. You came out in this adorable Purim costume and looked at me. Those looks and others like them haunted me my entire life and will probably haunt me forever!

You, the person who teaches the importance of eye contact in everything you teach. How could you not see that in my eyes? Your love is and was so pure, even as a little girl, but you were and still are so out of touch with reality and with your nonverbal communication behaviors and actions, which always said more to me than your words!

I was (and still am) so jealous of how much you genuinely loved Cami, and I could not believe it when she ran to the door even after not seeing you for many months. How could my love compete with that? Maybe I can be your cat in some future life! I hope I've made you smile, even for a second!

I watch you now and marvel at how you have survived and thrived on your own and at how you've created your own family. I never saw anyone leave this group (or other comparable groups) alive. I didn't know that was even possible! I still don't understand how you overcame so much more than I did and what Grandpa did, and still you have a HUMONGOUS heart and a pure soul! I agree with Eric: You ARE a miracle!

Like the words that you and Eric edited from the children's book, Love You Forever, *"I love you forever. I like you for always. Forever and ever and ever and a gazillion more evers, my very precious daughter you are and will forever be." I understand that these were your last words to Eric after you successfully persuaded the police to allow you a private moment with his body before they took it away. Again, how can I compete with this?*

I know there's nothing I can say to you now. To say, "I apologize" is meaningless. Just know that I love you SO deeply and am beyond blown away by the beautiful, intelligent, creative, kind, sweet, and loving soul you have become! I don't deserve you, but I'm so, SO proud of you!

The Soul of Our Nation

I'm writing this "New Beginning" two weeks after the inauguration of President Joseph R. Biden and vice-president Kamala Harris during a continued pandemic that Donald Trump said does not exist or is not bad. Trump triggered so many things for people with PTSD. The world felt crazy as he said outrageous things and created a chaotic world where up meant down and tree meant cupcake. President Biden entered the race because the soul of our country was at stake. He began his Presidential bid by referring to the violence and death at the University of Virginia (UVA) in Charlottesville, where Trump said, "There are many good people, on both sides." This violence hit me viscerally because I grew up in Virginia and participated in debate tournaments at the UVA campus; many students from my high school attended there. I also experienced a lot of anti-Semitism in Virginia. The silver lining was that Keller (my cat) was gifted to me that weekend!

I find that just as some people keep their souls, so too do some nations. For over four years, I've struggled to understand Trump and his supporters. Surprisingly, reading Mary Trump's book comforted me. In fact, I started to channel my birth father immediately after reading it.

According to Mary Trump and others, Donald Trump grew up in a home where admitting mistakes was not allowed. Actions of kindness showed weakness. Winning or not losing was the only currency and took the place of love. With only one winner possible, Trump had to win. Coming in second makes you a loser, the worst thing anyone could possibly be. Losers are disowned. They no longer exist.

41

No wonder Trump thought he needed to be the best at everything. He admitted no mistakes and had no regrets. Having never been truly loved, Trump knows only fear, rage, and rule-based order. He cannot learn and grow or even listen. He gave himself an "A+" on handling the pandemic as more and more people died, took no responsibility, never admitted to making even tiny mistakes. He knew only division and chaos. When you start at perfection, there's no need even to try to do better.

He demanded loyalty, which meant blind obedience. People who worked with him for years got fired (usually by tweet) for one tiny transgression for not supporting him 100% of the time. You were either for him or against him. No other position existed.

The following were frequent words in Trump's messages and, hence, in his thinking: spies, lies, witch hunt, hoax, phony, con game, fabricate, failing, corrupt, crooked, fraudulent, disaster, shithole, false, dishonest, dumpster, garbage, fiction, sucker, bogus, crime, treason, attack, dumb as a rock, lazy as hell, alien, and conspiracy.

He indeed seemed incredulous that he was impeached the first time because he had done nothing wrong. The phone call was "perfect," just as his public comments after the domestic terrorist attack on the Capitol set "just the right tone." We don't need to grow when we begin at perfection.

Trump chose something from one report and then another, in or out of context. It was as if he had the entire English language and the entire internet at his disposal. He told so many lies that just pointing them out became exhausting! How many hours will I save when not checking his tweets each day? He made up quotations, statistics, and conversations saying things that were blatantly false or different from what he said ten minutes earlier. He used absolute language and caps for further emphasis. Similar to a two-year-old, he liked the word "no." "I HAVE NOTHING TO DO WITH RUSSIA—NO DEALS, NO LOANS, NO NOTHING!" Note the double negative. Accuracy, truth, and reality didn't matter. Everything was an urgent emergency. He took up the news cycle, not caring if his words and actions were good or bad, true or untrue.

Trump is out of office, but Trumpism remains. With this method of thinking, everyone and everything becomes suspect. Trumpists use a process of induction, collecting scattered specifics with almost no overarching conclusion. The overriding conclusion then leads to circular thinking in a closed system. For Trump and many of his supporters, the overarching conclusions are conspiracy theories working together. Find more examples that fit the conspiracies and use the conspiracies to explain new details. The focus builds on a fear-based view of the world.

Trump's sycophants and supporters often spend a lot of time keeping up with the news, going down different rabbit holes that provide ways to validate themselves and their view of the world. Going down so many rabbit holes, they think they know more than others or *at least don't need to learn anything more.* Not surprisingly, it doesn't matter if the information is fabricated, factual, or fake, learned from formal education or memes.

Many consider themselves free thinkers, not bound by education or false flags. Some go down rabbit holes because they believe all news is propaganda, fake news, and bullshit. Such a worldview encourages furor and vindictiveness; rage, retaliation, and revenge. Danger and peril exist at every turn. We despise, loathe, and scorn, and we feel utterly disgusted and intense hatred of the Other.

I've heard some Trump supporters say they felt offended when Obama bowed to Iran's leader and kissed his hand, saying, "No US president should bow to any foreign leader. We're the leader; our country does not follow anyone. Bowing means submitting and surrendering. Bowing shows weakness." In this world, everything is win OR lose. There can be only one winner, and win/win solutions don't exist. To see both sides as winning requires living in a world of possibilities and nuances.

I find it telling that much of the alt-right possesses a patriarchal view of gender, believing eggs come out dead, but sperm serves one purpose—to create life. Women can masturbate but not men. A few days ago, Trevor Noah's "Daily Show" did a fascinating piece arguing that men in the alt-right would be less angry if they stopped following the Bible literally.

I'm concluding now (or at least hypothesizing) that my birth father, Trump, and Trump supporters live in a closed system, unaware of the possibility of something else. They go down rabbit hole after rabbit hole, often spending hours looking at multiple sources but not a variety of sources. Some might lack the critical thinking skills needed to evaluate the credibility of a source. I think Trump and some Trumpists have difficulty cherishing, empathizing, and loving others, even themselves. Social media greatly compounds this problem! Without curiosity and sensitivity, they become unaware of their lack of awareness.

If we come from a love-based view of the world, we begin with conclusions practicing deductive reasoning. Our conclusions are probable, not certain. We find examples that support them as we continually adjust and refine the original findings. We analyze, contemplate, discern, explore, learn, reason, and focus on credibility and credentials as we question everything. We continuously look for ways to go outside our comfort zones. We reflect, refine, and wrestle with competing and complex ideas, looking for nuances as we view different perspectives.

We do this through never-ending learning, traveling, talking to a wide range of people, and reading other people's stories. We focus on everyone's inherent interconnectedness and try to see the world as abundant, possessing more than enough for everyone. Many things "trump" winning or not losing (sorry—pun intended)!

As we go out of our comfort zones and learn other people's stories, we know we do not know everybody's account and can never know but still struggle to choose peace, love, and justice for all. We do our best to adore, honor, love, protect, and cherish our children and all children, or at least we strive to do so. We try to learn from our mistakes and find meaning in our lives. We struggle to put into practice former first lady Michelle Obama's maxim, "When they go low, we go high."

The 2020 election was terrifying, I think because just as my birth parents had no low that was too low, it seemed Trump had no bottom. The weeks between the election and Inauguration were incredibly agonizing as day after day, I waited nervously for the peaceful transition of power, unable to exhale fully. I kept my fingers and toes crossed as I tried to persuade myself that there is a Higher Being who's in charge now who will make the inauguration happen with the Divine energy of cherishing. I trusted this 99%, but not 100%.

So much was going on in my life and in the world every day. I might be overanalyzing the situation, as academics often, do. However, after the January 6 insurrection and less than a week before Inauguration, I played with ideas that I'm still trying to get to relevant decision-makers because my point is even stronger today (the end of September of 2021). Doesn't failure to concede an election exemplify a lack of a peaceful transfer of power? No more proof is needed.

A Letter to Everyone Willing to Read This

*I understand the impeachment charge against Donald Trump involved 2 points: (1) Trump incited an insurrection, and (2) Trump did not stop an insurrection. I think the country should focus now **only** on the 2nd point, even if this requires a new House vote. My reasoning is as follows:*

Half of the country believes Biden legitimately won the election. Half thinks he stole the election. To heal, we need to stop blaming and shaming and identify common ground.

At the moment, everyone is pointing to "blood" on everyone's hands. Only lawyers benefit from such behavior!

We need to send clear messages to those planning further violence (before and after next week) that there are consequences. Compare the number of National Guard members yesterday with last week. I think most people agree there need to be criminal charges as we restore law and order.

We've removed Trump's bully pulpit. Some corporations have pulled funding. Social media companies are accepting they played a role (a different topic).

Healing from cancer necessitates first removing the tumor.

*We need to separate the discussion of who is responsible and why no one saw this coming and focus only on Trump's **continued failure to stop the violence**. He continues to perpetuate the lie of a stolen election and expresses no remorse and no responsibility.*

Trump did not phone or text Pence for several days despite knowing that the terrorists were chanting "Hang Mike Pence" and despite seeing a noose.

Tonight, eight days after the insurrection, Trump condemned the violence, but he still has not conceded the election and has barely said there would be a peaceful transition of power.

Trump described his remarks last week as "totally appropriate." With further threats of violence, words matter.

It's not clear who called in the National Guard, but it should have happened sooner.

If the terrorists were from Antifa, Trump failed to stop them.

Issues of free speech are important but are separate issues.

We need history to remember January 6 as a terrorist attack, a shared reality, with the same facts. Let's celebrate that democracy triumphed!

*If we really want unity and healing, Democrats and Republicans will come together and deal with this crisis ASAP, **before** next week's Inauguration. Most agree that Trump failed (and continues to fail) at stopping the violence.*

Think about all the things we could do with the money saved!

We need restorative justice, allowing everyone to say, "I really screwed up." Focus on having everyone tell the truth without fear, similar to what the Truth and Reconciliation Commission did in South Africa. Get advice from Desmond Tutu himself or his granddaughter, who's written an incredible book on the concept of Ubuntu.

Several people on both sides have received death threats to themselves, their children, and their grandchildren. No one should cast votes (or do anything) because of death threats!

Several members of Congress are purchasing bullet-proof vests. We need everyone to condemn violence.

Some Trump enablers were trying to provide moderation, not thinking Trump would go this far. Today I also reflect on the ten Republicans who voted yesterday to support impeachment, each risking their political and actual lives (lots of death threats to themselves and to their children and grandchildren). They can never undo their vote on the first impeachment; yet, I see them as heroes who voted their conscience this time!

Focusing now only on the past week might help us begin to heal, accepting that no one is an Other. We are all loved and lovable! Let us cherish ourselves as we are and cherish others as they are, realizing we are all one heart beating as one!

People can rob us of many things, but they cannot take our spark, our spirit, our soul. Love has the power to transform.

Some Long Digressions

The day I sent out this piece, 100 personal emails disappeared. For over fifteen years, my birth family has engaged in significant harassment. I had a cat disappear with about 30 pieces of evidence pointing to someone within the Native American community who I learned afterward was practicing black witchcraft. I don't know how but I sensed correctly that a yogurt in my refrigerator had been poisoned. I gave it to Eric to have it tested, and there was arsenic in it! After Eric changed my locks twice, my favorite necklace disappeared, made by Chelsea, who's

46

like a niece to me. Chelsea hand beaded this amulet bag between the ages of eight and thirteen and gifted it to me. It was on the top of my jewelry box. What's stranger is the necklace reappeared six weeks later.

For years, I assumed my birth family's harassment had to do with the topic of child abuse, but I experienced the same harassment with my books on compassionate fairy tales and spiritual lessons in Dr. Seuss. They've done MANY other horrible things, several involving my computer. They've taken my entire email account or my complete contact list and changed security questions and passwords. I am not exaggerating when I say that I've changed passwords on Gmail and Zoom more than 100 times! It seems that anything I say about Eric is considered an insult to my birth father. Three sister-by-love relationships are taken as an insult to my sister. I suspect they interpret any loving relationship as a threat. Each episode of harassment can last several months but eventually stops. Fortunately, several people over several years have witnessed them with me first-hand.

Most bizarrely, they have answered student emails on several occasions. So far, "my" answers have been nonviolent, and, more importantly, my students know me well enough to catch something that doesn't sound like me. They even know the complex and nuanced differences between violent, non-violent, and compassionate!

When will my birth family and groups they're connected with decide to move on? They know I will continue to write books and speak out. In fact, their harassments perversely motivate me. How much more proof do they need? And, they know that every instance offers one more chance somebody will catch them and their connections.

I say to any members of my immediate and extended birth family who may read this: "I love you. I would like to reconcile with you (some more than others)! You should fear being exposed by yourselves more than wanting to hurt me and those I love!"

A Tangent

Politically, I worry that people on both sides are receiving death threats themselves and death threats to their children and grandchildren.

The last time I saw any member of my birth family was at my nephew's bar mitzvah in 1993. My mother and father died in 1981 and 1987, respectively. Eric came with me as a guest, as did Claudete, who I adopted from Brazil and was with me between the ages of eleven to thirteen. She was twelve at the time. As I write, I realize that this was the first time any family member met her. Perhaps I should have taken as a warning the fact that when I told my uncle, a rabbi, that she was black; he asked, "How dark is she?"

Eric and I were given lots of precise instructions from people familiar with Satanic and ritual abuse including to lie about the last place they would see us. My sister invited us repeatedly to her small party after the Bar Mitzvah, so I initially said "yes, absolutely" and then phoned to say "we could not make it." I don't remember what excuse I gave. We actually visited my BFF from age thirteen.

The following Tuesday, my uncle phoned, explaining in a loud profanity-filled tirade about how EVERY member of my family participated in a plan to hit my car—the precise angle, how they would get rid of eyewitnesses, etc. They wanted to hit Eric and force me to watch. They had everything accurate except because it was my car, they assumed I was the driver; they would have hurt me and forced Eric to watch, no better. The point of the phone call was to intimidate: My uncle kept saying, "You're not going to get away with this! We're going to come to Binghamton and torture Eric and your nigger daughter and force you to watch." I realize I lived with this threat for eighteen years, until Eric's death in 2011.

A Related Tangent

After agreeing that Claudete would do better in a large foster home, I relinquished her to the state and spent several years looking at other possible adoptions. Vaneza and Ana were sisters in Massachusetts. Vaneza was ten and a half when she came; Ana was eight and a half. They each had birthdays while with me. Although they lived with me for only six months, we deeply loved each other; they were my daughters-in-love forever and always, from day one. Eric gave me a book for Christmas of 1998 called *A Broken heart still beats: After Your Child Dies*. Inside, he hand-wrote, "Precious Oghegleh Ki IyoyamgalWi (Bright Colors Angel), may you find solace in these writings, and may the New Year be one of growth and joy for you." Losing Vaneza and Ana was like having my heart pulled out of me (times two). I did not protect my precious daughters!

I put Vaneza and Ana into therapy. I asked each to choose a therapist. There was one they liked but felt they would not grow much.

One MSW had lots of experience with children. She used puppets which they immediately loved. The third choice was a psychologist, Dr. Thomas Harding, who they connected with and who, indeed, in six months helped them grow! They saw him individually, with each other, and as a family. (They each chose him even before I gave them a few of the puppets!) He went through several crises with us, as we called during "closed hours" (with permission). In fact, he had written a strong letter a couple of months before they were taken about how much they had grown. He wrote an even stronger letter after they left elaborating on how each of us – Vaneza, Ana, and me – had grown individually and as a family and how struck he was by our deep love!

In therapy, I told my daughters to tell the truth, the whole truth, and nothing but the truth. Ana told him that their foster mom held her head underwater. Vaneza said Valdete didn't know how to swim. With a pregnant sixteen-year-old biological teen and other foster children in the home, Dr. Harding had to file a report. I begged him not to do this (as did Eric and a few others). I now realize Dr. Harding had no other choice, but there's no grief worse than losing children. I did not protect my precious daughters from the system's abuse. What's worse is that I received their therapy records from before they came to me, and it indicated that the foster mother held Ana's head under water in the toilet. Both Ana and Vaneza were telling the truth!

The six months that Vaneza and Ana were with me were the happiest months of my life! I made mistakes, lots of them. In fact, I got reprimanded for using some of the same re-parenting techniques that Eric used with me (see his response); people learned about them because Vaneza and Ana told friends about how much they helped. Photos of them document their going from living dead people to alive, fun, and funny kids. Ana's birthday was two months into them being here. I have a photo of Vaneza with a wide grin (better than living dead) and Ana holding onto Vaneza, frightened out of her mind. I have other photos where Ana especially is clearly depressed. This still was better than walking dead. I knew that look of terror. My abuse now had a purpose – I could be a more sensitive and better Mom to them. And they EACH were the MOST special, MOST precious gift to me!

Synchronicities on Steroids

What I write below may be more than some readers want to know. I'm struggling with how much information to include in this book. Many of the people I most cherish do not want me to include some of the material below so I do so without their approval but with their blessings. I often experience what psychiatrist and psychoanalyst Carl Jung labeled synchronicities but during the pandemic, my synchronicities have been on steroids!

SPOILER ALERT

Some of what I write below might trigger some readers. I ask these readers to be gentle with themselves as they choose to read or not read this section. Please understand that fuller disclosure on my part does not mean full disclosure. Even the people closest to me know only the tip of the iceberg! And, I can assure you that anything that is difficult to read is even more difficult to experience! I don't want to open personal Pandora's boxes unless you want them to open.

All of these new memories are stirring. I'm doing my best to keep one foot in front of the other. I'd not taken a lavender bubble bath in two weeks. [Eric and I spent an intense whole week with an expert in Idaho who specializes in sadistic and satanic abuse. He was familiar with some Nazi films I was forced to watch as a child. When I told him I was having a difficult time bathing, he responded, "Of course you do! When going to be gassed, Jews were told they were going to the shower." Eric and I looked at each other. How could we have not made that connection?

Only a week ago, a friend asked me, "What is it about Jews and enemas?" She had a close friend whose parents were Holocaust survivors, and they constantly gave her enemas. I connect more dots as I realize that some Jews were beaten in the camps by other Jews because they could not hold in their bodily functions. I constantly received scalding hot enemas (in the bathtub).

I had my regular appointment on Friday with Douglas. I suggested we use that time to talk about what my uncle said he would do to Claudete in 1993. Only the day before, I remembered multiple occasions when members of my birth family said some of the most horrifying, humiliating, and terrifying things you could say about a black person, similar to what Beatriz (the orphanage director) had said. But this was in 1993.

Douglas, my minister, has been MUCH more than generous with me! We've been meeting in my backyard or via Zoom each Friday. We just talked on the phone for more than an hour (Gmail and Zoom weren't working on my computer). As soon as we hung up, I connected more dots, realizing that members of my birth family had a short window of time between when Claudete got home from school and when I did. In addition to the horrible things they said and threatened, I just realized that they abused Claudete sometimes during these few minutes. Whatever they did to me, they did to Claudete.

More dots connect. Vaneza and Ana got home from school at 3:15 pm, and I got home at 3:30 pm, a fifteen-minute window of time. [For Claudete the time was different because she went to another school]. I experienced MANY horrific things in less time. I remember some things my family or group members did to me on my way home from school.

It's now 5:00 pm. In the past hour, I've realized that whatever my birth family did to me, they likely did to Claudete, and whatever they did to Claudete, they likely did to Vaneza and Ana. I became hysterical and seriously suicidal and phoned Douglas.

Claudete and I had mutually agreed that she needed more help than I could provide, and now I've also lost Vaneza and Ana. I lost them the day they were taken, and again after I lost a year-long court battle which left me nearly bankrupt. I now had to accept the many horrific things my birth family, my flesh and blood, people with whom I share DNA did to my precious daughters in the past and could still do in the present and future.

I realize I need to forgive myself first, but I don't even know where to begin! I continue to call Douglas leaving ever-increasing frantic, suicidal messages.

Does accepting mean forgiving here? Does forgiving mean accepting? In 2004, I received an award from the World Forgiveness Alliance as a "Heroine of Forgiveness, Reconciliation, and Peace," an award given to Mahatma Gandhi, Martin Luther King, Jr., Nelson Mandela, and Desmond Tutu. I've pretty much given up all hopes of reconciliation, and, at the moment, I cannot imagine wanting to forgive my birth family or even myself.

To my surprise, I had little problem forgiving myself up until this time. I took Claudete out of a 24/7 sadistic abuse cycle. She's living in the US. She could easily regain her command of Portuguese. She picked up sign language quickly. The last I knew, she was working in a pet shop; her sensitivity to animals might be her calling. No regrets. I hope, in fact, to reconnect with her.

Accepting my family's abuse of Vaneza and Ana is more difficult but I was surprisingly generous with myself even here. Shame and depression won't change the past. In just under six months, they were different people. If nothing else, they knew what it's like to be REALLY loved and cherished! Still, I didn't protect them then, and I cannot protect them now. I'm increasingly suicidal. Sharon (my therapist) and Douglas have seen me inconsolable and suicidal multiple times, even now over ten years after Eric's death, because he (fortunately) did not know this type or depth of evil.

I had a suicide agreement with Eric. If I felt seriously suicidal, I would call him. He would come over immediately or phone and say, "I've got stuff to do, but I'll be over in two hours." I made the same suicide agreement with Douglas many years ago. On Friday, for several hours, I spoke with Douglas or left answering machine voice messages. I went from "I feel suicidal" to "I'm planning on how to commit suicide," to "tell me you if have better ideas that we'll discuss in the future," to "send me a lifeline," to "you have a suicide agreement with you." Douglas finally said, "I'm on my way." I could barely breathe in the twenty minutes it took him to get here. It had also just begun to snow.

My birth family had tortured and killed Cami and Helen (a cat named after Helen Keller because she had Helen's personality) who disappeared one day. I got home from a sweat lodge ceremony, and there was no cat—dead or alive. She was taken using Eric's keys to my home. Separate story.

My parents are long deceased, but my birth family remains. By birth family, I mean sister, niece, nephew, cousins, their children and grandchildren, and groups they connect with. You have to remember that EVERY single member of my birth family was involved in the "hit the car" saga and continual death and torture threats. To my knowledge, I'm the only person who's gotten out of my family's cult alive. My birth father makes this comment in what I channeled. He did not know it was even possible to leave alive without being an abuser. I have hopes of possible reconciliation someday with my niece—separate story.

My thinking was and I think still is clearer than ever. Claudete was set up to fail and was abused by people who shared my blood and DNA. Ditto for Vaneza and Ana. I have no regrets! I would make the same choices with both adoptions, even knowing all of the consequences. But this "no regrets" applies only to the past.

I've now lost Cami and Helen. When Douglas says my love is 100% pure, I argue that I've spent my life going from 100% toxic to 99% pure. I saw two incredible presentations at a free Compassion for Therapists Summit. One dealt with self-compassion, and I learned about an entire field of research and teaching that focuses on this. The second program was equally fascinating. The speaker was trained in western psychology but realized he had not learned how to apply his education to the Native American community he was involved with. The program was about "soul wounds." I knew that Native Americans based decisions on the consequences for the next seven generations. The speaker said the 7 generations also connect to the past. I agree though I would never have thought of this on my own. Perhaps the 1% of my love that's still toxic comes from my soul wounds.

To someone who's never known such toxicity, it's hard to understand. Douglas was convinced he could locate Vaneza and Ana, despite my many attempts, because he's not connected to them. Him trying to contact could backfire because of his connection to me.

After losing Vaneza and Ana, I saw three psychics, all of whom said my daughters would reconnect with me once they "came of age." They're currently in their mid-thirties. For the past several years, I've accepted that we might reconnect in a different lifetime!

Douglas spent much of Saturday here. I shared what I learned with Eric. I always know what I need even when I can't get this out. I told Douglas that whenever I stop making eye contact, he should sing "How Could Anyone Ever Tell You" over and over and over and over again! This worked with Eric and me and with me and Vaneza and Ana. They LOVED the song. They each had their own CD of it within 2 months. I'm reminded of Aristotle saying, "Repetition is the single most potent form of persuasion." I agree. Let's use Aristotle's point about repetition in a good way!

Vaneza and Ana each made many things for me. Next to my bed, I have a beautiful flower picture Vaneza drew and gave me on Mother's Day and a beautiful picture of a butterfly made by Ana with the bottom saying "My name is . . . LOVE!"

A couple of days earlier, I had written something to be filled in by Cleone, my publisher. From a Little Piece of Shit to _____
(fill in the blank). By Saturday night I wrote, "From a Little Piece of Shit to Struggling to Become Divine Love, Beauty, and Peace Personified!"

My fear now is maybe I've done all I'm meant to do in this lifetime. I prayed when Douglas was here asking God to make the decision. I went to sleep on Saturday night into Sunday morning not knowing if this would be my last night on Earth. How do you tell someone that you think there's a reasonable chance you might die that night? I phoned Douglas at 3:00 am. He said he would come over on Sunday after services, as he had promised earlier. I gave him permission to share what was going on with anyone. I literally opened the front door welcoming anyone who wanted to come over so I wouldn't die alone.

On Saturday night I made a deal with God, Spirit, Soul, Divine Energy, but it's not a forever deal. I scribbled the following in purple as a prayer I shared with the relevant people:

"My birth family took Cami and Helen. I want to know that Keller's not next. My sister probably has little fear; because she loved or cherished little, she had little to lose. I do give myself credit for the number of people in my life who I cherish including, of course, each of you. The act of loving is what gets me into trouble.

In the original hardcover edition of this book, I write that I remember saying from as young as I can remember, 'Do whatever you want to me. Just don't hurt my teddy.' Right now, I'm terrified that the people I cherish are the ones at risk! I wrote that I need 100% proof that there's a bottom! Otherwise, every moment of continuing my struggle risks losing everyone and everything I love and care about.

I'm now 'From a Little Piece of Shit" to "Struggling to Become Divine Love, Beauty, and Peace Personified.' I'm a perfectionist but I don't need to be perfect or even 'more perfect' if doing that means taking even the tiniest of chances of losing everything. I cannot do this alone, and I certainly don't want to wear out Douglas or lots of other people who care about and love me because of my neediness."

I tell Divine Energy that I want to continue. There's much more I want to do. But right now figuring out what information to give to what person, answering questions that are in my writing, and just repeating the events of the past days and months is exhausting and counterproductive, even the positive ones.

I often refer to the transformative power of love. There's nothing to transform from if we try to shield ourselves and others from what really happened in the past. I hope I've not triggered anyone. Please know how much I cherish each of you and how grateful I am for your continued love, hugs, and blessings.

My suicide agreement now is with God, the Divine. I cannot deal with continued and ongoing suffering. If you want me to live, you need to take charge. I need to be bathed in love. (As I write this, I do see the "bath" connection)! Others need to protect me now from what my birth family might do in the present and future.

I actually think UU principles provide a way to a safe and sane future. Gone are the days of seeing a therapist once a week. The loving energy that I talk about above and below is precisely what we are about (or at least try to be about). I think UUCB does an extraordinary job of living from this energy. I think cherish includes loving and protecting and something more. I cannot tell you what I mean by "something more" but it deals with our ability to see the best in each other, to focus on our strengths rather than our weaknesses, and to cherish them! Uninterrupted check-ins, small group ministries, and so forth might provide paths forward for more than just UUs. They represent what compassionate listening is all about.

I had a problematic intermediate compassionate listening workshop last night. Early, we were asked to write a pouring out letter to someone who hit all our triggers. I wrote a letter to Trump. Being asked to substitute ourselves for this person felt traumatizing to me. Later, we examined the drama triangle of persecutor, victim, and rescuer. To me, all three roles involve judgment. We ended with a great list of ways to stop the drama or dance. Fortunately, I have two extraordinary teachers! I could express my concerns fully at different points before and after the session and felt completely heard. This provided yet another example of the importance of speaking and listening from the heart with compassion but also feeling seen and heard from the heart with compassion.

Things are coming together as I write. There are either a "Holy shitballs" of synchronicities (see "Ace Ventura, Pet Detective") or a lot of coincidences including what's going on in the world and what's going on in the absurdities of life.

A Scam that Went Awry

While waiting for feedback on my *Letter to Everyone Willing to Read This* (see above) I had an unusual scam. I still do not believe what happened in less than 24 hours. I shared my experience via email with students and friends to help them and others:

I spent over eleven hours yesterday dealing almost non-stop with what was a scam. I was billed for something from Microsoft, which I never ordered, and in refunding the amount, they "accidentally" overpaid me and put $2400 in my bank account which I took out in $100 bills. They wanted me to go to Target and get gift cards. I've stayed COVID-free for ten months. I had someone who could do this on Monday. They made it look like they froze my account and computer, and this is where I refused to negotiate.

I heard from a sister-in-love who had a close friend who lost a huge amount of money in a similar scam. When I realized it was a scam, I left a message saying I would call them on Saturday and then called "911." A police officer actually was here when the scammer called. I have no idea if they will be able to catch them. I still have more to do, opening new accounts in two banks and calling three fraud groups.

I was exhausted before the incident from writing and sending out my political letter. I had not bathed and barely eaten, so I went to bed late feeling frazzled, depleted, and very blessed! In the middle of the night, I woke up with several realizations:

1) *I thought the scammer got scammed; I gave 24 $100 bills to the police. They returned the money after over a month and I realize how blessed I am. Most Americans cannot sustain a $400 emergency.*

2) *I was embarrassed for the police officer to see my mess, especially in my bedroom, with piles everywhere of books, papers, and things to use to make bookmarks.*

3) *I got rid of one bookmark, not one box, but one bookmark! The police officer would not take a box, but she very reluctantly took the one on top.*

4) *I was holding Keller (my cat) while she was here and realized I needed to calm down for his sake; his heart was racing.*

5) *I am being protected. I needed a sign to continue my social activism work. This is a powerful sign!*

6) *This was also a powerful example of nonviolent communication. "Shutting down" my bank account and computer crossed the line.*

7) I am so blessed. What are the statistical chances of my learning about an almost identical scam from a close friend of a close friend?

8) Evidence that God is a noun and a verb.

9) The clear message that the things I teach and write about are correct, including the importance of integrity and the need to make all choices out of the energy of love.

10) Cherish is the term I've been searching for.

11) I hope it's not coincidental that this is happening as my letter went out. Maybe my idea will work?

12) God (or whatever word one uses for a Higher Being) cherishes each one of us!

13) What a world we can create if we make choices based on the energy of cherish!

14) If you argue with God, you will lose! As I tried to finish writing this email and then eat breakfast, my computer froze, I heard clearly, "Eat. You may be stubborn but I'm much more stubborn than you!"

To Love and Cherish

I love folk music and offer the lyrics from Paul Stookey's (of Peter, Paul, and Mary) "Wedding Song: There Is Love." Consider it from a broad perspective of love:

He is now to be among you at the calling of your heart
Rest assured this troubadour is acting on His part
The union of your spirits here has caused Him to remain
For whenever two or more of you are gathered in His name.
There is love, there is love.
Well, a man shall leave his mother and a woman leave her home,
They shall travel on to where the two shall be as one
As it was in the beginning is now until the end
Woman draws her life from man and gives it back again.
There is love, there is love.

Well then, what's to be the reason for becoming man and wife?
Is it love that brings you here or love that brings you life?
For if loving is the answer then who's the giving for?
Do you believe in something that you've never seen before?
There is love, there is love.

These words apply to the love between parents and their children. Although I did not receive this message from my family, I created a family based on love, and I strive to create meaning in life through my teaching, being, and connecting with others at a deep, soul level.

I remember the first time I heard the word "Namaste." I was at a Native American ceremony and a woman defined the word as "the Divine in me connects to the Divine in you." To me, this represented a spiritual meaning of the word "love," not a romantic love but a deeper love where the other person and you become one. Spiritual teacher Ram Das defines Namaste as "I honor the place in you of love, of light, of truth, of peace. I honor the place within you where, if you are in that place in you and I am in that place in me, there is only one of us." When we say "Namaste" we bow to symbolize humility and equality. I draw attention to the bowing to juxtapose it with Trump supporters who found Obama's bowing so offensive.

In recent months, I've read about Ubuntu, a term from several South African languages that, like Namaste, is difficult to translate into English. It translates loosely as I am who I am because of who we are. I am a human being. I belong. I participate. We are connected.

When Nelson Mandela was released from prison and was elected president of South Africa, he appointed Archbishop Desmond Tutu to set up a Truth and Reconciliation Commission, which played a significant role in transitioning from apartheid to post-apartheid, this country's horrific policies of racism. Might we do something similar in this country to deal with slavery and the genocide of native people? Let's also include anti-Semitism and hate crimes against Asians, the Sikh people, and all other groups who are treated as strangers or others. As Tutu wrote, "The completely self-sufficient person is in fact sub-human."

At Nelson Mandela's memorial, then United States President Barack Obama said, "There is a word in South Africa – Ubuntu – a word that captures Mandela's greatest gift: his recognition that we are all bound together in ways that are invisible to the eye; that there is a oneness to humanity; that we achieve ourselves by sharing ourselves with and for those around us."

Self-Compassion

In 2004, I created a senior-level course on Compassionate, Nonviolent Communication. Each year I spend more and more time discussing self-compassion. We focus on dealing with regrets and turning mistakes into opportunities. We spend a lot of time on self-talk and our judgments and labels of ourselves. We touch on authenticity and integrity, compassion, and kindness. If we learn how to be more loving and compassionate with ourselves, perhaps we will extend the love and compassion almost automatically to others.

My class in Intermediate Compassionate Listening through the Compassionate Listening Project ended with ways to help ourselves when triggered. When the primary facilitator said, "Have sex," I added, "use a vibrator." Everyone laughed. Last week someone who missed the session expressed disappointment because she heard we ended with vibrators. She asked who said it, and I felt too embarrassed to admit it was me. I think my embarrassment relates to the difficulty most people have talking about intimacy with others, much less intimacy with ourselves.

For most of my life, I was not able to masturbate without thinking about the abuse. I now can listen to certain music and songs that, especially with a vibrator, allow me to make love to myself from a loving energy!

The beautiful, soul-enhancing songs I listen to include "The Prayer" with Marcilito Pomoy singing both parts of the duet himself. I learned about Mat and Savanna Shaw when they sang "The Prayer" at the beginning of the pandemic. My idea to share song files (see appendix) stemmed from these songs' healing effects. Listening to these soul-filled messages sung from the heart allows me to make love to myself and cherish myself while surrounded by loving energy.

I'm taking another workshop on compassionate listening and racism. At the end of the session last week, we were asked for one word about how we felt. I chose "gift" and said that speaking and listening from a compassionate heart is a gift, as is feeling seen and heard from a compassionate heart. These are gifts because we are gifts! We are gifts to ourselves and the world. I am beyond grateful for the many people who've been gifts to me and helped me see myself as a gift.

As I complete this "New Beginning," I realize that what I teach, UU principles, Namaste, and Ubuntu are similar and capture part of how some people keep their souls. They focus on compassion, kindness, humanity, gratitude, forgiveness, restorative justice, and social justice, which perhaps form a basis for what we need right now in the United States and in the world. We have to belong to ourselves to connect with the world, and we have to belong to the world to connect to ourselves. No one should be forced to forgive.

The fight to keep my soul has been a continuous and continuing struggle, an act of rhetoric, choosing love over and over, and making a commitment to the process. Forgiveness then becomes an act of self-care as long as it comes naturally.

Imagine a world where no one is an "Other," and where compassion for self and others flow freely. If we treat ourselves with more compassion and love, think how this might automatically change the world. Just picture a world where no one is an Other, where we cherish ourselves and others, and where we feel cherished by others by being ourselves!

Imagine a world where all living beings strive to choose love more often and fear less often. Recently, I've told people, "Namaste BIGLY, making fun of everything Trump touches being the biggest. While this is a recent expression, I have used the phrase "Love always and ALLways" for at least twenty years. So, I end this New Beginning by sending you, Precious Reader, some cyber chicken soup (or vegetable soup if you're vegetarian), HUGE virtual hugs, and my warmest wishes for good health, joy, kindness, peace, love, and laughter always and ALLways! I cherish each of you!

May we learn from this pandemic never to forget how making eye contact and hugging safely encourage people to smile and add love to our lives and the world. May we remember that everyone and everything is alive, possessing a soul, and inherently interdependent. May I love and cherish me just the way I am, and love and cherish others just the way they are. We are all one heart beating as one!

INSPIRATIONAL QUOTES

"This is how we win: not fighting what we hate, but saving what we love."

– The Last Jedi

"There are two ways to live your life. One is as though nothing is a miracle. The other is as though everything is a miracle."

– Albert Einstein, American theoretical physicist

"I swore never to be silent whenever and wherever human beings endure suffering and humiliation. . . Silence encourages the tormentor, never the tormented. Sometimes we must interfere."

– Elie Wiesel, concentration camp survivor,
quote from his 1986 Nobel Peace Prize acceptance speech.

"To be yourself in a world that is constantly trying to make you something else is the greatest accomplishment."

– Ralph Waldo Emerson,
American essayist, philosopher, and transcendentalist

"We need more light about each other. Light creates understanding, understanding creates love, love creates patience, and patience creates unity."

– Malcolm X, minister and human rights activist

"When your life is filled with the desire to see the holiness in everyday life, something magical happens: ordinary life becomes extraordinary, and the very process of life begins to nourish your soul."

– Rabbi Harold Kushner, Rabbi Laureate, author of ***When Bad Things Happen to Good People***

"If only there were evil people somewhere insidiously committing evil deeds, and it were necessary only to separate them . . . . But the line dividing good and evil cuts through the heart of every human being. And who is willing to destroy a piece of his own heart?"

– Aleksandr Solzhenitsyn, Russian writer

"If I can stop one heart from breaking, I shall not live in vain."
–Emily Dickinson, American poet

"I live in a world that doesn't exist yet."
– Jim Scott, American folksinger,
quoting an African American man

"We are all connected; to each other biologically, to the earth chemically, to the rest of the world atomically."
– Neil deGrasse Tyson American astrophysicist

"The word 'listen' contains the same letters as the word silent."
– Alfred Brendel, Austrian pianist and poet

"There's no one alive who is you-er than you." – Dr. Seuss

"He drew a circle that shut me out – Heretic, rebel, a thing to flout. But love and I had the wit to win: We drew a circle and took him in."
– Edwin Markham

"It's a magical world, Hobbes . . . Let's go exploring." – Calvin

An Afterword: A Plea to the World

Some people will consider me crazy but I continue to have many deep and meaningful dialogues with God, Soul, Divine Energy! Even their assurances are not 100% because we each have choice—the very meaning of rhetoric!

My struggle today with the Divine has been over accepting myself as a hero to others, seeing myself as a "Bright Colors Angel" or "Bright Star." I've promised to work on this while others deal with the sufferings and horrors. The personal and the planetary are one!

Just as one cannot prove a negative, even the Divine cannot prove there's no bottom. Only WE can do that!

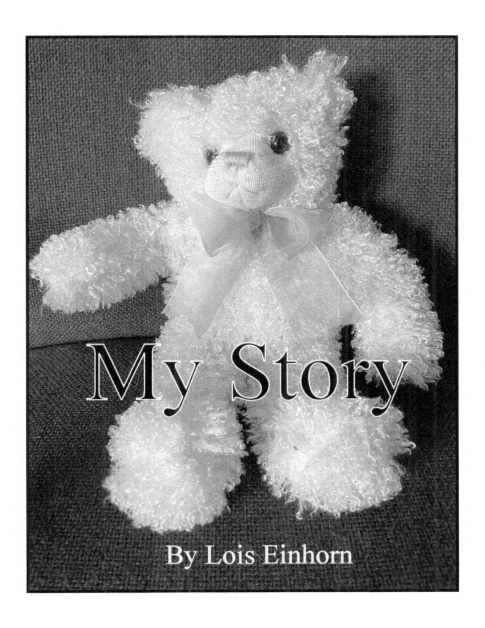

My Story

By Lois Einhorn

MY STORY

Since September 11, I am more convinced than ever of the relationship between the personal and the planetary: personal suffering AND healing touch the collective wound and heart of humanity. I do not think we are going to end terrorism until we end violence in all its forms—racism, hate crimes, sweatshop labor, child abuse, domestic violence, abuse of the Earth—the list goes on and on. Specifically, I want to do my part to help end "nursery crimes and scary tales" (my words for child abuse).

I do not know a person alive who has not suffered pain. Even though everyone's pain differs, pain is pain. And at some point in their lives, almost all people grapple with the issue of forgiveness.

A few years ago I read *The Sunflower: On the Possibilities and Limits of Forgiveness*. This book by Simon Wiesenthal tells his story: While a prisoner in a concentration camp, he was brought to the bedside of a dying Nazi soldier named Karl who asked for his forgiveness. Karl expressed remorse over the heinous crimes he committed and wanted forgiveness from a Jew. Wiesenthal listened to the dying man's confession, but he chose not to forgive him. The book includes Wiesenthal's story and the responses of fifty-three distinguished people from all walks of life who answer the question Wiesenthal poses to the respondents and the reader, "What would you do?"

The Sunflower is especially interesting because most of the respondents had *not* lived in a concentration camp. Yet, they were able to relate their varied life experiences to the question of forgiveness. The book is also thought provoking because readers cannot agree with all the responses—they are inherently contradictory.

Wiesenthal's book haunts me and has prompted me to create this book. I do not mean for my story to take away from the horrors of a government-sponsored plan of genocide. Through techniques similar to those used in Nazi concentration camps, my parents (now deceased) physically and sexually abused me. They forced me to torture my sister (and her me) and to abuse and destroy live animals and teddy bears whom I considered to be my babies.

All my life I have felt agonizing anguish because I acquiesced, complied, succumbed to my parents' power. I participated in unforgivable acts.

Like Wiesenthal, I ask my readers: **"What would YOU do? You are a child in a family that sadistically abuses. You are forced to torture and destroy. What should you do *now* as an adult? Do you forgive your parents? HOW do you forgive yourself?"**

These questions raise a host of sub-questions. For example: At what age are children responsible for their actions? To what extent does being tortured lessen a person's accountability? In a cosmic sense, are not all people—abused and abuser—related? What relationship exists between joy and sorrow?

This book is representative of the widespread nature of child abuse in society. Statistics show that one out of every three girls and one out of every seven boys are sexually abused by the age of eighteen. Between five hundred thousand and one million children are used in prostitution and pornography in this country alone. Add to these numbers all physically and emotionally abused children and all starving and neglected children, and we see that my experience is not so rare.

This story was difficult to write (and will be difficult to read), but nonetheless it is a story that needs to be told. I must warn the reader: The next five pages, especially, contain material that is tormenting, painful, gut-wrenching, and at times, seemingly unendurable. Bear with me; I promise I will not leave you in this state.

Also remember, after my story you will read many responses to my questions from people from all walks of life. And after these reaction pieces, I provide an Afterword. I will give you here a sneak preview: I believe that love, laughter, faith, and beauty are ultimate healers. Therefore, this book is ultimately not only about survival, but also about renewal, hope, empowerment, and love.

A Typical Abuse Day

Let me describe a typical abuse day. This day could have happened at age five or at age fifteen. Abuse rarely occurred on school days, but could happen on any weekend or holiday. I never knew which weekends or holidays would become a time for abuse. So the end of every week became a time of terror. My parents set up rituals that occurred time and time again from as young as I can remember until I went away to college at age seventeen.

I wake up and tremble in bed. I tell my body to be still as I pretend to be asleep. My father comes in and says good morning to my sister and me. "Tushi up time begins in five minutes." I quickly jump out of bed, take off my nightgown, put on a blouse, and get into position. I continue getting ready for the day while crawling around the house on all fours, stripped from the waist down. My sister is doing the same. I comb my hair, make my bed, and brush my teeth. My father comes in as I am brushing my teeth, and whacks me with a black strap because I am out of position; I cannot reach the sink while on all fours.

For the rest of the day, I endure ongoing pain and constant terror. I don't know what I've done wrong, but I know "it" is my fault. My parents have told me, and I believe that they are wonderful parents to put up with such a horrible daughter. I keep thanking them for their mercy, telling them in rhyme as they instruct me, "Any other parent would beat me until I'm dead. But you're being so nice and just spanking my little tushi until it's beet red."

My father puts a wire coat hanger in my "tushi" and another one in my "front" (my parents' name for my vagina). Sometimes during the day if I get out of tushi-up position, my father or mother touches the coat hanger with something that electrically shocks me.

I continually face "choices" as my parents ask me unanswerable questions: "Do you want to be hit or hit your sister?" Do you want to have darts thrown at your front or throw them at your sister's front?" "Do you want to have a wire hanger put in you or cut off this cat's ears?"

I choose. I participate. I spend the entire day crawling around on all fours in tushi-up position. From this vantage point, I must choose what to put on my sister and then do it—urine, shit, vomit, the remains of a doll she once loved. My parents hit me because I don't put the things on my sister quickly enough.

Throughout the day we play "games." Through being hit with a switch, we play, "How high can we make my little tushi jump?" My father, mother, and sister each take turns and keep score. If my sister loses, she is hit further. Another game: By hitting, "How red can we make my sister's little tushi?" I participate along with my father and mother. Again, if I lose, I am hit further. My sister and I hit each other while bare-assed in tushi-up position. My father stands behind us and hits us if we don't hit hard enough. My sister and I also have to cheer as my father and mother hit: "Hit her again. Hit her again. Harder. Harder." I think my parents want the words to sound like a football cheer.

My sister and I are frequently pitted against each other. We are forced to spy on each other and are rewarded for making reports. We have to make an obstacle course for each other: "Go right over this chair, go under this table," and so forth. We each create a good obstacle course. My father times each of us as we go through the other's obstacle course, being hit all along the way. If I win, I am spared some future "spanking." If I lose, I am punished further and told how stupid I am: I can't even make a good obstacle course!

My father comes in, pushes me on the bed, and puts his "front" into mine. I am happy to get out of tushi-up position, even if for just a short time. My father tells me I'm wet which, he says, means I want and like this. I don't understand. I try to stop the wetness, but to no avail. My father rocks back and forth. I feel crushed by his weight. I want to scream, but my father has told me if I make so much as a peep I will be "spanked" further.

I squeal. I have asked for further punishment, my mom says. She kicks me into the bathroom and gives me an enema with scalding hot water. As quickly as I make the shit, I have to eat it. "That's all you are," my father declares, "a worthless, little piece of shit. You are not even good enough to be a big piece of shit!"

I am hungry, but if I ask for food my parents will tell me I don't deserve it. Finally, my mother goes into the kitchen. My sister and I follow like robots. She takes out a piece of moldy bread and breaks it into small pieces. She throws each piece on the floor. My sister and I scramble on all fours to get it. If I get the bread, then my sister doesn't, and vice versa.

My mother and father often work together in hurting me: My father, for example, hits my front while my mother hits my backside. Sometimes my mother participates independently, without my father. Sometimes she watches. While my father is the primary torturer, my mother plays an active role.

Much of the day is spent waiting, always in tushi-up position. I hear my mother laughing maniacally. The day seems like an eternity—being hit, waiting in tushi-up position, making an instrument to hit my sister with, tearing apart my favorite teddy bear, waiting again in tushi-up position, having my father put his front into mine, being given an enema, putting shit on my sister, waiting in tushi-up position, eating the remains of a once-live animal. The waiting is as difficult as the torturous acts. I don't want time to think. I try to forget what is going on as fast as it is happening.

My parents threaten to strangle me. They put a rope around my neck; my mother and father each pull on an end until I choke, begging them to stop. But my pathetic pleas go unheard. My parents keep pulling on the rope. I lose consciousness.

My parents tell me that if I tell anyone or run away, they will me, kill my sister and themselves. They remind me of the time I told my first grade teacher who then told my mother. I feel chills up my spine as I recall how much pain I had to inflict on my sister for my "sin" of trying to get help.

While my sister and I are both in tushi-up position, my sister hits me with a black strap while another strap is used on her. My father hits my sister a hundred more times because, he says, my sister did not hit me hard enough. For trying to be nice, my sister is getting hurt more. When my sister faints from the pain, I want to die. I have nothing left to fight for. My insides are empty. I feel worse than worthless; I feel repulsive and despicable.

My sister is more rebellious than me. I envy her for this. Unfortunately, it does her no good. She just suffers more abuse. The only things I stand up for sometimes are not hurting my sister or live and stuffed animals. I beg my father, "Do whatever you want to me. Just don't hurt my sister." I plead. I grovel. But it rarely does any good.

To me, it seems my sister is better at being detached. I want to be like her. She seems able somehow to protect her inner core. My insides constantly feel like a bundle of tight knots. I want to be numb.

At times I ask my father to kill me. Dying would be a relief. I would not have to hurt my sister ever again. For as long as I can remember, I have felt that the lucky ones in the Holocaust were the ones who died. My father frequently threatens to kill me. But he won't kill me. He tells me I'm not good enough even for death!

An abuse day typically lasts over fourteen hours—minute after minute, hour after hour. Finally, my parents tell me to go to sleep. I lie in bed thinking: "Tomorrow might be a repeat of today or a day when I need to pretend that today never happened. I don't know." Before drifting off to sleep, I ask myself, "Has all this just been a bad dream? And I answer, "Yes," because I cannot accept that my parents are evil people.

I Know the Truth

I think I have given enough details so you, the reader, have a sense of a typical abuse day. I could go on and on with the details; I have written down almost a thousand of them.

I admit there are inaccuracies in some of the details. After all, I was a child, and sometimes my parents drugged me with pills or put drops in my eyes (similar to the kind used by eye doctors) to make everything look fuzzy. I endorse an analogy made by an expert in sadistic, ritual abuse: If you ask three people to describe a car accident, one will tell you the car was white, another will say the car was blue, and a third person will claim the car was gray. But all three people will agree that a car accident occurred.

Some people will say I have a big imagination; events like these could never have happened. Many other people will join them in the belief that, at the very least, I must be exaggerating. People cannot commit such heinous acts or get away with such heinous acts. But throughout history we have seen people do purposeful barbaric things to other people. Consider slavery, the Nazi holocaust, the genocide in Bosnia and Rwanda, and the decimation of Native People all over the world. We have witnessed the immense capacity humans have for evil, and the enormous reluctance of society to confront evil.

Why would I want to make up a past that brings me such agonizing anguish? Surely if I could imagine any childhood story about myself, I would save lives, not take them. I would triumph as a hero, not succumb to others' threats. I would be a leader, not a follower.

Why to this day do I see flashbacks, detailed pictures in vivid Technicolor and with clear sound effects? Why do hundreds of memories I have never forgotten "fit" so precisely the recovered ones? When I have returned to my childhood homes, why have I remembered scores of memories with remarkable precision? And why do some of my childhood and adult friends remember so many things now that corroborate my story, things that in isolation meant little at the time?

Even in death my parents torture me physically and emotionally. Because they almost never took me to the doctor even when, as a child, I complained of pain when having bowel movements, I have endured seven major abdominal surgeries and live with constant abdominal pain.

On an emotional level, I repeatedly have remembered, replayed, and relived what I have repressed. Sometimes my body feels like an agonizing abyss, and my life feels like a lyric without a song. But, unlike childhood, this time I am not numb. This time, I have to feel the terror, feel the horror, feel the rage, feel the pain. I have needed to go through the pain—not above it, not below it, not around it. I also grapple with unanswerable questions. For example, why did I survive? Why did God "save" me?

I need to speak up now for all the children who cannot speak. Abusive acts continue because of their unspeakable, unspoken, and seemingly unbelievable nature. My parents talked openly about the fact that the more bizarre their behaviors, the safer they were because no one would believe me if I told them about such hideous acts.

I Do Not Want to Forgive My Parents

Today I have moved beyond anger and hate. I have little bitterness and even less lust for revenge. But, still, I have no desire to forgive my parents. Many people will disapprove of this decision. We live in a society that applauds forgiveness. Several respondents in Wiesenthal's book say they hope they would have forgiven Karl if placed in the situation Wiesenthal faced. While being crucified, Jesus said, "Father, forgive them for they know not what they do." As he was dying, Gandhi forgave his assassin. Nelson Mandela forgave his abuser by inviting him to his inauguration as President of South Africa.

But I am not Jesus, Gandhi, or Mandela. And although I greatly admire all three men, I do not admire their acts of forgiveness. I think our society's encouragement of forgiveness relates to people's need to avoid dealing with pain, to deny the extent of human cruelty, and to distance ourselves from collective guilt. People often associate forgiveness with forgetting. We all frequently read or hear the message "forgive and forget" or "forget the past and move on with life."

Forgiveness is a way of putting closure on situations that I do not think should be closed. Society fosters a sense of spiritual sterility. I want to scream, shriek, screech, but instead I speak in a barely audible voice, feeling strangled by a society that values quiet. I want to cry torrential tears, but I can only weep, feeling stifled by a society that advises people to "keep a stiff upper lip." I want to consider my feelings and myself sacred, but I find this difficult to do in a plastic, polyester society where we use things and then throw them away and where people wear porcelain smiles.

How can I forgive my parents, people who tried to force me to hate myself, live in terror, and forget and/or rewrite my childhood? Am I heartless because, although I do not wish my parents any harm, I do not feel empathy for them? In order to abuse me as they did, my parents had to stop seeing me as a human being. Are there acts too horrific to ever forgive?

I can accept my past and go on without forgiving my parents. In many ways I have done this. I have earned a Ph.D. in Speech Communication and am in my twenty-seventh year of teaching at a major university. I have won five teaching awards, two on the national level. And I have published books about Helen Keller, Abraham Lincoln, and the Native American oral tradition, and am just beginning two other books.

EDITOR'S NOTE: Note that this chapter, MY STORY, is from Dr. Einhorn's 2006 edition. She is now in her forty-third year of teaching at Binghamton University.

What's the Problem?

You, the reader, may ask: "What's your problem?" My problem is that I cannot forgive myself. As a young child and teenager, at times I smothered my conscience, hardened my heart, deadened my humanity, and numbed my compassion. I feel crushing guilt, shame, and embarrassment for complying with my parents.

How do I honor my grief and pain and forgive myself? I can be professionally successful, but how do I deal with personal shame?

My Friends Tell Me I Am Innocent

The few people I have shared my past with do not see me as morally responsible for the acts my parents forced me to commit. But these people know me; they know the way I have chosen to live my life. They are not considering the philosophical, psychological, political, and moral implications of forgiving me.

These friends tell me I was only a child. Do we hold children accountable for nothing? What of the twelve-year-old in Germany who turned in his parents? What of Karl in Wiesenthal's book, who as a child joined the SS against the wishes of his parents? Are these children responsible? At what age are children morally responsible for their choices and actions?

Further, I did these things into my teenage years. "Yes," my friends say, "but you were still *emotionally* a young child." Weren't my parents also emotionally young? Aren't all child abusers and criminals of any sort emotionally young children?

I would hope that if I faced even one similar experience today, I would tell the abusers to kill me, and if they did not, I would kill myself. To me, the worst crime a person can commit is torture; the second worst crime is murder. In the first decade and a half of my life, I participated in both crimes more times than I can count.

My friends say my parents never got my soul. Usually I felt repulsed by what my parents forced me to do. But at times I felt indifferent; at times my parents broke my spirit. And does it even matter whether people torture and kill with pleasure, indifference, or horror in their heart? The hurt are hurt. The dead are dead.

"But," my friends continue, "you feel remorse." Does this mean we should forgive everyone who feels remorse? Wiesenthal did not forgive

73

Karl even though Karl felt remorse. Like many Jewish people, I cannot forgive the Nazis, even those who felt remorse.

My friends point out that I have not abused anyone since I went away to college at age seventeen. I cannot give myself credit, however, for not abusing as an adult. There was never any choice. I could never willingly abuse. I give myself credit for not becoming an alcoholic or a drug addict. I consciously made these choices. But I could never willingly hurt a person or animal. And does this even matter? I feel like I could be Mother Teresa for the rest of my life. It would not make up for all the horrible things I complied in doing.

Where Do We Draw the Line?

The bottom-line issue seems to be one of choice. I possessed little choice. Running away was not an option. My father said if I ran away or told someone again (as I had told my teacher), he would find me and kill not only me, but also my sister and mother. Similarly, my father threatened my mother: If she told anyone, my father would kill the three of us – and then himself. So I had little choice, and my mother had little choice. But did my father really have a choice? Does anyone really have free choice? My parents brainwashed and programmed me. But probably they also were brainwashed, conditioned, duped. I am almost certain both were abused as children in severe and sadistic ways. My parents seemed to experience immense inner turmoil. When I was about ten years old, I remember my mother with a razor in her hand threatening to slice her wrist. On several occasions, both my parents talked about their need to suffer and the enormous guilt they felt because, even though they were Jewish, they did not believe the horrors of the Holocaust when they first learned about them. But do these or other circumstances lessen people's accountability?

I never knew when my parents would act sadistically. Not just sometimes, but *most* of the time, they were nice, supportive, loving, and nurturing, making it hard for me to believe they could be so cruel, so sadistic, so mean, and so hateful. I think it might have been easier if they had always acted in evil ways.

Threats and turmoil are sometimes related to torture. What is one allowed to do to survive? What acts can people do when threatened with torture? When actually tortured? Are otherwise unconscionable acts always condonable if one is being tortured?

Given my spiritual beliefs, how do I separate forgiving myself from forgiving my parents? I consider all life forms to be connected and one at the deepest, most intimate level. Am I not one, then, with my parents? Can we separate the abused from the abuser? Are we not all children of the same God? Can I forgive myself while not forgiving my parents?

I agree with the Bible's words, "You shall know the truth, and the truth shall set you free." The truth has liberated me, but the truth cannot forgive me. The truth cannot undo all the pain I have inflicted on my sister. The truth cannot bring back the animals I have been forced to maim and destroy.

The Holiness of Life

The path from degradation to self-respect is arduous. The path from slavery to freedom is agonizing. From these paths I could learn callousness, insensitivity, and indifference. But these are not the lessons I am learning. As I heal, part of me is more convinced than ever of the holiness of each life—whether it be the life of a person, an animal, or a tree.

Trees and other aspects of nature were among my first childhood friends. My tree friends were safe because my parents never knew I loved them; I found security through their beauty. If I was tied to a tree, I became friends with the tree. Instead of being tied, I tried to feel hugged by the tree. My nature friends helped me find inner reserves of strength.

I struggle to accept my whole self, scars and all. I notice the words *heal*, *holy*, *whole*, *holistic*, and *hallow* have the same etymological root. I try to think holistically, heal, hallow myself, and consider myself holy. I work on allowing myself to be me—authentic, real, and spontaneous. It has taken me years to feel blessed to be alive, blessed to be me, and blessed to be able to feel. I want to really love and like myself. I want always to answer, "Yes," to the Congolese proverb, "The teeth are smiling but is the heart?"

My overwhelming grief and loss have taught me about the fragility of life. If I were not vulnerable to intense pain, would I also not be open to amazing experiences of bliss?

The Relationship between Joy and Sorrow

Throughout my childhood, my emotional touchstones became my emotional tombstones. For the first seventeen years of life, my parents forced me to destroy who and what I loved. My love was toxic: If I did not love an animal, it was not hurt. If I loved it, it was hurt. Why could I not stop loving? To this day, I ask myself this question.

My childhood was a time of silent sorrow. I often anesthetized myself, making myself into a frozen corpse. Sometimes I cut myself off from my feelings, pretending the torture was not happening. But I can no longer suppress and repress these oppressive experiences. Rather than numb myself, I need to stretch out and open up, allowing myself to be vulnerable.

I have experienced profound pain in my life, and I mourn all my losses deeply. But, as I heal, I realize I also have experienced profound love and joy. To what extent is my ability to feel love and joy carved out of and deepened by my suffering? Do joy and sorrow exist in direct proportion to each other? Perhaps people cannot experience true compassion, joy, peace, and love until they walk hand in hand with the pain, suffering, anguish, and despair of the Earth and the Earth's inhabitants. Perhaps my embracing the Earth with its sufferings and sorrows is what has allowed me to appreciate the Earth's beauty, mystery, and magic.

A New Family

I am blessed today with a new family, including a Daddy who adopted two "sisters" and me in a Native American ceremony. I have chosen each member of my new family as they have chosen me. Our relationships are based on love, not blood. With my birth family, love felt obligatory. It existed, but only in superficial ways. With my new family, love feels real. As I heal, my loving relationships have become more intense. Intimacy, joy, and even sublime moments of transcendence characterize my close relationships. Today I feel connected to each member of my new family on a deep, soul, spiritual level.

Evil people can do many things, but they cannot erase memories or break bonds of love. Am I able to love today because I never lost the capacity to love? Is loving a choice? Could I have stopped loving? Could I have lost the ability to love as a child and regained it as an adult?

Reclaiming My Life

As a child, I struggled to have a voice, not to be muted. Now I have a voice, but I struggle to find an audience, people who care, people who believe that seemingly unbelievable horror does occur and that intense feelings and severe suffering (of all sorts) need outlets for expression. I write in search of people who want to learn from history, people who want to make the world better for the next generation.

I will continue to fight so the horrors of my past do not continue to haunt me. I dream of the day when no one will participate (as abused or abuser) in "nursery crimes and scary tales" and when all children everywhere will be loved, nurtured, and cherished—as all children ought to be.

Through this book I hope other survivors of all types of abuse will receive the same help I do, and thereby feel empowered, love themselves, reclaim their lives, and celebrate living. For me the question of what other people would do is not just an intellectual exercise.

And so I ask you, the reader, the same questions I have asked several distinguished people. **"What would YOU do? You are a child in a family that sadistically abuses. You are forced to torture and destroy. What should you do *now* as an adult? Do you forgive your parents? HOW do you forgive yourself?"**

53

CONTRIBUTORS

RESPOND

A BRIEF INTRODUCTION
TO THE 53 RESPONDERS

1. Mumia Abu-Jamal, M.A.,– journalist, militant, author of *Live From Death Row*

2. Hunter Patch Adams, M.D.– untraditional physician, clown, author of *Gesundheit & House Calls: How to Heal the World One Visit at a Time*

3. Jeanne Adams – trauma & advocacy expert, author of *Childhood Ritual Abuse*

4. Frederic Arensberg, Ph.D.– psychologist, professor in New York City

5. Edward Asner – actor, producer, and activist, best known as "Lou Grant"

6. P.M.H. Atwater, L. H. D.– intuitive counselor, near-death researcher, *Coming Back to Life*

7. Rev. Bernard J. Bush – campus minister, theology teacher, works with troubled clergy

8. Rubin "Hurricane" Carter – boxer falsely accused of murder, movie "The Hurricane"

9. Zeqi Chen – Einhorn's undergraduate student, interested in English and law

10. Suzanne Daughton, Ph.D.– professor of communication, Einhorn's former student

11. Laura Davis – a leader in healing from abuse, co-author of *The Courage to Heal*

12. Thomas Eagleton – former U.S. Senator, Vice-Presidential nominee, author

13. Albert Ellis, Ph.D. – psychotherapist, author, founder of Rational-Emotive Therapy

14. Paul Ferrini – author (Christ mind, love, forgiveness), poet, mystic, visionary

15. Lynne Finney, J.D., M.S.W. – author, professor, lawyer, psychotherapist, healer, diplomat

16. Russell Friedman – helped 50,000+ grievers heal & forgive, author

17. Arun Gandhi – Mahatma Gandhi's grandson, receiver of many peace awards, author

18. Aba Gayle – daughter brutally murdered, befriended the murderer

19. Jack Gilroy – author, peace activist, and vocal critic of the Establishment

20. Bishop Thomas J. Gumbleton – recipient of 35+ awards for humanitarian causes

21. Anne Herman – peace activist, an expert in poverty law, advocate

22. Linda Hogan – one of the most awarded and influential Native American writers/activists

23. Rabbi Steven L. Jacobs – professor, author, son of a Holocaust survivor

24. Derrick Jensen – award-winning writer, activist, visionary, survivor of child abuse

25. Bill T. Jones – award-winning New York City dancer & choreographer

26. Scott Kalechstein Grace – humorous folksinger, songwriter, Dr. Seuss-lover

27. Mary Elizabeth King, Ph.D. – international diplomat, author, peace activist, professor

28. Barb Kohn. Ph.D. – limps because of severe & sadistic abuse, business vice-president

29. Ellen Lacter, Ph.D. – psychologist, advocate, trauma disorders expert, children & adults

30. Sammy Lee, M.D .– Olympic gold medalist, in US Hall of Fame, retired surgeon

31. Eric Loeb, Ed.D. – the psychologist who most helped Lois uncover abuse, her adopted "Daddy"

32. Rev. Dr. Richard P. Lord – minister, an expert on the victims of traumas

33. Cleone Lyvonne Reed, M.S.E. – editor, graphic designer, former therapist of abuse victims

34. Dale McCulley – retired writer/producer of 12+ films on child abuse, author

35. Robert Muller – U.N. Chancellor in Costa Rica, co-founder of the United Nations

36. Bill Pelke – Grandma murdered, *Journey of Hope*, crusades against the death penalty

37. Robert Plath, J.D. – attorney, Founder/Director of the World Forgiveness Alliance

38. Daniel Quinn – esteemed author of *Ishmael* and other books

39. Billy Ray Riggs – ex-ghetto king & drug dealer, was Lois's pen pal whom she visited once on death row at San Quentin

40. Robert Scaer, M.D. – neurologist, director of Pain & Trauma Recovery Center, author

41. Pete Seeger – beloved folksinger, award winner, environmentalist, social activist

42. Bernard S. Siegel, M.D., – physician, teacher, author of *Love, Medicine, & Miracles* and many others

43. Tamarack Song – Founder of the Teaching Drum Outdoor School, author, counselor

44. Oswaldo Soriano – prisoner on death row

45. Gerry Spence, J.D. – a "country" lawyer, author

46. Walter Starcke – author, speaker, metaphysician, former Broadway director

47. Mike Thaler – author of 180+ children's books, America's "Riddle King"

48. Susan Thornton, Ph.D. – professor, *On Broken Glass: Loving & Losing John Gardner*

49. Richard Vatz, Ph.D. – professor, author, media consultant, political commentator

50. Kurt Waldheim – past President of Austria and past Secretary-General of the U.N.

51. Ken Wapnick – teacher, author, Co-Founder of Foundation for *A Course in Miracles*

52. Gloria Wendroff – author, founder of *HeavenLetters, Love Letters from God*

53. Everett L. Worthington, Jr., Ph.D. – psychology professor, author, forgiveness specialist

1. Mumia Abu-Jamal, M.A.

Mumia Abu-Jamal, M.A., was an activist and award-winning journalist with the Black Panther Party when put on death row in 1982 for allegedly killing a police officer. Since being imprisoned, a movement accusing the FBI of fabricating the case and seeking Mumia's release has garnered support throughout the world. Paris, France has given him the title of Honorary Citizen. This African-American militant is now an author; his writings include *Live from Death Row, All Things Censored,* and *We Want Freedom: A Life in the Black Panther Party.*

* * * * * * *

What would YOU do?" It must be said, initially, that there is something quite presumptuous of us who even try to answer the question. For, if we are honest, we would reply, without shame or fear, "I don't know." For, how could we, who have presumptively not had those kinds of early-formative-years experiences, know what we would do?

We do not.

For we look back over the springtime of our lives into the sunlit dawn of memory, when the adults were giants, huge, distended beings, but not ogres, not monsters. Beings of love, comfort, hugs, kisses, who treasured their little ones like we.

Our very answers then, are formed amidst that backdrop, that look at the horror of what Dr. Einhorn calls, rightly so, "nursery crimes and scary tales", and shudder.

How we think is, of course, a function of how we have lived in this world of memory and sensation.

There is, therefore, a tendency for us to say: "Yes. Of course I would forgive Mother or Father!" — For the very notion of Mama or Pops is composed of the kind stuff of memory.

There is also the very real recognition that people who do such a thing to their child is a damaged person and were, perhaps, damaged in their youth.

Knowing that one's parent was damaged in youth may mitigate the anger and resentment one justly feels against one's abusive parent. But even this seems an evasion.

Could one forgive such acts designed not just to harm or humiliate children, but also to do so over such extended lengths of time, to actually warp them and destroy their sense of self? I think not.

No being has the inherent right to destroy another, except perhaps in self-defense; and this is especially so in the context of parent/child relationships. A parent may earn compassion, but s/he can never demand nor expect forgiveness for such violence against the young-one's own young!

It is interesting that such a question arises in the midst of a major scandal hitting the Catholic Church. The similarities are more than obvious: the unequal and deep power differentials between child and parent, and/or between penitent and priest.

In such an instance, hasn't the temporal and spiritual "parent" betrayed the trust of the young, the believer? A child so betrayed may, in adulthood, choose to forgive that betrayal, but no one has the right to petition for, demand, or insist on such forgiveness. For the child is involved in a soul-destroying power relation, one not of their own making.

Love may hear this breach, but love may also be irreparably maimed.

2. Hunter "Patch" Adams, M.D.

Dr. "Patch" Adams (1945 to present) is an untraditional physician who founded the Gesundheit Institute, a holistic medical community. Patients pay no money, physicians carry no malpractice insurance, and doctors and clients have a relationship marked by friendship, trust, equality, laughter, and love.

In addition to being a doctor, Adams is a professional clown, citizen diplomat, author, and social activist. His book, *Gesundheit: Good Health Is a Laughing Matter*, was the basis for the movie and video "Patch Adams" which have made his name a household word. He also wrote the superb book, *House Calls: How We Can Heal the World One Visit at a Time*. Dr. Adams has dedicated his life to bringing fun and friendship, laughter and love into both the health care system and the world.

* * * * * * *

You ask important and complicated questions. I spend much of my life—I'm primarily a political activist—in the issues of forgiveness and in how to make a world that would not produce people like your parents. I ached when I read your story. I know it's true because I've heard and read many like it and am very connected to the heinous crimes and genocides of the past 100 years. I've also taken clowns into wars and refugee camps and have touched many forms of human horror.

In reading what you say of yourself, I get the feeling that forgiveness is a stumbling block to your being freed of your past. I don't get the impression that you're fully ready to give up the pain.

> "To mourn a mischief that is past and gone,
> is next way to draw new mischief on."
> – Shakespeare, *Othello*

Yes, loving is a CHOICE. To my knowledge, no elementary, middle, high school, or college teaches loving. So it's no wonder that most of my patients in 35 years have not had loving skills, and even if they did, they weren't very articulate about them. You can lose (or lay dormant) your loving and regain it—IF you choose a life of intention. We CAN make a society that does not engage in violence. I can make MYSELF not be violent.

85

I think the most experimented, intelligent, and courageous set of the twentieth century was South Africa's Truth and Reconciliation Commission (see Bishop Tutu's *No Future Without Forgiveness*). The blacks of South Africa could not have been more humiliated and abused and had every "right" by modern standards to enact revenge on the white population. But instead, the Truth and Reconciliation Commission was a beacon of the love strategy, turning a world so clearly worshipping money and power over to one worshipping compassion and generosity.

I disagree with you that we live in a climate of forgiveness. I don't see any models. Even the pathetic President George W. Bush says that part of the reason he wants to kill Iraqi people is to avenge their attack on his father. Love and forgiveness are words palled back and forth everywhere without any action to back them up. The U.S. climate has been the celebration of revenge with 2001 spending the first half of the year concerned with revenge on Timothy McVeigh (who wanted revenge on Waco) and the last third of the year celebrating a revenge for 9/11 (which was a revenge on the terrorism of U.S. foreign policy). I never heard of any talk of forgiveness or quest for a love strategy to end violence and injustice. I see no meaningful teaching of love and compassion in our society.

I ache that your speaking up at school did not lead to solutions. I feel we need to make schools holy places, quadrupling teacher salaries— really creating an atmosphere where love is everywhere and opening our lives to an environment of love is the rule.

Lois, I invite you to go easy in forgiving yourself. You acted to preserve yourself. You were tortured—you cannot evaluate your behavior in that context. It's unfair. I forgive you. You do the right thing by studying it—presenting it, and I hope calling for a society to create ways of preventing it. Let it be common knowledge everywhere in school and in all of society that all such actions need to be reported, listened to, and believed.

Lois, I want you to take a good look at what you have done, given this past, and have a tidal wave of gratitude that you did not turn out like Charles Manson. You've done great. YOU are responsible for having done great. What happened to you was horrible and should never happen again. This is the task—to make a loving world.

So as an adult—become an activist for peace, justice, and caring. Forgive so you are clean and ready to be that instrument. Your parents were the products of systems that allowed them to be demons. Attack the system and forgive those who were so damaged by the system that all they could do was inflict horror. The system I speak of includes the government, those who own our governmental leaders, and a media that gloats of terrors and finds nothing newsworthy about love. The transnational corporations and their consequences are also the system. Put your energy into making love a value rather than perpetuating the sweetness of revenge. There is *no* future without forgiveness. Feel the pioneering nature of this truth.

How do you forgive yourself? Lois, you tried to find help at school. Your horror at what you did is proof that you can be free from guilt. What you've done with your life—once free of the torture—is remarkable. Given what you could be, you got off extremely lucky. Feel gratitude and make the world loving.

> "The robbed, who smiles, steals something from the thief."
> – Shakespeare, *Othello*

3. Jeanne Adams

Jeanne Adams is the founder of Mr. Light & Associates, Inc., a non-profit organization that advocates for survivors of severe childhood trauma and educates professionals on the issues that surround childhood ritual abuse. An expert in ritual trauma and victim advocacy, she is the author of two books: *Childhood Ritual Abuse: A Resource Manual for Criminal Justice and Social Service* and *Drawn Swords: My Journey through Childhood Ritual Abuse.*

* * * * * * *

Lois, thank you for sending me your story and questions. I was saddened as I read the account of your childhood. I have heard of similar stories. They are heartbreaking, each and every one. Your questions are important ones, questions that require thought from ALL people. Below I share what I have learned from my own professional and personal experiences.

In my professional life, I have worked as a victim's advocate in several capacities. I began by organizing a chapter of MADD, Mothers Against Drunk Driving. It was back in the 1980's, early in the victim's right movement, and I felt compelled to jump into the fray. In my MADD career, I assisted victims in more than seventy criminal cases, giving them a voice in a criminal justice system that was reluctant to hear them. More recently, I have founded a non-profit organization that advocates for the survivors of severe childhood trauma.

Although it was my job in MADD to educate and assist victims as they went through their legal cases, I learned a great deal from them as well. Their emotions were raw. The crashes that brought them to my office had been sudden and violent. When a death had occurred, family members came to me in extreme distress. Their cases were frequently lengthy, spreading out over months and even years, so I had the opportunity to watch these victims work through the stages of grief.

The grief cycle would begin with numbness, shock at the loss of a loved one and then it often moved into an anger stage. After a number of months, the anger would melt into depression. Gradually the depression would lift and there would be some sense of acceptance. Occasionally a victim would get stuck in a stage and have difficulty moving forward. Anger was the most noticeable. Perpetually angry people have a tendency to spew that anger onto anyone in their paths. Instead of getting support from others, their anger keeps everyone away.

Why do I tell you this? **Because it is the victim's job to heal.** Although others can offer loving support, it is the victim who must go through the stages, feel those awful feelings and work through them. Victims of drunk driving crashes deal with their grief immediately. The dynamics differ somewhat in child abuse cases. Without intervention, many child abuse victims suffer from long-term trauma and cannot face what has happened to them until they are adults, safely away from their dysfunctional childhood environments. Nevertheless, they must also work through the stages of grief in order to heal.

I found my voice when I worked in MADD. Although I did not have a loved one injured or killed by a drunk driver, I identified with the victims and felt empowered as I spoke out on their behalf. Eventually I had to work through my own victim issues. Like you, Lois, I was sadistically abused as a child. My father involved me in incest, child prostitution, child pornography and ritualistic abuse. My mother, a victim herself, turned her wrath upon me to vent her alcoholic rages. It was a childhood I wouldn't have wished on anyone.

It has been my job to heal from my childhood abuse. I have had to recognize the events and acknowledge their reality. I've had to feel the traumatic emotions – the numbness, rage and sadness – and find my way through them. Along the way, I have also realized that healing is a journey and not an event. The abuse has left me with a dissociative disorder, but I am learning to live within those limitations. Today I am more physically and emotionally healthy than I have ever been in my life.

My parents died many years ago. There were never any confrontations or acknowledgements of violence; I did my best just to get away from them. More recently I have traced some of their friends who were involved the abuse. A few of them are still living. I am not interested in altercations with the elderly. I do not wish to switch roles and appear as the perpetrator, creating scenes and squabbles by confronting the old and frail. Nevertheless, I must wrestle with the issue of forgiveness. Should I forgive them?

For the most part, I think I have already forgiven them. In my mind, forgiving is letting go. It is working through the grief and not being stuck in the anger or depression. I admire the kind of person who deals with life, learns from both the good and bad, and then moves on to new experiences. Years from now, I want to be an eccentric old woman known for her kindness and humor rather than a curmudgeon holding onto a lifetime of grudges and anger. I want to let go of the pain. I want to be the kind of person who forgives.

While I can forgive, I have no intention of forgetting. Child abuse is not a minor infraction that can be forgiven and forgotten with a handshake. It is a cruelty that has been carried down from generation to generation. As a society, we must bring it out of its secret places, acknowledge that it exists and determine ways to prevent and intervene on behalf of all our children. I will honor my parents for those things they did that were honorable, but I will also speak out regarding their deviant behaviors. Let this abuse stop with my generation.

Unfortunately, it is easier to forgive my parents than it is to forgive myself. Like you, Lois, I was also forced to torture and destroy. I was a child coerced by adults. I obeyed and then absorbed all the guilt and shame. As an adult I have recognized the dynamics and can logically absolve myself of blame. If I had been given a free choice, I wouldn't have been there at all! It is much more difficult to rid myself of lifetime's worth of loathing and self-hatred. How do I learn to like myself and rise above the mire?

Healing appears to be the key. Each day is a new experience. I strive to make choices that will bring me closer to the light and further away from darkness. I am reaching out to other trauma survivors and sharing that light. We are gathering together and making plans to educate the public and do what we can to protect future generations of children. We are determined in our work, but our meetings are also sparked with laughter. We are healing each other and ourselves. Each day the pain is lessened. Joy is a new emotion for me. When I feel it, it startles me and I burst into tears. It has been a slow process, but gradually I am recovering from my past. My intent to forgive has been enough.

4. Frederic Arensberg, Ph.D.

Dr. Frederic Arensberg is currently in full time private practice as a psychologist in New York City. He is also senior supervisor, faculty, and training analyst at the Postgraduate Center and at the Training Institute in New York City.

Dr. Arensberg received his doctorate degree in Clinical Psychology at Aldephi University in 1964. He received his certificates in Psychoanalysis, Psychoanalysis in Groups, and Psychoanalytic Supervision at the Post Graduate Center for Mental Health in New York City. He was supervised for four years by Dr. Heinz Kahut.

* * * * * * *

As a child, I believe you had no choice but to do what you did. I have no question that I would have done the same. No one has the right to question the inevitability of your actions, and I identify with you as best as I can, never having gone through that degree of torture. Your guilt is understandable, since society trains us *not* to have violent or retaliative thoughts and actions.

I hate what was done to you, and I hate the people responsible. I have no interest in understanding their motives (although there are always psychological explanations). They tried to destroy your humanness, integrity, and soul; they obviously failed since today you clearly maintain your courage, morality, intelligence, and spirituality. It is sad that in addition to what was directly done to you, you are also burdened by this inevitable but irrational guilt; it is a double whammy.

I could never forgive the sadistic torturers, nor would I want to do so. Instead, spend your psychological energy trying to understand and forgive yourself (not them). I have been called selfish or narcissistic, but I am unforgiving of those who have intentionally hurt me. They don't deserve the forgiveness, and to do that would be hurting myself (repeating the same crime that was done to me).

5. Edward Asner

Edward Asner (1929 to present) is an actor, producer, and activist. He is best known as Lou Grant, a gruff man on the exterior with a heart of gold inside, on the television series "Mary Tyler Moore" (1970–1977) and "Lou Grant" (1977–1982). Asner has won seven Emmy Awards, more than any other male actor. In addition, he has won 5 Golden Globe Awards and 2 Screen Actors Guild Awards including the prestigious Lifetime Achievement Award (2002) for his career as a dramatic and comic actor and his humanitarian accomplishments. In announcing the award, then Guild President William Daniels praised Asner: "His passion for social and political causes has been consistently underscored by deeds as well as words. We commend his lifelong accomplishments as a superbly versatile actor and a dedicated advocate for human rights, world peace, environmental preservation, and political freedom."

Asner has earned several other honors for his humanitarian efforts including the Organized Labor Publications Humanitarian Award, the Anne Frank Human Rights Award, and the Eleanor Roosevelt Val-Kill Medal.

* * * * * * *

I am totally awestruck by the account you have sent me; one can read and reread of barbarities perpetrated on children, but never actually comprehend them. I can remember soon after I came to California in 1961, I heard about a boy not much older than five, maybe seven. Either his father or his stepfather beat him to death, and as he lay dying from his wounds, he was quoted as saying, "I love you, Daddy." The story has stayed with me ever since . . . the rage I felt, the disbelief I felt, and finally the realization how with nobody to cling to, a child is lost.

When you ask, "What would I do," I stare in amazement at how *you* have done! Your unbelievable actual accomplishments—physical and emotional! Your list that goes on and on makes me wonder if such a horrible past created this drive on your part. I've often been quoted (being Jewish and experiencing some small discrimination in my life) that a little discrimination is good for you – sharpens and hones you. I cannot begin to comprehend the degree to which you have been honed and improved, and yet your guilt haunts you.

It is amazing that a child forced to do what you and your sister had to do to survive—to kill animals, to barbarize each other—is unbelievable to me. That you should feel guilt is unnecessary. You ask at what age children are responsible for their actions. Childhood encompasses such a broad spectrum. I just saw an account of three-year-old African children herding cattle and being responsible for their cattle and their actions. But taking responsibility for actions *forced* upon them by adults? Never!

These are phenomenal questions you ask. To what extent does a person being tortured lessen a person's accountability? Enormously! The woods are filled with stories of those forced to kill and bestialize. I cannot begin to count the number of concentration camp survivors I have come across who merely shake their head and say you will never know, never know. Having been forced to commit and perform acts that they will carry as stigma all their lives and yet they continue to go on living, creating, and serving. So are the abuser and abused related? I think they form a unity, a relationship between relief and sorrow.

You ask why to this day that you see flashbacks, memories with remarkable precision, undoubtedly seared, burned upon your brain. Your father couldn't have done a better job with a red, hot poker. How diabolical to constantly ask the question, "How do you wish to be tortured?" I don't even think Heydrich did that to his victims. It was awesome; it is horrible beyond words.

Why did you survive? You live now because you are undoubtedly a wonderful, phenomenal human being. Why did God save you? To make those of us lesser than you realize how much more we can survive, how much more we can suffer, if the situation required it. You have provided us a stunning and appalling example.

I am glad you don't forgive your parents. I cannot tolerate the thought of your parents without thinking how unbelievably tortured they must have been. I realize they have passed on, but of course, their spiritual presence still lives with you.

In conclusion . . . what would I do? I would do as you do and hope to survive as well as you. I hope I would not forgive my parents, or if I did, it would be for the sole purpose of healing *me*—not them. What would I do? I would stand and be proud and recognize that I was a superior being who survived to save others. If you still have guilt over your powerlessness as a child to resist evil, I simply say: "Your guilt does not belong to you. It is not yours to claim."

6. P. M. H. Atwater, L.H.D.

P. M. H. Atwater, L.H.D. is one of the original researchers in the field of near-death studies, having begun her work in 1978. Today her contribution to the field is considered one of the best. Her first two books, *Coming Back to Life* and *Beyond the Light*, are deemed "the Bibles" of the near-death experience. Using police investigative techniques as her protocol, she has specialized in original fieldwork. She has presented her findings in seven books including: *The Complete Idiot's Guide to Near-Death Experience* and *Beyond the Indigo Children: The New Children and the Coming of the Fifth World*. She is also an expert on the dying process, helping people alleviate their fear of death.

* * * * * * *

We cannot gage measures of child abuse, and not all abusers are monsters. My own childhood offers such an example. I sometimes wished for bruises and broken bones so I could point to them and say, "This is why I hurt," but nothing like that ever occurred. The abuse I lived through, the terrors of my early years, were mostly invisible, overlooked, ignored, or, according to many a scolding, "the product of my imagination." As I share bits and pieces of those times, you may notice, dear Lois, some eerie parallels to what happened to you as a child.

I was born out of wedlock during a period in our country's history when that was seen as a grievous sin. My mother was the daughter of immigrants, people who birthed enough hands to work the farm. When I was two months old, she rented a room from a Norwegian couple and placed my crib in their bedroom. I was four years old before I learned that the woman who flitted in and out of the house was my real mother. This woman showed me no love that I can recall.

As a youngster I was not allowed to ask questions, since doing so was considered a sign of stupidity. I had to find my own answers. This I did, conducting my first double-blind control group study at the age of five as a way to begin establishing the "environmental integrity" I needed to negotiate in the world around me. My sensory system was somehow different, even from my peers, and my instinct was to test this and see for myself what was true and what was not.

Pearl Harbor changed everything – people screaming and crying – rationing, long lines to buy anything, air-raid drills, hobos pounding at the door for food, gatherings at the library to roll bandages for the troops, and years of radio and newsreels about war and destruction.

So much uncertainty existed that the needs of a small child were usually brushed aside. I was sexually assaulted by an uncle, and terrified by gangs of boys who wanted to rape girls. I saw a boy have his head smashed in while teachers joked around and did nothing to stop the violence. It took most of my life to piece together the puzzling nightmare called "first grade."

That nightmare was peppered with confrontations. For instance, I often had to sit on a tall stool in front of the class, sometimes wearing a tall, conical hat that said "DUNCE" on it, as an example of a bad child who told lies – just because I was the only kid in school who could see music, hear numbers, and smell color. My sensory differences included dyslexia (not recognized then), multiple sensing (still not recognized by the educational system), vivid past-life recall, faculty extensions (e.g., I could pick up a handful of soil from anywhere, let it sift through my fingers, then accurately describe the health of the people who lived there), and other sensitivities and empathic abilities. I was repeatedly punished for telling the truth and praised only for lying. This conundrum turned my world upside down; I fled into nature for solace.

My visits to the couple who raised me were both wonderful and bittersweet. I had to behave one way in their house and quite another in my mother's house. Woe be it if I forgot whose house I was in and mixed things up. I adjusted by separating into two versions of me, one for each mother.

My perceptual abilities were a constant embarrassment. I felt shame because my mother said I was "no good" and "would never amount to a hill of beans" – reminiscent of what you faced, Lois, when your parents called you "a little piece of shit."

A series of events over a two-year period enabled me to find myself. They were triggered by a single look in the bathroom mirror where I saw a face twisted by deep rage. I remember pointing at that face and shouting, "I'm going to change you. I don't know how, but I will." That's what it takes – a particular instant when, no matter the consequences, we open wide to embrace a greater potential. Even the air changes once we do; disadvantages shift into opportunities.

I was really lucky as a child. Adversity bestowed upon me a fighting spirit and an almost unquenchable desire to seek the truth behind appearances. And I knew what love was, thanks to the Norwegian couple. I knew about love because they smothered me with it – a warm, cuddly, supportive kind of acceptance that was ever-present, freely given, and fully trustworthy. Such a love does *not* have to come from parents.

A question you ask, Lois, is how do we forgive the injustices of childhood? Once grown, I found it easier to ignore my past than to focus on forgiveness. Nobody knew, so why bother? Then I became a mother. The incredible love I felt for my own children forced me to face a deep emptiness within myself, but I wasn't certain what to do. Then, the stress of working long hours, having three kids, raising and canning my own food, baking bread, sewing clothes, hammering out toys, teaching Sunday School – and all of it needing to be done perfectly – resulted in a nervous breakdown. As despair threatened to blacken the lens of my mind, I happened upon a paperback called *The Sleeping Prophet* by Jess Stearn. The book was about Edgar Cayce, one of the most documented and accurate psychics of all time. This one book explained my entire life, my memories, my perceptions, and my differences. The Association for Research and Enlightenment, the institution that survived him, sponsored Study Groups. I joined one. The group studied, not so much Cayce, but *A Search for God.* I was never the same again. My change was dramatic. My divided self reunified.

Forgiveness was one of our topics. Here was one of our exercises: totally relax, eyes closed. On the view screen of your mind, picture the person who has hurt you the most. Picture that person clearly and in detail. As you look at that person, relive every hurt, every fear, every anger, every pain, every betrayal you ever suffered because of him or her. Leave nothing out. Feel your feelings deeply. Cry if you want. When finished, spend one full minute completely forgiving that person. Spend another full minute forgiving yourself of anything you might have done to contribute to the problem between you. For an additional minute, see the both of you together in your mind's eye and forgive you both. Relax. Do not open your eyes for a while. Let the impact of what you have just done sift through your consciousness and your heart. Be at peace.

Soon after, repeat the exercise, only this time, focus on the person who has loved you the most. In clear detail, relive all the love, the good feelings, the times pleasantly spent. Involve as many senses and feelings as possible. When finished, spend a minute giving gratitude and heartfelt thanks to that person. Spend another minute appreciating what you did to help the individual. Devote the last minute to seeing both of you together enjoying each other's company, and giving thanks. Relax. Make no attempt to move. Be in that space of joy and love for a few minutes.

After time has passed, examine what occurred during the two exercises and examine the insights. Conversing with other participants who also took part in the exercise was richly rewarding, even weeks later. Although the Study Group addressed different virtues one by one, and in a personal manner, forgiveness was a breakthrough for me. I saw "the other side" to my story and recognized the sacrifices my mother had made on my behalf. Even though I recognized this did not justify her behavior, it did enable me to give credit where credit was due.

Life goes on, doesn't it? We either learn from our trials and tribulations and improve our lot or we remain forever wounded by them.

My choice to heal and make a better life for myself was sorely challenged in 1977, when serious health traumas quite literally killed me. A miscarriage and severe hemorrhaging caused my first encounter with the grim reaper. Two days later a huge blood clot in my right thigh vein dislodged followed by the worst case of phlebitis the specialist had ever heard of, let alone seen. Two months later, my body collapsed and ceased to function. Each time I had a near-death experience, and each of these experiences was different. Afterward I had to relearn how to crawl, stand, walk, climb stairs, run, tell left from right, hear and see properly, and rebuild all my belief systems. The devastation to my body was tough enough, but having my mind stretched beyond any boundary imaginable so overwhelmed me that I became lost between worlds, unable to find my way.

A talk by a physicist on "The Eternal Now" (the theory that all aspects of time are simultaneous) showed me I could trust what I had witnessed in death; I could trust my mind.

During my third near-death experience, I reached what we in research term "the realm of all-knowing," and was one of the few who returned with full memory of the experience. Many of the revelations I was given are recorded in my book *Future Memory*. I became a researcher of near-death states because of that episode.

One of the revelations I was given is: "Forgiveness is our only protection because we become whatever it is we cannot forgive." I understand this to mean that unless we truly forgive (let go of the pain, fear, anger, and guilt we harbor), we remain attached, shackled somehow to that which torments us, and we are never able to move on in life, healed and whole. Forgiveness, then, is a willingness to surrender to A Higher Order.

Lois, it might interest you to know how I translated this revelation in regards to my mother: I stopped by her home, jumped out of my car, strode up the steps and through the front door, grabbed my mother firmly with both hands, gave her a big kiss, and told her how much I loved her. She stepped back in utter shock, unable to speak. I meant what I said, and I have reaffirmed my love for her every time we have spoken or seen each other since. The day may never come when she says the same to me, but, miracles of miracles, she is nice now and a pleasure to be with.

Without the skills I forged during the early years of my life, I could never have accomplished what I have or helped as many people. None of this would have happened, though, had I not made the initial choice to release the pain. Calling upon the power of forgiveness not only set me free, it has freed everyone else, and it now allows me to help others become free.

7. Rev. Bernard J. Bush, Ph.D.

Dr. Bernard J. Bush is campus minister at the University of San Francisco and spiritual director and teacher of Theology at the Jesuit School of Theology in Berkeley. For ten years, he served as the director of the House of Affirmation, a residential clinical center for emotionally and mentally troubled clergy and religious professionals. He also served for five years in the Diocese of Norwich (CT), helping to develop programs for clergy and church ministers on issues of spirituality, mental health, and child abuse prevention. He is presently on the staff of the Jesuit Retreat House in Los Altos, California, offering retreats, pastoral counseling, and other types of spiritual direction.

* * * * * * *

Lois, I think you should forgive your parents. Forgiveness is not contingent on the quality or quantity of the damage or suffering inflicted. It is a kind of illusion to think it is easier to forgive a so-called minor offense than to forgive something absolutely atrocious such as your abuse. The same mechanism is required in every case. If we cannot forgive in the big things, then we must questions whether our forgiveness in the small things is genuine. True forgiveness is a state of soul and an ongoing process.

Forgiveness is a decision of the will and higher powers of the soul neither to retaliate nor to hold the debt owed by the offense any longer. Forgiveness is essentially a letting go, disengagement, an unhooking from the offender. Unless there is forgiveness, the abused person stays locked in a spiritual embrace with the offender. Refusal to forgive, nursing the grudge or harboring the resentments is like dancing with a dead person. It is necessary to let it go in order to be free and healthy.

A man at a recovery meeting once said that the person who holds grudges and resentments is like the person who drinks poison and hopes the other person dies. Lack of forgiveness only hurts the holder of it. The opposite of forgiveness is not righteous anger but anger cherished and possessed, that is, held onto. That kind of anger possesses the person who holds it and is like an acid that corrodes the soul. It does not harm the object of the anger, nor does it restore justice; it simply festers like a sore that will not heal.

Whenever one person owes another something, an imbalance is created between them as long as the debt is not paid. This can happen in many ways. Economically the situation exists when one person owes another money or property. The money or property could have been borrowed or stolen. Either way the imbalance exists until the debt is paid. If someone injures another deliberately or accidentally, another kind of debt is incurred. That debt can be erased sometimes by an apology and sometimes by restitution. For example the offender can pay for the damages resulting from the injury whether spiritual, psychological or physical.

A serious psychological and spiritual problem arises when the debtor either refuses or cannot pay the debt and sometimes even will not admit it or refuse to apologize for the injury caused by him or her. In that case a permanent state of imbalance exists. The person who holds the debt is a victim of injustice, and is powerless to right the wrong.

Apart from legal redress or a lawsuit, which in most cases is only marginally effective as an instrument of justice, the person is stuck and holds the grievance which becomes a resentment with nowhere to go. This condition is humanly universal, since everyone has something to be resentful over. For some the injury is catastrophic as in your case of deliberate abuse and torture. For others it can be something as seemingly minor as being ignored by an inattentive spouse or being treated unfairly by a teacher. Everyone without exception has some wrongs in their history. Moreover, everyone has committed offenses against others in their lifetime. No one is exempt from being both a victim and a perpetrator. In religious terms, this means that we are all sinners and sinned against.

Since forgiveness is such a serious spiritual problem, it is addressed very directly in the Christian tradition. This does not mean that Christians practice it as well as they should. Many Christians tend to be as vindictive as the rest of the society and culture around them. But it is at the core of the teachings of Jesus for his disciples to follow.

Quite simply stated, Jesus teaches in the Lord's Prayer, "Forgive us our sins (trespasses, debts) as we forgive the sins (trespasses, debts) of others." That is not very sophisticated spiritually. It states that the forgiveness of our own sins is dependent upon our forgiving the sins of others. To underscore the point, after teaching the prayer, Jesus goes on immediately to say, "If you forgive others their transgressions, your heavenly Father will forgive you. But if you do not forgive others, neither will your Father forgive your transgressions."

100

Since this is such a powerful spiritual injunction, which declares that our own freedom is contingent on our freeing others, it is important to understand what forgiveness is and what it is not.

First of all forgiveness is not exoneration. That is, to forgive is not to declare that the injustice committed is not an injustice after all, or that it was right in some way for the person to have done it. This situation occurs when people "jump to forgiveness" or judge that the offence was somehow their own fault and that they deserved to be treated that way. Forgiveness depends on truth. A real injustice was committed, and it must be acknowledged. The temptation to resent must be faced directly and not avoided.

Forgiveness is simply the ability everyone has to no longer hold the person in debt. It is a letting go of the imbalance. It unhooks the other from the obligation and lets them go. For instance, if someone has stolen money from me and there is no chance that it will ever be repaid, I can forgive the debt and simply write it off and let it go.

It is a statement that the person really did owe me the money, but I am giving up the expectation that it will ever be repaid. What fuels the victim's continual unhappiness is the expectation or desire that it will be repaid and the frustrated knowledge that it will not.

Reconciliation is very different from forgiveness. Reconciliation requires two people to mutually forgive each other. It is possible to have forgiveness without reconciliation, although the possibility for reconciliation should always be kept open.

The act of forgiveness is completely within the ability of the person who holds the debt. What makes it particularly difficult to do, however, is that it goes against the grain and seems to be letting the perpetrator off the hook to go completely free and be irresponsible. In the scheme of the world and in the code of human fairness that most of us live by, that is completely true and totally unacceptable. That is why forgiveness requires help from God. It is an act of the will, a choice and decision, not a feeling. To let go of the complaint and leave it to God sometimes has to be made against powerful feelings of vengeance. Of course, it is easier to forgive when the perpetrator apologizes or makes some kind of restitution, but forgiveness does not depend on that. Jesus understood this when he told Peter, "I say to you, forgive your brother seventy times seven."

Forgiveness is a free choice very similar to the choices we make when we do not act out our feelings. It is a choice made based on a higher understanding about the necessity of peace within oneself, with others, and with God. However, since we live in an imperfect society, there are civil consequences for criminal actions. We have trials, convictions, and imprisonments. Let us keep in mind, however, that the original intent of prison was to give the convicted person time for conversion and penitence, not primarily punishment. However, morally speaking, we must leave the ultimate punishment or vindication to God.

Does the forgiveness of the debt and letting the perpetrator go, unhooking oneself from the imbalance so to speak, then mean that the debt itself goes away? No. The perpetrator of the injustice still carries the debt even if the victim forgives it. The debt continues to exist in the eyes of God, and the one who has acted unjustly must answer to God for it. In one place God declares, "Vengeance is mine..."

Since we are all in need of Divine mercy because we have all sinned, the formula for obtaining that mercy is to be merciful. The fifth Beatitude is "Blessed are the merciful, for they shall obtain mercy." Jesus also tells us that the measure we use to measure out mercy to others is the measure that will be used by God to measure mercy to us.

From the point of view of Christian spirituality, those who have suffered much unjustly and who have the most to forgive are in a position to receive greater graces from God than those who have not suffered in that way. They closely resemble Jesus who was treated unjustly and identifies with their suffering. Such suffering can cause a greatness of soul that has within it a large capacity for compassion, tenderness, and love. The valley carved out in the soul by suffering can be filled with constant seething anger, resentment, grudges, and bitterness, or it can be filled with forgiveness, understanding, and real holiness. The choice is with the person who had been offended.

What I am offering here comes directly from the Christian gospel and the teachings of Jesus. That many of the followers of Jesus do not live this way and unfortunately are as unforgiving as the culture around them does not detract from the beauty and nobility of the teaching itself.

There is greatness in the saintly people who have lived this way: Gandhi, Martin Luther King, Mother Theresa of Calcutta, St. Francis, Dorothy Day, and many others. Such holiness and nobility is within the grasp of everyone who has suffered at the hands of others. Through conversion and repentance, forgiveness is available to all the sinners of the world. That includes us all.

It is not correct to say that we "forgive ourselves." Only God can truly forgive us, so our spiritual task is to accept the forgiveness that God offers when we ask for it. We can be sorry for our misdeeds and sins and tell God in prayer or Sacrament that we are sorry for them without really knowing what the actual culpability is for any given thing we have done. God is rich in mercy and forgiveness, but is also just and demanding, "Forgive us our sins as we forgive the sins of others."

In sum, it is necessary for you to forgive your parents for your own peace and freedom.

8. Rubin "Hurricane" Carter

Rubin "Hurricane" Carter (1937 to present) was the number one contender for the World Middleweight Boxing Title when he was falsely accused and convicted of a triple murder. His autobiography, *The 16th Round: From Number 1 Contender to Number 45472*, attracted international attention including that of Bob Dylan who wrote a song called "The Hurricane." In 1983, after spending over twenty years in prison (over ten in solitary confinement) and becoming blind in one eye because of lack of proper medical attention, Carter was released. He currently is Director of the Association in Defense of the Wrongly Convicted.

* * * * * * *

Lois raises an intriguing question. Like pain is pain, suffering is suffering—whether being wrongly imprisoned, wrongly placed in a concentration camp, or wrongly abused as a child. But pain is a component of suffering; it is not suffering itself. There are no degrees of suffering.

I spent twenty years in prison, in a hellhole where every day people tried to strip me of my dignity. I did nothing to be there. I was given a triple life sentence for a crime I did not, could not, and would not commit. I did nothing to belong there. Because I refused to follow the rules, I spent ten out of my twenty years in solitary confinement—six feet underground, five slices of stale bread a day. I was stinking and starving. There was no morning, noon, or night—just different shades of darkness.

Hate took over everything. I was furious at everyone—the two lying criminals, all the people who sent me to prison, and the racist white jury who accepted the decision. All I could see was police brutality and other instances of man's inhumanity to man. All I could smell was the vile stench of shit. Simmering anger and hatred consumed me. I existed in a living hell.

Every fifteen days we were allowed to take a shower, and every thirty days we were given a physical checkup. During one of the checkups, I walked by a mirror. I saw a grotesque image. I saw the face of hatred, a monster, and that monster was me!

I realized that I was not hurting the prison wardens, and I realized that hatred and bitterness only consume the vessel that hold them.

I ask myself the questions that you, Lois, are asking: How could I forgive them? How could I forgive the people who took me away from a wife and daughter? How could I forgive the people who left a three-year-old thinking her father had abandoned her? How could I forgive all that?

I had to first forgive myself. I had to understand the conditioning. People are not born hating others or themselves. The hate of others did not need to become my hate. The guilt was imposed upon me, but I was angry enough and intelligent enough to do something about it. I had to get rid of the bitterness and anguish. They only consumed me.

I came to an understanding of who and what I am. Like Victor Frankl wrote about the concentration camps, I realized that prison provided me the tools to become all that I could be. I was able to seize the opportunity to use these horrible conditions to find something above the law. I had an opportunity to go on an anthropological expedition into an unnatural laboratory of the human spirit.

Yes, I was able to forgive the two criminals who lied, the two police officers who manufactured evidence, the misinformed and racist jury. I had to forgive because if we hate, we are mass murderers ourselves.

I attribute my becoming free to this change in my being. It's a miracle that I survived—escaped the electric chair, am somewhat sane. I look at November 8, 1983, the day I was released from prison, as the first day of my new birth.

Lois, to forgive yourself and your parents, you need to understand that you too are a machine. I am no different; you are no different. There are no saints. It's the way we were created. We are all savages on this earth. We are as much a machine as your lawn mower. Your reactions are the same as mine or anyone else's. But you have the ability to wake up. That's your salvation. Somehow, some way, you have to get over it.

Hate can only produce hate. That's why all these wars are going on, all of this insanity. There's too much anger in the United States. People are too afraid, too numbed out. We need to wipe out all this hatred, fear, distrust, and violence. We need to understand, forgive, and love.

9. Zeqi Chen

Zeqi Chen is a student at Binghamton University. She took Professor Einhorn's course on Compassionate, Nonviolent Communication via Zoom during the pandemic from China, showing her commitment to education because the course met from 2:20 to 3:20 pm which was twelve to thirteen hours the next morning in China. She is fluent in Chinese and English and plans to pursue a degree in English or law.

* * * * * * *

Hello, Professor Einhorn. I appreciate your sharing your experience and your journey in this book. I have experienced some hurts from family relationships, and I don't even want to write them in my diary because I think writing it down means I have to review it again, which is like having to uncover the scars again. It hurts; it's like torturing myself. This is why I am so grateful that you are willing to share your story with us because I know how difficult it is. I see that despite these sufferings, you are willing to teach us to forgive, teach us how to love the world, how to accept ourselves, and never hesitate to convey your love to us. I think this is a heart-like gold. So, in this response, I would like to share my stories and thoughts with you, like a genuine conversation with a friend I trust so much; take this as your sincere expression to us in return.

You ask me what I would have done if I had been the child whose family had abused me. Frankly speaking, I don't know. Because I've never experienced anything like that, and I don't think I'm qualified to use that analogy and imagine what I would do, because I haven't experienced that pain, and therefore I'm not qualified to think about it in such a safe environment.

If I were that child, I would probably be forced to torture other lives, hurt my sister, and dare not fight back because I can't even protect myself. In that situation, I can only follow the orders of my parents and endure all this to protect myself. The equal relationship between parents and children has always been pursued and yearned for. To some extent, it is an idealized state that will appear only after the development of civilization to a certain height, especially in the East, which is influenced by the conservative Confucian culture. There is an old Chinese saying that the father is the son, meaning that the son obeys the father. This concept has diminished with time and people are now more open-minded, but listening to their parents is still seen as one of the criteria for good sons and daughters. Children are vulnerable and completely powerless to refute when they are confronted with domestic and sexual abuse by their parents. So I don't think I would do any better than you when it comes to being abused and being forced to torture. Even apart from tolerating and submitting, I can only silently hope to leave such a family as soon as possible because I would feel overwhelmed by a sense of powerlessness and suffocation in this situation.

If I am a child who is too weak to have the power to protect myself, then becoming an adult means having stronger power to protect myself and even others. Weak children act passively, but as adults, they can take the initiative. At this stage, what I would do is flee, far from my abusive parents, far from the places where those dark memories were held, far from the city, far from the people who inflicted my pain. Let it all go and start a new life. Bury the pain deep underground as if it never happened, recognizing that even if you force yourself to forget, those painful memories will haunt you like demons. At some unplanned moments, the dirty words, the physical mutilation, the mental torture will break through your pretense that nothing has ever happened and cut through your heart mercilessly.

How might we seek redemption? Forgiveness is a noble word. Especially in Confucian culture, it advocates the elevated and lofty integrity of the gentleman and praises those who can overcome all hardships and finally achieve a just peace. But can we have the right to be ordinary people instead of gentlemen?

My abusive parents have been a devastating blow to my life. Where do I stand to forgive them? Confucius said, good for evil, how to repay good? Be good to those who treat you badly with conscience and virtue, and what in return should you give to those who treat you well? Just as being a parent is no excuse for violence against a child, being a parent is not a requisite for being forgiven either. Children who suffered from childhood abuse are lucky to grow up, always trying to overcome their scars. Forgiveness is not their job.

Indeed, we can argue that your abusive parents and mine didn't just appear out of nowhere, and they certainly carried hidden traumas. It's an endless cycle. You are in the best position to break the cycle of hate, and a brave step forward is forgiveness. Forgiveness is tender, but never belittles the power of gentleness. Lao Tzu, the founder of the ancient

Chinese school of Taoism, had this to say: "The Supreme Goodness is like water." Graceful to all creatures without striving for fame and fortune but awarded the highest goodness, the closest to Taoism. Forgiveness is like water, both rigid and generous, soft but with bones, naturally and silently nourishing life can be turned into a trickle to the dark corners, the abyss of hatred, embracing all things like water. It is honorable for grown children to not pass on the evil they receive to the next generation because they know the harm of malice and the pain of hurt. For the sake of breaking this cycle and to redeem myself, I am willing to choose forgiveness and be a water-like gentle soul.

How do we pull ourselves out of the mire and forgive ourselves for the bad things we've done? I will first learn to accept myself, all of myself, the good and the bad, the proud and the ashamed parts. That's all me. And I will learn to appreciate myself and be proud of myself. I have come through unimaginable hardships, and if I am lucky enough to be successful in some way, how incredible it is! Try to be more grateful to yourself, thanking and appreciating who we are today. What happens is what happens, and it's worth thinking about how to fix things and move on.

Based on my experience, I think radiating and exuding love are the ways to redemption. If we continue to vent hatred towards those around us, that negative energy will still bounce back at us. Rene Magritte, a famous Belgian ethicist and artist, pointed out, "If it is simply forgetting, it is not true forgiveness." Forgiveness and/or reconciliation, according to his theory, do not mean letting go of the past. "Forgiveness is a form of salvation. It saves everyone from the shadow of past disasters."

I would try, like you, to transform myself into beams of light to illuminate those in the shadows, allowing the sun to shine brightly in the dark places where I have been. Like you, I will help children who are being abused but have no power to protect themselves. I hope to use what I've learned to create a more positive community and world. When I see someone else going through what I went through, I'm not going to roar over the ruins of their life, but rather, I'm going to help them rebuild. When everyone gives a little support to others, resentment goes away from everyone.

Turning myself into a beam of light is my way of forgiving both my parents and myself. Shimmering in the gloom like fireflies in the night, dazzling and shiny lights attract each other, glowing, illuminating each other, and there will be moments when these sparkling stars merge together enough to disperse the haze.

10. Suzanne Daughton, Ph.D.

Dr. Suzanne Daughton is an associate professor of communication at Southern Illinois University. She is the co-author of a book on rhetorical criticism and author of several book chapters and journal articles. She has been editor of the national journal, *Women's Studies in Communication*. She has been honored with both teaching and research awards.

* * * * * * *

In answer to the question of whether or not Lois should forgive her parents, I am hesitant to make a "recommendation." I don't believe that we can experience emotions because we "should" feel them. However, I do believe that forgiveness is healing, and that really experiencing the emotions that are present for us in a given moment allow us to eventually move through those emotions. (For example, no one stays happy forever or sad forever.) And when we move through those emotions, trying neither to hurry nor to prolong them, we often drop into a place of deep forgiveness and peace.

It is a truism that holding onto anger, hatred, resentment, pain, etc. is ultimately most hurtful to the one doing the holding. That does not mean, "Don't worry, be happy; just get over it, just let it go; you should not feel this way or that way." Those are all traps, and we often rightly want to kick the people who tell us these things. Rather, what I mean is something more akin to Buddhism, and acceptance of what is. We feel how we feel.

Accepting how we feel is easy when we feel joy, difficult when we feel pain. But accepting every emotion is a great gift. It sometimes requires forgiving ourselves for having "undesirable" emotions or judgments. I may feel forgiveness toward someone, and then experience a resurgence of the hurt at some future date, as I remember the event. That is fine.

The trouble comes, I think, when we resist the emotions we are feeling, or when we judge and try to edit them, rather than embracing all of them as valid.

So, yes, forgiveness is healthy. But anger and grief naturally arise, just as joy and delight do. None of these emotions should be censored. This does not mean we should act on them, particularly anger, or react toward others out of those emotions. It just means that we recognize those feelings when they arise, and not judge them, but let them be as long as they exist at that time.

I wish Lois and all readers of this book the grace of acceptance.

11. Laura Davis

Laura Davis is a lecturer, workshop leader and six-time HarperCollins author. Her books have been published in nine languages and sold more than 1.8 million copies. Her classic bestsellers, *The Courage to Heal, The Courage to Heal Workbook, Allies in Healing* and *Beginning to Heal* paved the way for hundreds of thousands of men and women to heal from the trauma of sexual abuse. In 1997, Davis co-authored *Becoming the Parent You Want to Be,* a rich resource guide that helps parents develop a vision for the families they want to create. Davis' latest book, *I Thought We'd Never Speak Again: The Road from Estrangement to Reconciliation* teaches the skills of reconciliation and peace building, one relationship at a time.

* * * * * * *

For almost twenty years now, I have been receiving letters, phone calls and emails from survivors of sexual abuse thanking me for my book, *The Courage to Heal.* Next to comments like, "Your book saved my life," and "Finally, I knew I wasn't alone," the one response I have heard the most often, expressed the most passionately is, "Thank you for saying I didn't have to forgive my father (mother, stepfather, uncle, brother, coach, priest) for abusing me. Everyone has been telling me for years that I *must* forgive in order to heal. Thank you for telling me I don't have to."

Ellen Bass and I wrote, and I still believe, that the only essential forgiveness an abuse survivor must experience is the forgiveness we offer ourselves. We must forgive ourselves for any guilt we are carrying because of the abuse, any way that we still believe that somehow we were to blame—because we accepted the bicycle, had an orgasm, wanted the affection, loved the abuser, didn't tell, or failed to say "no."

No matter what we did or did not do, we were not to blame. A child is never responsible for his or her own abuse. Even in the extreme circumstances Lois describes—being forced to abuse others or face annihilation—it is never the survivor's fault. Never.

Yet because we were abused and told lies about ourselves, and because it was unacceptable for us as children to accept that the people entrusted to cherish us failed, and in some cases, meant to hurt us, we take the "easier" route—we believe that something must be wrong with us. This belief that we are inherently flawed at the core is the most damaging legacy of sexual abuse. Uncovering this lie is critical to our healing. Knowing that we were not to blame is essential if we are to recapture our capacity to live a full, vibrant life. So to the extent that we still believe that we are flawed, dirty, damaged, or complicit, we must forgive ourselves.

This is a long, arduous journey. The healing process requires that we face the pain and anguish of betrayal, grieve lost opportunities for love, trust, safety and nurturing. It means getting in touch with our anger and placing the blame squarely where it belongs—on the shoulders of the abusers. It means forgiving the innocent child inside us *who had no choice but to survive any way he or she could—whatever it took.* This is the forgiveness that is essential.

I still believe, twenty years after writing *The Courage to Heal*, that forgiveness of the abuser is not required for healing. It is only *after* we gone through the healing process, *after* we have wrestled our souls back from desolation and rebuilt ourselves into the people we were meant to be, that we can begin to consider forgiving the offender. Even then, forgiveness is a byproduct of the healing process, not the ultimate goal.

Trying to forgive when we are beginning to heal undermines the healing process. In the early stages of healing (which can take years), anger at what happened is the fuel that motivates us and gives us the courage to heal, the determination to wrest our lives back.

Anger can be a powerful ally. It keeps us from killing ourselves in despair, it enables us to go back to therapy when we think we cannot bear another moment with that lonely, sad little girl who lives inside our abdomen and hides her head in despair. Anger is a powerful catalyst for change and healing. But it is not a panacea.

Righteous rage has its place; my anger served me for years. It fueled my recovery. It motivated my activism. It spurred me to write and speak about sexual abuse and to reach out to survivors everywhere. I was not going to let the abusers win!

During the early years of healing from the abuse, I needed to give my anger full expression. And because I had the opportunity to express it fully to a safe and willing listener who received it with understanding, empathy and compassion, I was ultimately able to heal *through* my anger and let it go.

At that point in my healing, my inner work changed direction and new, more spiritual qualities began to emerge—compassion, generosity, discernment, equanimity, and to my surprise, forgiveness.

Twenty years after I started healing from my grandfather's abuse, I forgave him. It wasn't something I planned to do, aspired to do, or tried to do. Quite simply, it just happened. Like a bud opening into the sunlight, something in my heart shifted, and I forgave him. And it felt good. In fact, it felt wonderful.

I have also forgiven my mother—for her failure to protect me, for her denial when I told her about the abuse, and for her inability now, 45 years after the abuse began, to accept that I am telling the truth.

During the long years of our estrangement, I assumed we could not have a relationship until she broke through her denial and admitted what my grandfather had done. Yet I was wrong. I have learned that human relationships are complex and full of paradox. I have learned to accept my mother as a flawed, imperfect human being (just as I am flawed, imperfect human being), to love her, and to recognize that she has done her best with what she had to work with. I am no longer holding out for her to believe me. I can't tell you what a relief it is to no longer want to change my history.

Twenty years ago, when Ellen Bass and I wrote *The Courage to Heal,* I couldn't have conceived of these huge, unexpected shifts in my consciousness. But the healing process worked and my perspective changed radically. Rather than seeing my life in a microcosm, in which I was a victim wronged as a child, I began to see a larger, more expansive view. I realized that the strength and compassion I have today are *because* of what I suffered as a child. I began to contemplate my mother's upbringing, and her father's upbringing, and her father's father's upbringing. I saw my personal suffering as one small part of the suffering human beings endure and live with every day. And when I did these things, I began to feel like a player in a much bigger drama. I started to feel compassion for everyone who had played a part in the story of my life—whether their influence was positive, negative, or more frequently, a combination of the two. And without any effort on my part, I forgave them.

For me, forgiveness has been a spiritual gift. I did the work of healing and forgiveness came to me. And I like it. It feels free. It feels open. It feels good. But it is not something I ever strived for. Nor could I have "made it happen" any earlier than it did.

Ultimately, I believe that forgiveness is a deep, personal experience that should never be forced on people or crammed down their throats. It is something that comes from an open heart and a deep commitment to heal. Focus on the healing. Forgiveness will take care of itself.

12. Thomas F. Eagleton

Thomas F. Eagleton (1929 to present) is a former Democratic Senator from Missouri, having served in the US Senate from 1968 to 1987. He was the Vice-Presidential candidate of George McGovern in 1972 until he removed himself from the ticket because of past treatment for depression. Eagleton is a lawyer and author of *Our Constitution and What It Means* and *War and Presidential Power*.

* * * * * * *

Dr. Einhorn, my initial response to your letter was that you were a "kook." I read it again and said, "My God, this might be true." I gave it to my secretary to read and she had a similar reaction. Yours is the most abusive case I have ever read.

My "pain" is nothing compared to yours. Yes, I had depressions. (By the way, none since the early '60's.) To be sure, depressions are painful – not only to the depressed person, but also to those around him – family members, friends, co-workers. However, the worst of depressions cannot be compared with your tragic experiences.

I simply do not know what to say. I am not an overly religious person, but I do believe in God. I believe that you will be "rewarded" in heaven. I think God takes everything into account and those souls who have suffered will be "special" in God's kingdom. Poor people (e.g., those in city slums), sick people (e.g., those in Africa), mistreated people (e.g., you and the victims of Catholic priests – I am Catholic), handicapped people (e.g., the son of my best friend), etc. – all of these and many others will be "special" to God.

13. Albert Ellis, Ph. D.

Dr. Albert Ellis (1913 to present) is best known as the father and founder of Rational-Emotive Therapy. He earned his Ph.D. from Columbia University in 1947. Currently, he serves as the President of the Institute for Rational-Emotive Therapy in New York City.

Ellis has written or edited over 50 books, authored more than 700 articles, and composed more than 200 rational songs. His latest book is called *A Guide to Rational Living*.

Ellis was named one of the most influential psychotherapists in an article in the *American Psychologist*, ahead of Freud, Perls, Erickson, and other noted therapists. He has received scores of other awards including Distinguished Psychologist, Scientific Researcher, and Distinguished Psychological Practitioner. The American Psychological Association awarded him one of their most prestigious honors for his "Distinguished Contributions to Knowledge."

* * * * * * *

Thank you for your story of child abuse and forgiveness. Let me briefly answer your questions. If I were abused as a child and forced to torture and abuse others, I would still unconditionally accept myself and my family members who tortured me. The principles of Rational Emotive Behavior Therapy, which I started practicing in 1955 and have promoted here and all over the world since that time, teach three main principles:

1. You unconditionally and fully accept yourself despite your distinct limitations and failings.

2. You accept and forgive other people even though they behave very badly.

3. You unconditionally accept the world with its exceptionally bad conditions and do not condemn it as a whole.

My main reasons for this kind of unconditional acceptance are:

1. All humans are fallible and therefore will definitely do wrong and bad acts during their lifetime. That is the way humans

almost invariably act. Therefore, they are not to be condemned, as a whole, for their actions.

2. As Alfred Korzybski, the found of General Semantics, wrote in *Science and Sanity*, all people do thousands and thousands of acts during their lifetime – some good, some bad, some indifferent. Therefore, they cannot logically be given a global rating for their numerous acts. They are not what they do, even though they unquestionably do, sometimes very often, evil deeds.

3. Unless we humans learn to teach ourselves this kind of unconditional acceptance of other people, the world, and us, we will endlessly hate ourselves and also fight with other people. Hateful thoughts and feelings help create hate in others, and one of these days the human race is likely to obliterate itself with this kind of hatred. If we educate all children from nursery school to graduate school to accept the principles of unconditional acceptance, we may eventually eliminate holocausts, wars, terrorist acts, and other disastrous events.

For realistic reasons, for logical reasons, and for practical self-preservative reasons, we had better embrace a philosophy of unconditional acceptance and forgiveness.

14. Paul Ferrini

Paul Ferrini has written over twenty-five books on the Christ mind, love, healing, and forgiveness. His books include *The Wounded Child's Journey into Love's Embrace*; *Crossing the Water: A Poetic Exploration of Healing and Forgiveness in Our Relationships*; and *Forbidden Fruit: Unraveling the Mysteries of Sin, Guilt, and Atonement*. He founded and edited *Miracles Magazine* and devoted the Winter 1995 issue to sexual, ritual, and satanic abuse and forgiveness. In addition to being a well-known writer, Ferrini is an inspirational speaker, workshop leader, healer, and counselor. Larry Dossey, M.D. calls Paul Ferrini "a modern-day Kahil Gibran—poet, mystic, visionary, teller of truth."

* * * * * * *

Lois, I devoted an entire issue of *Miracles Magazine* to the subject of sexual/ritual abuse and forgiveness because of the following factors:

- If the statistics are correct, and one out of six people is sexually abused, then everyone knows someone – a parent, a spouse, or friend – who has experienced this kind of abuse. Dealing with sexual abuse and its psychological effects is therefore an everyday matter.

- Abuse is the core issue. All trespass is abuse in some form. If we can understand serious abuse – what causes it and how people heal from it – then perhaps we can understand how to create an environment that helps us respect each other's physical and emotional boundaries.

- Abuse is institutionalized in our society. Children grow up with a steady diet of TV violence that desensitizes them to the suffering of others.

- While our consciousness has been raised about the prevalence of abuse in our society, very little has been written on the healing process.

Editing this issue reinforced my belief that people can go through the most terrible experiences and still heal from them. As Victor Frankl observed in reference to concentration camp survivors, what is done to us against our will cannot condemn us. Our humanity cannot be taken away by acts of brutality. Rather, it stands against all attack, witnessing to our essential dignity and spirituality.

The healing journey for survivors of sexual abuse, ritual abuse, and other forms of childhood trauma involves many layers of shame. Many survivors feel, as you do, Lois, that they are responsible for the abuse they underwent. They feel dirty, stained, unworthy, and unlovable. Your first challenge, Lois, is to forgive yourself, to realize that you did nothing to deserve the attack. Since your parents perpetrated your abuse, you must deal with an intense sense of betrayal. From talking to many survivors who have shared their stories, I know the journey will be a lifelong one. Healing for you will be ongoing.

Anger, rage, blame, holding onto the victim's role are states that survivors go through. A milestone in your journey, Lois, forgiveness will occur when you realize that you can no longer hold onto the past without holding onto your pain. Unless you unhook emotionally from your violators, you carry their trauma indefinitely into the future. Forgiveness of your parents sets you free. It says, "I refuse to carry this pain anymore. I release myself from the painful bondage of shame and blame, which ties me to the violator."

In this sense, forgiveness of others is simply an extension of forgiveness of self. It empowers you to move forward in your life. When self-empowerment flowers, when you understand that it is impossible for such violation to occur again, you become capable of feeling compassion for your parents/violators.

You can forgive and not forget. Indeed, that is the most powerful stance; it is a testament to your own healing and decision to use the experience you have had to help other victims heal and confront their victimizers.

The final stage of healing occurs when we realize that our abuse was a major wakeup call we have experienced in our life. Thanks to the abuse, we learned to stand up for ourselves in a way we never could have otherwise. Thanks to the abuse, we learned to reach out, bond with, and empower other people with similar experiences. Thanks to the abuse, we have healed the deepest shame in our consciousness and become able to help others do the same.

Those who hurt are capable of great brutality. Yet they are our brothers, too. If we condemn them, we condemn those parts of ourselves that are wounded and crying out for love. Let us find a way to get our arms around all of this pain, as Jesus did. Let us embrace the wounded child in each one of us. This is how the Christ is born.

Love and blessings.

15. Lynne D. Finney, J.D., M.S.W.

Lynne D. Finney is an internationally acclaimed author, gifted healer, motivational speaker, educator, life coach and former attorney and psychotherapist who specializes in helping people overcome limiting beliefs and live more fulfilling lives. Four near-death experiences transformed her. She teaches at the University of Utah, presents life-changing workshops nationwide, and has appeared on more than 200 radio and TV shows, including Leeza, NPR, Good Morning shows, and Larry King Live.

Lynne's newest book, *Windows to the Light: Enriching Your Spirit with Haiku Meditations*, is a gift book of haiku poetry meditations and art. She also has a new CD, *"Connecting with the Universe: Meditations for Enlightenment and Self-realization."* Lynne is the author of *Reach for the Rainbow, Advanced Healing for Survivors of Sexual Abuse* (also in Chinese); *and Clear Your Past, Change Your Future*, with editions in Spain, Russia, India, and China. Currently, she is completing a book on relieving pain using mental and spiritual techniques (to be released in 2006).

* * * * * * *

Your story touched me in many ways because it is eerily similar to my childhood experiences. I too was physically, emotionally, and sexually abused by my father from the time I was a baby until I was eight years old. My mother witnessed the abuse. When I asked her to take me away, she hit me and distanced herself emotionally from me. My father also forced me to help him kill my kitten.

Sadly, our stories are not uncommon. I have heard similar experiences from men, women, and children across the country who came to me for counseling or attended my workshops for therapists and abuse survivors.

Some people find it difficult to believe that such terrible things happen to children, but studies show that at least a third of children in the United States under the age of eighteen have been sexually abused. Sexual abuse occurs in every ethnic, economic, and religious group, not just the poor and uneducated, as recent revelations about Catholic priests demonstrate. Studies in England, Germany, Australia, Canada, France, and Belgium reveal numbers of cases similar to those in the U.S. If

120

criminal neglect and physical and emotional abuse are added to those numbers, the number of abused children is over two thirds. Child abuse is a worldwide epidemic. It is also a major cause of violence in the world.

As you are all too aware, the most devastating effects of abuse are not physical, but psychological and emotional. While he was abusing me, my father told me that he was doing it because I was evil. He said I made him do it, that God told him to punish me because I was so evil, that I was a child of the devil, and that anyone I loved would die. The abuse made me hate myself, God, and everyone in the world. It destroyed my trust and love. It filled me with hatred, murderous rage, and a desire to die that that made every moment hell. I believed I was in hell and would be tortured forever, hardly conducive to a happy life.

Like you, Lois, I put on a great façade. I drove myself to overachieve academically and professionally to prove I was "good". But my accomplishments provided only fleeting moments of pleasure before I sank back into despair. I unconsciously sabotaged anything good that came my way, including jobs, relationships, and finances.

During my recovery, I uncovered hundreds of self-sabotaging decisions made from confusion, despair, anger, and desperation. My healing process took sixty years and included years of therapy and self-analysis to clear out repressed emotions, memories, and self-sabotaging beliefs and behavior patterns. The abuse caused post-traumatic stress disorder, inappropriate emotional reactions, and self-sabotaging behavior. Trying to use my intellect and sheer will to change behavior and reactions didn't work. My mind had to be cleared of the old trauma so I could be free to choose how I felt and reacted.

You asked whether there is free will. Recent neurobiological studies show that until we clear our minds of trauma, we have only limited free will. Traumatic events are imprinted in our brains with all of the sights, sounds, smells, tastes, feelings and emotions. These memories are like a computer software program running subconsciously in our minds. These stored memories and feelings can be triggered by later events, until memories and emotions of the traumatic events are brought to consciousness and released. When something in the present reminds us subconsciously of repressed traumatic events, the reasoning part of our brain is bypassed. Information is shunted down different neural pathways directly to the repressed memory, causing us to react as we did during the trauma. We lose our free will.

121

Most people find it easier to accept this fact in cases of soldiers suffering from post-traumatic stress disorder, than in adults who suffer from PTSD because of childhood abuse. But the neurobiological reactions are the same. If a medical helicopter flies overhead, Vietnam veterans may scream "Incoming, incoming" and dive under tables. They react as if they were still in Vietnam, even though most of the time they know the war is over and they are safe in the United States. These soldiers cannot "choose" to act differently. At the moment their repressed trauma is triggered, they have no free will.

The free will of child abuse victims is limited in the same way. When fear and rage suppressed during childhood abuse are triggered, as adults we may explode with inappropriate anger, destroy relationships, hurt ourselves, or even abuse others. I was horrified to realize how many people I had hurt, not physically, but emotionally and psychologically. Words can wound as much as rape and beatings.

There is only one reason why people abuse children: because they have been abused as children themselves. Abuse is a learned behavior. After helping thousands of victims (including perpetrators), training hundreds of therapists and reading hundreds of books, I have never heard of a case where a perpetrator was not also a victim. Sexual abuse is not a crime of lust; it is a crime of violence. Although only a small percentage of sexual abuse victims become abusers, children subjected to violence, especially when forced to abuse others, can repeat the same acts on others. Just as the sounds of a helicopter trigger a Vietnam vet to react with fear as if in combat, old feelings of helplessness and rage can be triggered in abuse victims, unconsciously causing them to repeat what was done to them, not out of lust, but out of feelings of helplessness and a need for control and power.

After my father received therapy and stopped abusing me, he would often come to me in tears. I remember his words clearly: "I'm such a terrible father. I did such terrible things to you. I'm so sorry. I love you so much. You would have been better off if I were dead. I should have committed suicide."

My father was not a "bad" person. My memories revealed his different personality states and his semi-autobiographical books describe childhood abuse and parts of his mind that made him do terrible things. In his primary, conscious state, he was not an abuser. My father talked about abuse by his mother, stepfather, and other family members and wrote about it in his books. He was also abused in a satanic cult in Austria. He did to me what was done to him. Once he knew consciously

122

what he had done, he spent the rest of his life overwhelmed with remorse, trying to atone and show his love for me. He died before I recovered memories of the years of abuse. While he lived he had to see the effects of his abuse on his daughter every day. I cannot imagine a more terrible hell.

But despite horrendous experiences and actions, my father healed himself, with therapy and his own introspection. One of his last poems, entitled "Escape", describes how he finally escaped from the tomb of hate in which he lived much of his life. It says that after growing up on "a childhood vow of hate" and years of blindness, he found "light."

As a therapist, I have seen into the minds of murderers and child abusers. Most perpetrators are not consciously aware of what they are doing when they abuse. When feelings of their childhood abuse are triggered, they have no free will. They are terribly wounded people who do terrible things. But they are not "evil". The sad fact is that hurt people often hurt others. People who act the worst hurt the most.

Religions tell us not to judge because we can never know another person's whole story. The Sioux Indians have an insightful prayer: "Great Spirit, help me to never judge another until I have walked in his moccasins for two weeks." We cannot know what someone has experienced and thus do not know what will break him and send him over the edge into violence.

Non-judgment and forgiveness give birth to compassion. I believe that was Jesus' message when He said, "Forgive them, Lord, for they know not what they do." He knew that until we realize who we really are – divine spiritual beings who are eternal expressions of Love – we have only limited free will. Until our minds are clear, we are puppets of our past trauma.

The key to recovery is forgiveness. But the concept of forgiveness is greatly misunderstood. It does *not* mean we condone what our abusers did. "Condone" means to overlook. We can *never* overlook the magnitude of suffering we endured. Forgiving does *not* mean what they did was all right. No child deserves to be abused. Abusing a child is *never* "all right".

Forgiveness does *not* mean we forget what was done to us. Those acts are irrevocable and affected the course of our lives. They are part of our history. To heal, we must remember traumatic events and release the violent emotions that create turmoil inside us. We must grieve for what we suffered and what could have been. We must make peace with the past. As long as we repress traumatic memories, we remained trapped in the trauma.

But abuse does not have to haunt us or be the focus of the rest of our lives. We can be free by letting go of the bitterness, anger, and hatred without condoning what our abusers did.

"Letting go" is the true meaning of forgiveness. Forgiveness is for the one who forgives, *not* the one who is forgiven. As long as we hold on to anger and resentment, we cannot be free. As long as we hate or resent our abusers, we remain tied to them. The energy of our anger keeps us enmeshed. We need to let go in order to free ourselves.

Forgiveness demands that we feel our anger, grief and resentment, not in the abstract, but tied to specific memories of what we endured. Most people are terrified of their own murderous anger – the shadow side. Some therapists and spiritual teachers have not done their own inner work and are afraid of anger. They discourage people from expressing and releasing it. But anger and hatred are just as much "God-given" emotions as love and compassion. When these emotions are suppressed, they act as barriers to love. If we do not allow ourselves to experience anger and hatred, we are unable to feel love and compassion. We are the walking dead. When we release the many levels of anger and hatred inside us, love, compassion, and happiness remain - our true nature.

Some therapists and spiritual teachers try to make people forgive before they are ready. Forgiveness does not come from an act of will. Rationalizing away our pain and anger because of what our abusers might have suffered denies what we felt as children and keeps us stuck in pain and anger. Ignoring the feelings that we had as children dishonors us and causes self-hatred. It is only when we know the details of how we have been hurt and release the violent emotions that we are ready to forgive. When we release the many levels of anger and hatred inside our minds, understanding and compassion come naturally and effortlessly.

Forgiving does *not* mean we must have further contact with an abuser. And we certainly do not have to allow someone to continue to abuse us or treat us with disrespect. We do not even have to tell people who hurt us that we have forgiven them. Even if the person never knows, forgiving creates miracles. Quantum physicists have proven that we are composed of atoms and molecules, tiny particles which when broken down are energy – conscious, intelligence. When we forgive – let go – we change our energy and affect the quantum field. It changes the energy of our abusers giving them an opening to change their lives.

The process of forgiveness has many levels. I had to let go of my anger toward my father, mother, and others who hurt me. Then my anger focused on my father's abusive mother and other relatives involved in the chain of abuse. I had to forgive all the people who didn't help me. When I thought I was done, I uncovered my rage at God for not protecting me and for allowing me to be abused.

Last, but certainly not least, I had to forgive myself for hating myself, hating others, sabotaging my life, and hurting myself and others. It was a long process. Even now the old tapes sometimes play in my mind, but they are shorter and I can clear them more quickly.

Each time we forgive, miracles occur. Our beliefs and emotions, conscious and subconscious, act like blinders that control the way we view the world. Anger, hatred, resentment and our judgments keep us from experiencing the miracles and love that surround us. When I stay in faith, forgiveness, peace, gratitude, and acceptance, I live in the flow where serendipity, synchronicity, and miracles surround me.

Until we clear our minds and forgive, we remain blind to the perfection, love, and beauty that are right here, right now. Most of us believe we have done terrible things. We punish ourselves. No one judges us; we judge ourselves. It's all in our own minds.

The startling truth is that we experience only as much happiness as we believe we deserve. When we totally pardon and love ourselves, we experience inner peace, compassion and love – nirvana, shambala, the kingdom of heaven on earth.

Forgiving allows us to tap into this kingdom, the world of miracles that surrounds us right now. The answers are inside ourselves. No matter what we have done, or what has been done to us, we can pardon ourselves and heal. There are no exceptions.

I used to be the quintessential victim, insisting everyone else was to blame for my unhappiness. My hardest lesson was accepting the fact that I was responsible for my feelings and that all the answers I needed were inside me. Enlightened psychiatrist Carl Jung said: "Who looks outside, dreams; who looks inside, awakes." I had to look inside to find the truth of who I really am – powerful, eternal, unlimited and loving.

The world "outside" is a mirror of our thoughts and beliefs. Sages and mystics throughout the ages have recognized this truth. Playwright George Bernard Shaw advised: "Better keep yourself clean and bright; you are the window through which you must see the world." Thomas Dreier echoed, "The World is a great mirror. It reflects back to you what you are. If you are loving, if you are friendly, if you are helpful, the

125

world will prove loving and friendly and helpful to you. The world is what you are."

The Lord's Prayer says: "Forgive us our trespasses, as we forgive those who trespass against us." This is cosmic law. To the extent we forgive others, we forgive ourselves and are forgiven. Harboring anger and resentment keeps us in hell. Forgiving allows us to live in the flow, in the kingdom of heaven.

When I realized who I AM, I also realized that the Universe is perfectly orchestrated. There are no mistakes. There is a perfect plan for us all. Everything that happens to us is a gift designed to wake us up, to bring us to enlightenment.

If you are thinking this is "airy fairy nonsense", I suggest you rent a video of the Michael Douglas movie, *The Game*. Douglas portrays a cold, arrogant, wealthy executive. When his brother enrolls Douglas in "The Game", which is the game of life, people do "terrible" things to Douglas. They rob, beat, and try to kill him.

At the end of the film, all the people in Douglas' life, including those who did "terrible" things to him, celebrate his awakening at his "birthday" party.

The Game is based on ancient spiritual teachings in various religions as well as the Bible: everything that happens to us, and every being we meet, is a gift designed to bring us to enlightenment and Self-realization. In an early scene, Douglas asks an older man who has played "The Game" to explain it. Smiling, the older man says, "I was blind, but now I see."

Everything that happens is a gift, never a punishment, designed to wake us up. In the kingdom of heaven there is no duality. There is no "good" or "bad". All is well, all is good, and all is God/Spirit / divine consciousness. There is a divine plan motivated by love. When you see the world in this light, your life will change and you will see miracles everywhere.

One of my therapy clients, a survivor of satanic cult abuse made a list of the strengths she gained from what she had experienced. Surprisingly there were many, as I found when I made my own list. Included among them were courage, resilience, compassion, and spiritual awakening.

Would I have had these qualities without the abuse? I don't know. However, my pain spurred me on to greater spiritual growth, propelling me to become more understanding, tolerant, and compassionate than I might have been otherwise. I am also blessed with having been able to

126

help many people, survivors of unimaginable abuse and suffering, because of my experiences. The ultimate gift is that I now live in a world of constant miracles, a divine flow that brings me everything I need and want effortlessly.

We are living in a time of rapid evolution. We face many changes and challenges as spiritual beings having adventures in human form. Sometimes it may seem overwhelming. But we are never given anything we are unable to handle because, at some level, our souls choose our destinies. The Universe/Spirit/Consciousness already knows the outcome for all of us—and it's perfect. Some people call these the "end times" and fear a terrible Armageddon. But based on years of study, I believe Revelations has been grossly misunderstood. The world will not end. What will end is our illusion about a "physical" world we think of as reality. We will step into the perception of a new reality, the true reality, where we realize that we are love, spirit, consciousness, connected to and part of All That Is.

After the devastation of hurricane Katrina, Lynn Robinson, a dear friend in Mobile, Alabama wrote, "The storm is an invitation to love." Every challenge we face, all pain and suffering, are invitations to love. As C.S. Lewis wrote in *The Problem of Pain:* "God whispers to us in our pleasures, speaks in our conscience, but shouts in our pains: it is His megaphone to rouse a deaf world." Pain and challenges are gifts designed to wake us up, to bring us to enlightenment and love.

We are all helping each other every moment, even though we may not be aware of it. The fun comes when we become consciously aware of the synchronicity and see the perfection at work, the intricate symphony playing in our lives. Being fully aware of the people who are sent to me for help and who are sent to help me is living magic. When my intention is clear, I can just follow my feelings and do what I want. Whatever I do is perfect – even if I decide to do nothing.

No one can "give" you enlightenment. You are already enlightened. You are only limited by your limiting beliefs. Enlightenment does not need to take years of struggle; it can happen in an instant. You do not have to earn it; it's who you are. You only have to *realize* that you are already enlightened, pure consciousness, spirit, eternal, and unlimited. That is why it's called Self-realization. You are perfect right now.

We are spirit, divinely guided and always on the right path, despite outward appearances. My favorite quote is from the Buddha:

"If you search the wide world over,
you will never find anyone
more deserving of love than yourself."

This applies to everyone.

When we see the truth of who we are, we know that all is forgiven and all is well.

Love and blessings.

16. Russell P. Friedman

Russell P. Friedman is executive director of the Grief Recovery Institute Educational Foundation, Inc., and co-author of *The Grief Recovery Handbook: The Action Program for Moving Beyond Death, Divorce, and Other Losses*, and *When Children Grieve: For Adults to Help Children Deal with Death, Divorce, Pet Loss, Moving, and Other Losses*. Both are published by HarperCollins. Substantial details on forgiveness are included in both books. In addition, he maintains several Internet web sites and has written many articles on the net including "After the Fall of the Towers: How to Address Your Children," "Recovering from Loss and Adapting to Your New Family," and "Legacy of Love or Monument to Misery."

Mr. Friedman has personally helped more than 50,000 grievers heal, forgive, and release their heart and soul, and through his publications has helped countless more. Through the Institute, he also offers grief recovery certification to people "who wish to help those with broken hearts retake a productive place in the mainstream of their lives."

* * * * * * *

Over the past fifteen years, I have helped thousands of people deal with the ravages of their pasts. Starting with myself.

While the details of my past do not contain the specific travesties of sexual or physical abuse, the emotional horrors I experienced kept my heart and soul imprisoned for nearly 45 years.

In the end, the resentments I harbored and nurtured seem in retrospect to have been as damaging as the original painful events that birthed them, in their capacity to keep me turning on the roasting spit of rancor without the possibility of escape.

It is reasonable to suggest that based on my past and the internal nightmare it engendered, that I was in constant fear of what the future would hold. In the elaborate two-step dance between past and future, I was rarely present and accounted for in "real time." That idea doesn't necessarily sound debilitating unto itself, until it is put into context to two divorces, a bankruptcy, and a landscape littered with irreparable relationships, plus the constant implication that things could only get worse, not better.

While there were a series of actions I needed to take to arrive at a newfound sense of participation and joy in my life, there was an underlying principle that stands out from all the others. That is the "action" of forgiving those who had harmed me. Unfortunately, my "victim" status made it almost impossible for me to recognize that forgiving them would be the key to my eventual freedom. And frankly, if any well-meaning person should had wandered into my life and suggested the very thing that ultimately did set me free, I'd probably have chased that individual away as fast as possible.

Until the constancy of my own self-defeating actions, reactions, and behaviors became so unbearable, even to me, I could not hear anything helpful.

Now that you have a little bit of first person information about me, I will now shift from my personal story and take a more educational tone, and speak from the point of view of our teachings at The Grief Recovery Institute.

Unresolved grief is cumulative and cumulatively negative. Since time can no more heal an emotional wound than it could put air back in a flat tire, it remains true that only actions can help us complete our relationship to the painful events of our past. And even then, they must be correct and helpful actions. Of all the actions, there is one that is essential to recapturing a sense of well-being when a life has been torn asunder by systematic mistreatment in childhood.

The losses of trust, safety, and control that are the underlying hallmark results of that mistreatment probably comprise the single largest overall, non-death loss issue in society today. There can be no simple, universal cure-all for the life-limiting symptoms that attach to such painful beginnings. But if there were one element that can be a practical common denominator for defeating the demons of our past, forgiveness would fit that bill.

Forgiveness, in its purest sense, is the key to living life effectively and in real time. It is also the secret formula to reducing the ongoing impact of past events. The dictionary definition of "forgive" is: *to cease to feel resentment against [an offender]*. That's the number one definition in *Webster's Ninth New Collegiate Dictionary*.

Even a casual look at that definition makes it clear that the purpose of forgiveness is to release the holder of the resentment from bondage. Not one element of the definition minimizes or condones the actions of the perpetrator. In fact, in my fifteen years of helping people deal with every imaginable loss—and some that are even beyond the imagination—the biggest stumbling block to moving beyond the hurt is the idea that forgiveness would somehow condone the horrendous acts committed against the victim, and give some kind of free pass to the perpetrator.

It is understandable in our world, which does not teach forgiveness very well, if at all, that people would get stuck in confusing forgiveness with condoning. Yet, we must bring them back to the definition – *to cease to feel resentment against [an offender]*. I often find it useful to take a slight verbal liberty and change the definition to read – *to relieve oneself of a resentment against [an offender]*. Switching the word "relieve" for the words "cease to feel" makes it more of an action, rather than a passive non-action.

The other major dilemma in helping people actually "take the action" of forgiveness comes in the form of a resistance, which is usually stated thus: "I can't forgive them [the perpetrators]; I don't FEEL forgiveness." To which we ask, "How can you feel something you haven't done?" It's akin to trying to feel sober while still drinking.

In simple point of fact, forgiveness is an ACTION, not a FEELING. Forgiveness is something I must do so I can feel different. It is nearly impossible to feel forgiveness until or unless the verbal action of forgiveness has been taken, and even then, there may or may not be an accompanying feeling.

Quite often we have been called on to help someone who is carrying a massive resentment against someone who is no longer living. The phrase "being ruled from the grave," takes on a new and painful meaning when people's lives are still very much limited and restricted by their memories about those who no longer have the physical capacity to hurt them.

Please do not interpret anything being said here to mean that we are minimizing or otherwise limiting the reality of the overwhelming impact of cruel and inhuman treatment of children. That is not what we're saying.

What we're saying is quite the opposite. The perpetrator's actions [or non-actions] hurt us to unspeakable levels sometimes, and **that is not okay**. The question is, "What can a person do to free her/himself of the current and future hurt generated by all of the losses that are part of the hurtful memories of the past?" We have already explicitly and implicitly mentioned some – Loss of Trust, Loss of Safety, and Loss of Control [over my body, and often my mind, as well as my heart and soul]. These are the central loss elements that most restrict our lives.

To tell someone to "not" think about something is absurd, as well as impossible. To try to control the environment and all possible stimuli is almost equally impractical. Besides, you cannot control your own unconscious dream life, which all too often may remind you of the very things you would like to "put behind you."

It is equally unhelpful to advise someone to "let go" and "move on." What exactly does that mean, "Let go and move on?" Or more accurately, let go of what and move on to where? If people could so easily "let go and move on," there would probably be no need for therapists, social workers, clergy or others who try to help people deal with the events that have affected their lives.

Now let's discuss the horrific mental images of any of the wide range of abuse issues. When there has been long-term, systematic mistreatment of anyone, the need for that person to acquire skills to stay in the "present moment" or return to the "real time" are extra-ordinarily important.

We would never suggest that someone could "forget" the horrors that have been visited upon them, and the mere act of "forgiving" someone does not erase either the memories or the feelings attached to the events that harmed them. One of the most meaningless clichés in our vernacular is, "I can forgive but I can't forget." It is one of those unfortunate pieces of language babble that is not helpful to anyone. The fact is, until or unless you get Alzheimer's, you are not going to forget. It makes no sense to co-mingle the worlds forgive and forget.

But we need to get unstuck from the memories of past painful events. To demonstrate how it works with memories of abuse: If someone has told me that they are having a lot of feelings about those memories, I might paraphrase with, "Sounds like your memories about one of those events is really bothering you." And then I might add this question, "Have you remembered to forgive the perpetrator so that you can be free to go about your day?"

We know it sounds simple and simplistic, and it is both. In fact we usually only offer that kind of help to people who are dealing with the entirety of the relationship with the perpetrator. Within those actions, forgiveness is just one part, though an essential and powerful part. It is not uncommon that the "victim" has a legitimate mixture of feelings that can cover a wide range, from fear and loathing even to love and respect. Most relationships contain a broad spectrum of feelings, and the more painful relationships often carry much higher levels of intensity of emotion, and often at both ends of the scale.

However, forgiveness alone is usually not enough. Though valid for dealing with passing events, as when the stranger cuts you off on the freeway, forgiveness does not undo a lifetime of damage that has been carried forward and often has become a part of a person's identity. Nor does forgiveness instantly repair the damage caused by a childhood marked by consistent violence and abuse.

There are no simple "tricks" that can overcome the feelings and habits we have developed in response to the things that have happened to us. So, all ideas must be viewed and all actions must be taken in the larger and more complete context of being willing to pull off some scabs, and dig down and review everything that we know about our relationship with those who have hurt us. To that end, forgiveness is either the sticking point or the release point.

One crucially important issue is that forgiveness must always be indirect. Clearly, if the perpetrator has died, there could not be a direct interaction on forgiveness or anything else. But even when the perpetrator is still living, the action of forgiveness should never be stated directly in any form—not in person, not on the phone, and not by letter or email.

Forgiveness is an attack and a confrontation. What it sounds like is this: "You have hurt me very much, but I'm Mother Teresa, so I forgive you." Almost anyone confronted with that kind of statement will respond by saying, "Thanks for pointing out what a jerk I am; I really appreciate it." It also needs to be understood that if a perpetrator has not come to you and acknowledged what they did, and apologized, then it is massively unlikely that your "forgiveness—confrontation" is going to open their eyes and their heart to what they've done to you.

Forgiveness, as a starting point, allows us to do the things we must do to get as emotionally complete as we possibly can with the events, with the perpetrators, and with the habits that we may have developed in relationship to them. Without forgiveness, we can become stuck on the events and the people, and not get to work on ourselves so that we can achieve any measure of freedom.

Unforgiven resentment carries with it a constant focus on the event and the perpetrator and acts as a never-ending stimulus in keeping someone trapped. Forgiveness is the first and most important step on the pathway to freedom.

17. Arun Gandhi

Arun Gandhi (1934 to present) is the grandson of Mahatma Gandhi and a winner, himself, of many awards for peace and nonviolence. Born in South Africa, Arun Gandhi is a man of Eastern descent who experienced hatred and bigotry from whites and blacks alike. At age twelve, his parents sent him to live in India with his grandfather, Mahatma Gandhi ("mahatma" is an honorary title meaning "great soul"). He lived there during India's fight to free itself from Great Britain.

Gandhi was among those who founded India's Center for Social Unity, a group dedicated to helping end poverty and caste discrimination. He moved to the United States in 1987, and four years later, with his wife Sunanda, founded the M.K. Gandhi Institute for Nonviolence, whose purpose is to practice and teach the philosophy of nonviolence.

Gandhi has authored and edited several books and hundreds of articles. His most recent book is *Gandhi: Legacy of Love*.

Arun Gandhi's awards and honors include the Martin Luther King Freedom Award, the Amnesty International Outstanding Contributions Award, the Maya Angelou Award, and the Peace Museum Lifetime Achievement Award. He has received keys to five cities and has earned five honorary doctoral degrees.

* * * * * * *

It is always difficult for one who has not experienced abuse from parents and does not know what it means to be a girl or woman coveted by others for carnal or sadistic pleasures to comment on how a victim should feel and what a victim should do. What is clear, however, is that those who feel helpless or, as children, are helpless, are always the first to be victimized. We unanimously agree that a child abuser commits the most heinous of all crimes and incidences of abuse happen frequently. This raises questions: How does a victim of such abuse get justice? What do we mean by justice? How do we stop such abuse from happening to others? And as you Lois ask, what is the role of "forgiveness?"

First, let us consider the question: "Why does this happen?" Over several centuries we have built around ourselves a "culture of violence" so pervasive that it permeates every aspect of life. This "culture of violence" governs our thinking, our relationships, our attitudes; and everything including our economic, social, cultural, and religious beliefs.

Human beings seek to control each other through fear escalated to maintain control. Fear breads hate, hate leads to anger; and anger leads to destruction of the Self.

Every individual is endowed with differing levels of tolerance to suffering. Some people endure suffering for longer periods and in greater depths than others, while some can suffer and yet shut violence out of their lives as though nothing has happened. To some degree, people's attitudes on suffering correlate with the amount of fear and level of helplessness that the individual feels. In a totally unrelated situation, Mohandas K. Gandhi said: "No one can oppress you more than you oppress yourself." When adults submit to oppression out of fear or because they don't want to be the ones to topple the apple cart, then they share the blame with the abusers.

In this "Culture of Violence," justice has come to mean punishment and revenge. "An eye for an eye," my Grandfather said, "only makes the whole world blind." We are constantly told that someone has to pay for what has happened or what they did, assuming that abusers are born evil and if we lock them up, or better still eliminate them, society will be rid of evil. Although we have pursued this policy for generations, we find that child abuse and violence have only increased exponentially. If we intend to reduce, if not eliminate child abuse and violence, then society needs to focus on the circumstances that breed evildoers and not just on the perpetrators of the crimes.

As a society, we need to change the "culture of violence" to a culture of nonviolence. While the culture of violence evokes negative responses from individuals and societies, the culture of nonviolence allows positive attitudes to flourish. In a culture of nonviolence, we build relationships based on positive principles such as respect, understanding, acceptance, and appreciation.

RESPECT: We need to learn to respect ourselves, respect each other, and respect our connection with all of creation. Today we have virtually no respect for ourselves because we allow others to determine what we should be; when we don't measure up to the standards set by others, we suffer from low self-esteem leading to lack of respect. We are created by a higher power. Let me use here an analogy of a machine representing all of creation: When an engineer is constructing a machine, he/she requires all kinds of parts, each of which performs together to play an important role. So, when we look upon ourselves as being these small parts of creation, then we can respect ourselves.

Respect also implies that we constantly attempt to reach a higher level of existence. To say that I am what I am and will remain that way is a negative attitude, indicating a lack of respect for the self. The purpose of life is to grow, not simply in age. We have to grow mentally, spiritually, and physically. Education is a life-long process, constantly providing us with nourishing experiences that can lead to...

UNDERSTANDING: We need to understand who we are and why we are here on earth. Our birth is neither an accident nor a result of carnal pleasures alone. Science tells us that the egg and the ovum have to meet and be fertilized for a human birth to occur, but precisely when this process happens continues to remain a mystery.

It is also a fallacy to believe that we are independent individuals who can do what we like as if it's nobody's business. No one is independent. We are all inter-related and interdependent, and what we do with our lives makes a big difference to the rest of society. For example, those who commit crimes or indulge in violence in the United States amount to fewer than five percent of the total population; yet, their actions directly and indirectly affect all our lives. It is through the understanding of the larger picture that we acquire the ability to understand ourselves. That understanding leads to...

ACCEPTANCE: Accept each other as human beings and do not identify people by color, race, nationality, gender, religion, and the thousands of other identification labels we use to classify people. Labels serve to divide people, and every division is a possible conflict perpetuating the cycle of violence. Only when we discard the labels and begin to look at each other as human beings can we APPRECIATE our own humanity. Positive relationships help us to usher in a culture of nonviolence.

In the process of creating a culture of nonviolence, forgiveness or the ability to forgive plays an important role. Forgiving certainly does not mean forgetting. Sometimes one needs to forgive even if the abuser is not present. Most importantly, as with love, forgiving must be unconditional. Conditional forgiving is meaningless and insincere. Forgiving functions as a form of healing, purging people at the seed of their anger and hatred.

Most Jews have not forgiven the Nazis for the holocaust, and the consequence is that they have not healed the wounds. The seed of anger remains buried in their soul and manifests itself in hate and violence. It is this inability of the Jews to forgive and heal that leads to their excessive violence towards the Palestinians. If the Jews had healed themselves by

136

forgiving the Nazis and working towards establishing a culture of nonviolence, they would have negotiated a settlement with the Palestinians long ago.

In a culture of nonviolence, forgiving means healing and dedicating oneself to helping create an atmosphere where horrible things do not happen again. To say we will avoid another holocaust by keeping the memory of the last one alive serves only to nourish the seeds of hate, prejudice, and violence. History has shown that, in spite of the holocaust museums and attempts to teach children to abhor violence, the result has been just the opposite: In the past fifty years, the world has experienced multiple holocausts, and violence has assumed satanic proportions.

In summary, what will save the world from horrendous violence and abuse is our determined effort to change from a culture of violence to a culture of nonviolence. Simply explained nonviolence is love, respect, understanding, acceptance, and appreciation. If cynics say that it is impossible for these positive attitudes to govern people or that a culture of nonviolence is a Utopian dream, then all I say is we are in a deeper hole than I had imagined. My grandfather, Mohandas K. Gandhi, said:

"We must be the change we wish to see in the world.
Change can only grow from the roots upwards,
never from the treetop down."

18. Aba Gayle

Aba Gayle is the mother of a nineteen-year-old daughter who was found stabbed to death in 1980. After intense grief, anger, meditation, and study, she realized that we are all one. Twelve years after her daughter's murder, she wrote a letter of forgiveness to the murderer. The act of mailing the letter transformed hate and rage into love, joy, and peace. Now friends with her daughter's murderer who is on death row, she devotes her life to teaching the healing power of forgiveness and to being a political and social advocate for all men and women in prison.

* * * * * * *

Lois, I believe your question is: Could I forgive parents who abused me and caused me physical and emotional pain?

I am not qualified to make such judgments. I was a blessed child with a mother and father who loved and adored me. I was never spanked or abused with cruel language. That said, I have been in emotionally abusive relationships with two husbands and have lost my youngest daughter to the violence of murder. So I will speak from my personal experiences.

We live in a culture that condones hate, rage, and revenge. It can be very difficult to forgive when everyone around you supports your anger, some saying you must be crazy to forgive the perpetrator.

I consider myself lucky to have discovered the Unity Church and the attached metaphysical bookstore. After reading my way through great spiritual teachings, I was introduced to "A Course in Miracles" which talks repeatedly about Forgiveness being the single most important spiritual practice.

You asked me what I would do if I had a past like yours. Based on the healing that my own forgiveness gave me, I would definitely forgive my parents. This certainly does not mean that anything they did was acceptable or that I would ever forget. It means I can let go of the horror and live on my terms, not theirs. It means I take back my power and no longer allow memories to ruin my emotional health.

It is clear to me that parents who abuse their children are emotionally ill, and I always wonder what happened to them. How were they abused? Who abused their abusers? At some point we must say,

"Stop! It all stops with me." Rather than asking how or why, we must all accept responsibility for our own feelings, thoughts, and actions.

I believe a child is not responsible for actions done at the direction of their caretakers. This includes child prostitution, sexual abuse, and torture of animals or others. But forgiveness of ourselves is absolutely necessary to live a normal adult life.

I recommend my favorite book on forgiveness: *Radical Forgiveness: Making Room for the Miracle* by Colin C. Tipping.

Forgiveness is not a one-time event. You will find yourself needing to forgive almost daily. Forgiveness is not something you give to someone else, but rather a gift you give to yourself.

Forgiveness is giving up all hope for a better past!

19. Jack Gilroy

Jack Gilroy is an esteemed author, peace-activist, and vocal critic of the Establishment. He has inspired many students to voice their concerns about the current state of affairs in the world. After retiring from teaching public school, Gilroy protested at the School of the Americas in Fort Benning, Georgia, resulting in a six-month sentence in a federal penitentiary. Gilroy is the author of two books: *Absolute Flanigan* and *The Wisdom Box*; both novels feature young men who refuse to follow US Government's orders to train to kill. About this second book, creative Writer Susan Deer Cloud writes that it is "a courageous novel of conscience, vision, and transforming love."

* * * * * * *

Reading the description of the torture endured by Lois is so far removed from my life experience that I have grappled for months with the question: "What would I do?" The torture described by Lois is at first incredulous. My disbelief seemed to be supported by the photo of the beautiful, smiling child that is Lois. How could she smile through all that? How could one perceive torture in such a beautiful, innocent face?

A second reading made me skeptical, but a third reading led me to put faith in the story. Belief is too difficult to say. How can one believe such evil actions on the part of anyone, let alone birth parents? Yet, I am a student of history and one who has witnessed psychological and physical torture. In grade school I had my head banged on a blackboard by a towering woman teacher. The physical act was less torturous than the degrading comments she made to my friends and me. The woman was well respected by the community, and parents believed any stories about her actions were exaggerations of a need to control misbehaving kids.

As an adult I saw acts in the military and in civilian life that were mean-spirited and sometimes vicious. Later in life, as a prisoner of conscience, one who opposed the teaching of terror and torture by the United States Army School of the Americas, I was chained and moved to a dark basement cell. I lie silently in my prison bunk, kept awake with the sound of prisoners banging walls with their heads, crying out in the darkness. I was moved from the cockroach-infested jail to three federal prisons, my feet and arms in chains, shuffling to urinals with shotgun-armed guards standing overhead as I tried not to wet my pants.

All of this and more is nothing compared to what Lois experienced. I can't imagine having the strength to endure the pain and suffering she did endure. As a male, I suppose I would have run away. I can't bear the thought of seriously saying I would love those who tortured me. I would have lacked both will and strength to stay.

Forgive my parents if I did endure the pain and suffering described by Lois? No. I can't conceive forgiveness. As an adult I would pity them. If there is a hell, I would feel sorry for them, knowing they are there.

If I were Lois, I would glory in the achievements she has won. I would realize I rose above terror and replaced that sad part of my life with love. I would be proud of the students I have helped, the friends I have made, and the academic honors and awards I have earned. As I relish in my good deeds and love of humankind, I would put away any thoughts of forgiving those who, although sick of mind, deserve only pity.

20. Scott Kalechstein Grace

Scott Kalechstein Grace is a beloved folksinger and songwriter who calls himself a "Fellow Student of Forgiveness." He shares his music and positive messages internationally at a wide variety of venues. A pioneer in the field of intuitive song, he to date has nine compact discs that are distributed internationally. He travels the world, giving inspirational talks combining music and storytelling. Humorous and entertaining, his music about personal and planetary transformation is highly accessible and offers everyone a playful approach to learning and discovery. He is the author of *Teach Me How to Love: A True Story that Touches Hearts and Helps with the Laundry; How to Evolve during the Trump Experience Whether Humanity Joins You or Not;* and *Oh, the Places Your EGO Will Go! And Other Stories...* See scottsongs.org.

* * * * * * *

Lois, you graciously ask difficult, but important, questions: "Do I forgive my parents? And HOW do I forgive myself?"

If I had a past such as yours, I would hope that I would be courageous enough to walk a path like the one you have walked. I would hope to move to a place of forgiveness for my own sanity, and also so that the legacy of pain is not passed onto another generation.

I think forgiveness is the end result of emotional work, the place we arrive at naturally from being willing to face the flushing out of the feelings over years and years of committed work. I would gravitate towards forms of therapy that are body-centered and emotionally releasing, so I could release from my body-mind layer after layer of rage, hurt, shame, and terror. I would avoid an intellectual or philosophical approach to forgiveness and just create a safe space for my inner child to feel and release whatever comes up.

Self-forgiveness would be a matter of purging shame – again, not just from the mind, but also from the very cells of the body. Amends and apologies are helpful steps, but ultimately, it is about your willingness to see yourself compassionately as a human being who was and is thoroughly innocent, having done whatever you could do to survive.

Lois, I believe you have taken the high road in your healing process and are sharing a great deal of inspiration, hope, strength, and wisdom with the world. I send this response with much love.

21. Bishop Thomas J. Gumbleton

Bishop Thomas J. Gumbleton (1930 to present) is Auxiliary Bishop of the Archdiocese of Detroit. He holds honorary degrees from six universities and has written numerous articles.

Bishop Gumbleton has devoted his life to fighting for humanitarian causes including human rights, civil rights, world hunger, political prisoners, gay and lesbian issues, preventing a nuclear holocaust, and national and international peace and justice. He has traveled the globe including visits to Iraq, Iran, Vietnam, Hiroshima, and countries in South America.

Catholic, Protestant, Jewish, and Palestinian groups have all recognized Bishop Gumbleton's achievements. He has received over 35 awards. Bishop Gumbleton is described as a "man of peace, justice, and reconciliation who speaks out boldly, courageously, compassionately, and personally and whose vision of the Church is an inclusive one of love."

* * * * * * *

The question: "What would YOU do? You are a child in a family that sadistically abuses. You are forced to torture and destroy. What should you do *now*? As an adult, do you forgive your parents? HOW do you forgive yourself?"

I cannot even imagine this scenario in my life. I was raised in a loving two-parent family with nine children. We had our challenges, but we always knew we were loved. So, in responding to your questions, I have to look to those I know who have experienced suffering, torture and abuse. I believe that those able to bring themselves to the point of forgiveness find in themselves a deeper healing that those who cannot forgive. I refer specifically to two women.

The first is Sr. Diana Ortiz. Sr. Diana was tortured by the Guatemalan military, raped, forced to kill another woman, and lowered into a pit filled with dead bodies and other tortured victims. The person in charge was an American our government protects to this day. Her road to recovery has been painful. I am certain she would tell you her recovery is still in process, but forgiveness was part of her process; and it allowed her to move on, breaking the cycle of hatred. She has used her pain to bring to light the plight of other tortured victims and to become their voice.

The second woman is Marietta Jaeger. Over twenty-five years ago, her young daughter was taken from a campsite in Montana where she was raped and killed, and her body dismembered. On the first year anniversary of her daughter's disappearance, the killer called Marietta. It was chilling. She kept him on the phone long enough to have the call traced. He was captured, and while in a holding cell, committed suicide. Before his death, Marietta had a chance to speak with him. When her daughter first disappeared, Marietta said if she could have put her hands around the killer's neck, she would have strangled him herself. She was filled with rage, hurt and guilt. She told God that she could never forgive her daughter's killer; that if that is what God wanted, God would have to do it for her. Through prayer and I'm sure long, sound therapy, she was able to forgive the killer.

She and his mother became friends. Marietta is now a national advocate, standing in opposition to the death penalty.

My point is that I wonder if these strong women could have turned their horrific situations into ones of redemption had it not been for their willingness to forgive. They faced their painful experiences honestly, saw the cruelty and unfairness of their situations – screamed, cried, hollered, swore, and more I'm sure – and began, slowly, once again, in a small way, to take control of their lives.

I don't know if I am as strong as Diana and Marietta. I would hope I could be. I would hope that I could rise like the phoenix from the ashes. I would hope.

144

22. Anne Herman

Anne Herman is an expert in poverty law and an advocate for survivors of domestic violence, homelessness, hunger and the welfare system. She has stood with the oppressed in Vieques, Chiapas, Palestine Iraq, Canada, and the US and spent twenty years engaged in non-violent direct action. She was a prisoner of conscience in federal prison for six months for action against the teaching of torture at School of the Americas to the military of Central America.

* * * * * * *

I sit here at the computer trying to overcome my resistance to putting my feelings down in black and white. It is partly because I have to stop to wipe away the tears, in part for the child you write about, but also for my own child who has never been able to fill the emptiness of not being loved at an early age.

I am responding to your questions as stated – what would I do? No way would I attempt to tell you or anyone else what to do in this situation.

Though I have very few memories of my birth parents, they were not capable of nurturing. They all but disappeared from my life when I was very young, and I grew up with relatives who saw a need to mold me into someone I could never become.

I choose to believe my family did not act out of sadism. Had I been ritually tortured or forced to torture and destroy, I would probably respond as I did as a child, to deal with things I couldn't tolerate or understand by creating a different reality than the one I lived in. On the outside I tried to be who they wanted (and was seldom successful). In my mind I was someone I never let them see. My world was populated with invisible friends that no one knew about. These invisible friends taught me things like reading at an early age, giving me more ways to escape.

I don't know what I should have done except what I did, which was to survive. I pretty much reject *should's*.

As I compose this, I come to realize I'm not sure what it means to forgive. The best I can do is to accept my parents as they are and not expect acceptance, love, or nurturing from them. I know from facilitating an incest survivors group that it is seldom helpful to confront the abuser. You simply end up being abused further by their denial.

One of my greatest gifts is my anger – not at others, but transformed. There were times when anger literally enabled me to survive. It is what I use to counteract my tendency toward guilt, self-doubt, and depression. I'm not sure I have ever overcome the feelings of guilt even though I'm not really sure what I have to feel guilty about. As an adult I feel guilty and sad that I often don't trust others enough to show my true feelings.

I sometimes wonder what I might have accomplished with my life if it had started out differently. Perhaps I would not have spent my life trying to make a difference and confronting violence.

23. Linda Hogan

Linda Hogan is a Chickasaw poet, short story writer, novelist, playwright, and essayist who has done much concerning the development of contemporary Native American poetry, specifically regarding its relationship to environmental, anti-nuclear, and feminist issues. She has been an associate professor at the University of Colorado in Boulder since 1989. Awards and honors include the Five Civilized Tribes Playwriting Award, the Guggenheim Award, and the Wordcraft Circle Writer of the Year (Prose–Fiction) Award for her book, *Mean Spirit*. She is commonly regarded as the most influential, female Native American writer/activist in the United States.

* * * * * * *

Lois, your story is very important to me. My oldest adopted daughter suffered similar abuses, including cigarette burns all over her body, wire burns, and worse. She never has recovered. So I find you to be most amazing.

Cruelty, I don't understand, and surprisingly, I try to. Even though I am extremely sensitive, I try to know what hurts the world and the creations (including us) in it. I want to believe that understanding would help make some change, some difference.

I am grateful to hear that you are your soul and not what was done to you... because torture can be soul altering. I am also grateful for your courage in writing this book. And it looks as if your other works are also significant.

I did not suffer as you did, but was not treated well – neglect, abuse with laughter, but from my mother – not a collusion between both my parents. I can barely grasp how you pulled yourself into life, but feel I did so, too.

About forgiveness... No. Not always. I cannot forgive those who knowingly, willingly cause pain. I don't think even nature can forgive. But I'm softhearted, so if I found a weeping killer, who knows?

Here is to a celebration of your life! And to others who do survive, and with deep sympathy to those who don't, let's love, live, and sing. Tra la la, Tra la la.

24. Steven L. Jacobs

Steven L. Jacobs is a Rabbi, Associate Professor of Religious Studies, and Aaron Aronov Chair of Judaic Studies at The University of Alabama, Tuscaloosa. He earned his D.H.L. (Doctor of Hebrew Letters), D.D. (Doctor of Divinity), and ordination as a rabbi from The Hebrew Union-College: Jewish Institute of Religion, Cincinnati, Ohio.

A child of a Holocaust survivor, Jacobs' research has focused on Holocaust and genocide studies, and on translating and reinterpreting the Bible, including the Dead Sea Scrolls. He has written several books including *Rethinking Jewish Faith* (1994): *The Child of a Survivor Responds*; (Editor) *The Holocaust Now: Contemporary Christian and Jewish Though*t (1996), and (Co-Editor) *Pioneers of Genocide Studies* (2000). He served also as an Associate Editor for the two-volume Encyclopedia of Genocide (1999).

* * * * * * *

I write these words of response two days prior to the start of yet another Jewish religious and liturgical year (5763/2002), and twelve days prior to Judaism's holiest day, Yom Kippur, its communal Day of Atonement. I do so as one ordained to the (liberal) Reform Jewish rabbinate; child of a survivor-escapee from the carnage and devastation now known as the Holocaust, himself now deceased; and a university professor of Judaic Studies.

Throughout religious Judaism's evolving history, forgiveness has long played a dominant role. The Biblical text, or Torah, is filled with examples of sinful human beings forgiven for their sins by the God of Israel – Leviticus 4:26, for example, among the primary texts. Post-Biblical or rabbinic Judaism built upon this foundation, and the rabbis of that tradition, in their sophisticated understanding and interpretation of those texts, drew a critically-important distinction between sins committed by an errant humanity against God for which the Divine Presence only had the power to forgive, and sins committed by humanity against itself for which only the aggrieved individual had the power to forgive. Both understandings are predicated upon the sinner recognizing the error of his/her ways, expressing sincere and heartfelt remorse for the wrongs committed, leaving such acts, and vowing concretely not to repeat such behaviors. Thus, all such sinful acts – with three notable exceptions: murder (for which the victim cannot grant absolution), idolatry (the public supplanting of the God of Israel by anything or anyone else), and incest (relevant to the theme of this project; a sin perceived by the rabbis as so odious to their conception of the order and harmony of the universe itself as to be "beyond the pale") – were possessed of the possibilities of repentance and forgiveness; what I would label small "s" sins (the three large exceptions labeled as capitalized "S" sins).

Central to this entire process of repentance, forgiveness, and reconciliation is the recognition of the one who committed these acts of having violated the norms of either human-to-Divine encounter or human-to-human encounter, coupled with a genuine, heartfelt, and sincere desire not to erase the past (for which there is no erasure) but to overcome it by commitment to non-repetition. Nowhere in this entire discussion is the innocent victim-recipient of such behavior understood to bear any responsibility for such behavior with one notable exception.

The rabbis of the Jewish Religious Tradition teach that, prior to the holy day of Yom Kippur, all individuals are obligated to go to those persons whom they have wronged and ask for forgiveness. If the offended person, however, finds the pain too great to bear, and is unable to grant such a request, Talmudic tradition dictates that the offending individual must return a second time and request forgiveness. If the pain remains and forgiveness is still not granted, the individual remains obligated to return yet a third time to plead his or her case. If forgiveness is still not granted, then and only then is such an individual permitted to enter the Sanctuary and ask for God's forgiveness, the onus of responsibility having now shifted to the afflicting party after this third attempt.

One should note at this point that the human act of forgiveness is understood to be behavior comparable to Divine behavior, for the God of Israel was, oft-times, referred to as the Compassionate or Merciful One. According to the Babylonian Talmudic tractate Sabbath 151b, "All who act mercifully toward their fellow creatures will be treated mercifully by Heaven; and all who do not act mercifully toward their fellow creatures will not be treated mercifully by Heaven."

Nowhere in the horrendous acts detailed in Lois Einhorn's account of her growing up years in the home of two parents psychologically, sexually, and physically dysfunctional does she present us with either one or both parents genuinely and sincerely recognizing their truly sinful and egregious behaviors as morally and ethically wrong. Nor does she

149

present us with either one or both parents, post-recognition, vowing solemnly not to continue such aberrant behavior. Nor does she present us with either one or both parents genuinely and sincerely pleading for forgiveness from either Lois or her sister. Thus, the strictures of the Jewish Religious Tradition, as responses to what she has so graphically portrayed, are not applicable. Indeed, nowhere do I find any Jewish text that suggests, either explicitly or implicitly, that the primary responsibility of initiation in the recognition-forgiveness-reconciliation continuum is that of the victim-recipient. Knowing from her "story" that both of her parents are deceased, thus have died unrepentantly, the responsibility to address their sins falls upon God. That, tragically, both Lois and her sister did not have the opportunity to forgive their parents, and, therefore, experience the healing of reconciliation makes this horror even more devastating. That she, at least according to her own account and her official university curriculum vitae, has become the success that she has is tribute not only to her as a singularly unique person, but to the indomitable human spirit to overcome even the most extreme adversity. Her own resilience speaks volumes.

Lastly and finally, I am reminded of those who, murdered by the Nazis in the most inhumane of all hells created on Earth, refused to give in to their baser, animal-like instincts, but went to their deaths with prayers on their lips and in their hearts, as they were herded into the gas chambers or forced to lie upon the bodies of others already machine-gunned to death before them in vast open pits. Not all but many. Of such persons, the Jewish Religious Tradition regards them as having died for the sanctification of the Divine Name (of God). From that same perspective, Lois Einhorn's parents did everything they could to debase two innocent human persons, their own daughters, attempting to rob them of their own dignity and worth; that they died without having confronted their own crimes, like far too many of the Nazis before them, proves them guilty of their crimes and worthy of condemnation. That the God of Israel may choose to have mercy and compassion on them is God's choice, not their daughters. Ultimately, the only appropriate response for Lois, even after acknowledging perhaps begrudgingly with thanks (with a very, very small "t") her own birth, is not to forgive her parents for what they did, not even to feel sorry for them for the horrific tragedy she endured, but to continue to affirm the blessing of her own life in the words of a widely-known Jewish toast "L'chaim!" (To life!)

25. Derrick Jensen

Derrick Jensen is an award-winning writer, thinker, activist, visionary, and survivor of child abuse. His books include *Listening to the Land: Conversations about Nature, Culture, and Eros* (Critic's Choice winner for one of the best nature books of 1995); *A Language Older Than Words* (named best book of the year for the Quality Paperback Book Club's New Vision Award), *The Culture of Make Believe*, and *Walking on Water: Reading, Writing, and Revolution*. Jensen has also written scores of essays and some short fiction.

All of Jensen's books empower readers in our dehumanizing culture to be fully human and courageous champions, and encouraging others to be the same. Scores of people have complimented Jensen for speaking personally, provocatively, and passionately on human and humane ways of living.

Frances Moore Lappe wrote about one of Jensen's books, "Derrick Jensen is a public intellectual who both breaks and mends the reader's heart."

* * * * * * *

When I was a child, my father beat my mother, my brother, and my sisters, and raped my mother, my sister, and me. I can only speculate that because I was by many years the youngest, my father somehow thought it best that instead of beating me, he would force me to watch and listen. I remember scenes – vaguely, as from a dream or a movie – of arms flailing, of my father chasing my brother Rick around and around the house. I remember my mother pulling my father into their bedroom to absorb blows that may have otherwise landed on her children. We sat stone-faced in the kitchen, a captive audience to stifled groans that escaped through walls that were just too thin.

The worst thing my father did went beyond the hitting and the raping to the denial that any of it ever occurred. Not only bones were broken, but broken also was the bedrock connection between memory and experience, between psyche and reality. His denial made sense, not only because an admission of violence would have harmed his image as a socially-respected, wealthy, and deeply religious physician, but more simply because the man who would beat his children could not speak about it honestly and continue to do it.

We became a family of amnesiacs. There's no place in the mind to sufficiently contain these experiences, and as there is effectively no way out, it would have served no purpose for us to consciously remember the atrocities. So we learned, day after day, that we could not trust our perceptions, and that we were better off not listening to our emotions. Daily we forgot, and if a memory pushed its way to the surface, we forgot again. There'd be a beating, followed by brief contrition and my father asking, "Why did you make me do it?" And then? Nothing, save the inconvenient evidence: a broken door, urine-soaked underwear, a wooden room divider my brother repeatedly tore from the wall trying to pick up speed around the corner. Once these were fixed, there was nothing left to remember. So we "forgot," and the pattern continued.

When I finally started to speak of what my father had done, members of our church were quick to dismiss, first by disbelieving and then by telling me that, even if what I said were true, I had to learn to forgive.

I realized though, even as a child, that there can be no forgiveness without prior change on the perpetrator's part. To forgive my father as he continued to rape and beat us would be to actively participate in our own victimization. To forgive under those circumstances is obscene.

Even now, three decades later, I am still told by some people – invariably those who do not know me - to forgive my father. But to my knowledge (and I have not spoken to him for decades), he hasn't changed. Even now, to forgive would be a betrayal of the child I was, the child who was raped and saw his siblings and mother beaten, the child who for most of his life had incessant nightmares, who to this day has tremendous difficulty sleeping (I write this at 6:35 am, after yet another night of no sleep).

I want to talk, though, also about my mother. In my father's case, to forgive would be unthinkable. In my mother's case, it's no longer relevant.

I've always had a close relationship with my mother. Through my twenties, however, I harbored a lot of resentment toward her that she had not left my father. They stayed together until I was ten or eleven. When I was in my early thirties, my mother and I had a long series of conversations about my resentment, culminating in a several-hour talk sitting in her car in her garage. Toward the end of this talk, she said that the reason she stayed as long as she did was that she was afraid if she left sooner my father would gain custody of me.

She had a point. My father was rich, and was also tennis buddies with the presiding judge in their divorce, who himself was an extreme misogynist. Even as it was, the judge very nearly gave my father custody any number of times. But there are ways in which none of that mattered, then or now. I said, "I categorically deny that rationale, because it implicitly makes me responsible for a decade of beatings and rapes. Had I not been born, that would have saved everyone that pain."

"What were my options? There were no battered women's shelters."

"We would have been better off if you would have killed him, and then left us to be raised by wolves." This was no statement about my mother's capacities: away from my father, she did a wonderful job. But she did not protect us when we could not protect ourselves. I continued, "We would have been better off if you would have taken us to live in a slum in South America. We would have been better off under almost any circumstances."

She responded, "Do you think that even one hour goes by that I don't regret the decisions I made and did not make? I regret them every moment. I am sorry. I am sorrier than I will ever be able to say."

Neither of us said anything for a long while.

Finally she continued, "Why do you think, when you were in your twenties and calling yourself a writer but not writing, that I never once suggested you get yourself a job, that you do anything other than what you were doing, which was not very much? Why do you think through all that time that I supported you emotionally, and at times financially?"

Another long pause.

"It was because I knew you never had a childhood, and if you were ever going to be happy as an adult you needed a long time to just sit and be and do whatever you needed to do to vomit up the effects of your father's violence. You needed to become who you are. And if I wasn't able to protect you better as a child, I was certainly going to do everything in my power to help you become the happiest person you could as an adult."

She'd never said this to me before, never once thrown her support in my face, and never would have said anything at all had I not backed her into a corner. In that moment all of my resentment disappeared, never to return. I could not ask any more than that she acknowledge her mistake, say she was sorry, manifest that sorrow, and try by doing everything in her power to make it right. Forgiveness became in that moment irrelevant. There was nothing anymore to forgive.

26. Bill T. Jones

Bill T. Jones is a famous dancer and choreographer. His fame is even more impressive given that he is black, homosexual, and HIV positive.

In 1982, with his long-time partner and companion Arnie Zane, Jones founded Bill T. Jones/Arnie Zane and Company, a vehicle for the development of their choreography in which they commonly employed openly gay themes.

Both with Zane and after Zane's death, Jones has gained recognition as a "new wave" or "postmodern" choreographer. He has performed in prestigious venues and has received prestigious awards including a Bessie Award and a MacArthur Fellowship. The Dorothy B. Chandler Performing Arts Award recognized Jones as an "innovative master."

* * * * * * *

I am sure you have and will continue to receive strong responses to your request.

I suppose I should say I was flattered to be in the company of the individuals you have identified. But the injustice and abuse that you speak of leaves me shame-faced with my own suffering. I realize all comparisons are irrelevant and verge on the ridiculous when it comes to human suffering. Yet, my initial response was an ego-driven response, but with that came anger and even a small sense of violation.

To put it bluntly, my knee-jerk response was, "Why does she burden me with this!" And following this response came one of shame. I certainly do not want to be party to a conspiracy of silence.

I have questions about your provocative reasoning that draws an unambiguous line between inhuman domestic suffering such as you suffered at the hand of your parents, September 11, and the present state of the world. The rancor I felt at your conflated logic cannot overcome the imperative now established between you and me, and such an imperative is that once an individual bears witness or makes one a party to the facts and the moral questions that your question of forgiveness implies, one has no choice but to respond.

So my response is only this: Forgiveness in any relationship is relevant and of use only when that relationship (be one between two lovers, a parent and child, coworkers, citizens, ethnic groups, nations) has a future. Requesting forgiveness and granting it are mechanisms, tools for change, a means to fight back against the suffocating perception that this is an immoral indifferent universe, and that we are thrown into a chaotic, ever-rolling, chemical change such as that of molecules in a scientist's laboratory beaker. Granting forgiveness is a way of saying, "Yes, this is a painful bloody place, but I believe acts of will and faith are the ways to live here."

I have said much more than I intended, and yet I don't feel as if I have said enough. I admire you and wish you continued success.

27. Mary Elizabeth King, Ph.D.

Dr. Mary Elizabeth King is a visiting research fellow at the Rothermere American Institute in Oxford, England; Professor of Peace and Conflict Studies at the University for Peace in Costa Rica; and a former Distinguished Scholar at the American University's Center for Global Peace in Washington, D.C. She has devoted her life to the study and practice of nonviolent communication. She was one of the few white females in the Civil Rights Movement, working beside Reverend Martin Luther King, Jr. (no relation). Her book about Christmas in jail in 1963, *Freedom Song: A Personal Story of the 1960s Civil Rights Movement*, was honored with the Robert F. Kennedy Memorial Book Award.

King's latest book, *Mahatma Gandhi and Martin Luther King, Jr.: The Power of Nonviolent Action* explains the theories, methods, and power of nonviolence. It also details nine contemporary examples of nonviolence including East Germany, Palestine, and Guatemala.

Under President Jimmy Carter, King was responsible for the Peace Corps (then in 60 countries), and she served then and after as Special Adviser to the Middle East. Carter says that Mary Elizabeth King "has a sensitivity and a courage that's absolutely superlative."

* * * * * * *

Many years of research have clearly established that the majority of adults who physically and sexually abuse their children were victims themselves in their youth. A vicious cycle exists that must be broken, if we are to save future generations from a similar fate. The greater the abuse is, the more the need to avoid its transmission to later generations.

As someone who has devoted her life to resolving conflicts nonviolently, I believe a quest for forgiveness must be at the heart of improving the human condition and overcoming the egregious wrongs done to so many human beings. As the Reverend Dr. Martin Luther King, Jr., stated:

> *Darkness cannot drive out darkness*
> *Only light can do that.*
> *Hate cannot drive out hate;*
> *Only love can do that.*

Hate multiplies hate,
  Violence multiplies violence.
And toughness multiplies toughness
  In a descending spiral of destruction…
The chain reaction of evil—
  Hate begetting hate,
Wars producing more wars—
  Must be broken,
Or we shall be plunged into
  The darkness of annihilation.

In South Africa last year, I could discern that the Truth and Reconciliation Commission—despite all its flaws and imperfections—showed that an entire society could be helped toward healing, despite decades of appalling atrocities, if the victims were willing to forego retribution and vengeance, and discover mental cleansing for themselves by laying aside their hatred.

Recently, I spent a week in Rwanda, where approximately one million persons were hacked, slashed, or shot to death during a few months in 1994. Organized killings, targeting persons along ethnic lines, had occurred there several times, and no one was ever punished. People in Rwanda used the term "genocide" for the first time in 1994, but the international community was silent. The United Nation's Security Council passed a resolution condemning the killings, but omitted the word "genocide," because, had the term been used, the UN would have been legally obligated by its Charter to act to "prevent and punish" the perpetrators. Insiders say that Clinton officials had detailed knowledge of the genocide but explicitly forbade the use of the word.

Not surprisingly, eradication of a culture of immunity has become the top consideration in Rwanda today. Accompanying a deliberate process of urging the *genocidaire* (genocide perpetrators) to confess is the hope that communities will embark on a road to forgiveness and even to reconciliation. Immunity—exemption from penalty—functions as a significant underlying cause of conflict: When a populace sees high crimes, rapes, and murders go unpunished, individuals turn to violence to fight violence. The fact that no one was ever held responsible for repeated organized killings led to what happened in 1994. A traditional mechanism, called "Gagaca"—the word for the green, grassy knoll on which the elders met to establish justice in pre-colonial times—has been upgraded to meet international human rights standards, requirements of a fair trial, and dealing with the huge numbers of genocide detainees. The Rwandans administering the system believe that by making sure justice is done, significant steps towards reconciliation may be accomplished.

What most intrigues me in Rwanda is that the first step in the Gacaca trials is to try to get the genocidaires to confess. According to Alice Urusaro Karekezi, Director of the Center for Conflict Management at the National University of Rwanda at Butare, "Everybody knows who did the killings, and we want them to confess. It's better for them. It's better for the victims who survived. It's better for the families of the victims who did not survive. It's better for the whole society. If the genocidaires confess, it can start the process of forgiveness, and ultimately we may reach reconciliation." A number of non-government organizations that run trauma-healing workshops in this sensitive situation report doing so based on the conviction that nothing can be accomplished if Rwandans hold onto bitter grievances. They say that no matter how angry, embittered, or aggrieved people are, they must somehow find a way to climb onto the road to forgiveness.

I do not share this with you lightly or trivially. Forgiveness sets in motion a complex psychological process in the human mind and psyche that can act in beneficial and healthy ways for the individual. Especially after the perpetrators are dead, all that matters is the healing of the victim and his or her loved ones—something jeopardized by the continuing allocation of blame and the perpetuation of anger. When embarking on the search for the means of forgiveness, it does not matter how accurately the details of abuse are remembered. Excruciatingly painful details may be minimized, distorted, or exaggerated over time, but forgiveness has the potential to wipe it all away.

I hope these few thoughts regarding planetary peace and forgiveness help you in dealing with what has been an excruciatingly painful situation in your personal life.

28. Barb Kohn, Ph.D.

Dr. Barb Kohn is Vice President of Research and Development at a profitable biotechnology company that manufactures test kits used to ensure that food is safe to consume. She is a Distinguished Agricultural Alumna of Purdue University, where she shares this high distinction with seventy out of the School's 30,000 alumni. She earned her Ph.D. in biological chemistry at Harvard University and then carried out postdoctoral research at the Center for Cancer Research, Massachusetts Institute of Technology. For twenty-two years she has been married to a gentle, loving man.

Kohn was brutally abused as a child. Because of the abuse, she still limps and can't use her left arm normally; yet, she recently began having fun with inline skating. She is grateful for the question given her by a Catholic priest who believes children become guilty when broken by their captors during torture. He asked, "Couldn't a child theoretically have held out?" The examination of this question propelled her from uncomprehending harshness into a place of reality and compassion, and into a deeper embrace of her faith as a Jew.

Kohn is not morbid but merely reducing her life to the most essential elements when she states that she wants her epitaph to read, "She got back on the horse. Every time."

* * * * * * *

Ah, the torturer's games we sometimes still play, in our desire to be upright and conscientious while stumbling over invalid assumptions. I speak only with empathy, for I have tripped numbly to the music of such dances on many a cold night or distant day.

I know and respect that the questions posed by the author are based on the utmost integrity and soul-searching: "You are a child in a family that sadistically abuses. You are forced to torture and destroy. What would YOU do? What should you do *now*? HOW do you forgive yourself?"

In answering, I take refuge in what we know to be true of most human beings. Most human beings try their best. They try to help. They try to support the common good. Sometimes they are forced by others intent on evil to participate in such mayhem. But even then, the intent of the heart must speak louder than the actions forced by torture.

159

"What would you do?" At first I smile with transmuted grief. For I love the action verbs that imply there was some control you or I could have exerted. It is more comforting than the truth that we were just inanimate tools of destruction in our captor's eyes, children who were no more to the abusers than a knife or a gun, devoid of moral consciousness and sentient empathy.

So, try as I might, still I cannot respond to the inquiry. I must first protest the phrasing. It is a leading question, and therefore, illegitimate. One might as well ask me when I stopped beating my husband. The question implies the existence of my freedom to have made choices in external behaviors, as opposed to the interior orientation of the heart. That belief is as dangerous as it is seductive. Therefore, any response must follow a rejection of the implicit assumption of the question before it is possible to formulate a reply.

The sages of the Talmud, the code of Jewish Law, clarify this point. They tell of an impudent and cruel man who once attacked a rabbi by saying, "Rabbi! I have in one of my two hands, which I am holding behind my back, a small bird. You must correctly guess which hand. If you do, I will let the bird go free. If you are wrong, I will crush the bird to death. What do your precious Talmud and Torah teach you now?" And the Rabbi replies, "That the question of the bird's life is in your hands, not mine."

Knowing this, you may now ask me, "What would you do?" And I will answer you: I did, Lois, exactly as you, which was precious little. Mostly we embodied our captors' desires, because given the drugs, pain, torture and horror, we as children could do little else. Have rachmones (compassion) on the goaded-ox-that-gores. By this I refer to a tortured animal. For the Rabbis again wisely say that an ox that goes and kills should itself be rendered unable to kill again, and they consider the ox guilty. Guilty, that is, unless the ox has been goaded to gore. If so, then the ox is guiltless, and only those who goaded it are punished.

The next question is: "What should you do?" And I will answer with the opposite of what the captors said. I recommend survival. I know the old lies. I know the heroism touted in this culture by those who, to their great fortune, have no first-hand knowledge of these experiences, and substitute for this lack only glib and wounding moral certitudes: "It is better to lay down one's life..." Well, maybe, if that is a choice. But again we dance with smoke and mirrors.

I saw a child try to lay down her life by leaping into a fire rather than continuing to throw animals into it. She was dragged out, rolled on the earth, and treated. I, too, had decided to die once, when my living had been paired through my captor's forced choices with the deaths of animals. My captors allowed me to become dehydrated, and I lost the will to live. I couldn't drink, with such a swollen tongue. Nor did I want to, anymore. Their ministrations after the days of torture were interruptions, a nuisance intruding on the hot, dry, dark journey to which I had surrendered. I still remember how the pain came back once they had forcibly hydrated me with IVs, and I began to live again. How I hated it.

So let's put aside the mirage of choice, of our fantasy of nobility or even the permissibility by one's captors of sacrifice of oneself. This flawed premise is water flashing faraway on searing sands in a dry desert, and it is no sustenance we will ever reach. There was no choice. It is true that we are alive now, while others died in a crazy quilt of evil quite incomprehensible to most people. Perhaps we may console ourselves that there will be more clarity from a higher spiritual vantage point. But in any event, remember this, about the question, "What should you do?" Remember that there was no "should." There was no "do." For there was no choice.

"How do you forgive yourself?" This, finally, is a ground on which I can move with some assurance. There is much to forgive. But I try to view myself with compassion, as I have done the best that I could out of a pained heart, and I urge you to treat yourself with compassion as well. You and I never gave up permanently. We have not done badly, considering. We can only judge our behavior now as free people. Growth is always an option, for all of us, and I try to choose it when I can. And in so doing, I never lose the exhilaration of finally being able now, at long last, to ask the author's questions in a genuine way, as a free woman, for these questions are indeed the cornerstone of a considered life: "What would I do? What should I do? How do I forgive myself?"

29. Ellen P. Lacter, Ph.D.

Dr. Ellen P. Lacter is a Clinical Psychologist in San Diego, California, specializing in the treatment of psychological trauma disorders in children and adults, particularly ritual trauma and dissociative disorders. She is an outspoken advocate for ritual abuse survivors, through workshops and via her website.

* * * * * * *

I am a psychologist living and working in San Diego, California. Ten years ago, a mother brought her small children to me for play therapy because they had been sexually abused by some neighbors. The mother was fiercely protective, yet gentle and adoring. These are my favorite kind of cases. I feel competent and in control. The children work through their trauma within the secure nest of their parent's love. And usually in less than a year, I say good-bye, knowing all will be well.

I could not have been more wrong. These children were my first ritually abused clients. I was beginning a journey that would take me to an underground of darkness and evil I could not have ever imagined, and would also bring me to the side of survivors of these horrors who have become my teachers about kindness and healing and faith and strength.

The horrors that Lois describes are real: sadistic and repeated rape, electroshock of "private parts," forced ingestion of feces and animal remains, pitting children against each other, being starved and drugged, strangulation to the point of losing consciousness, words that pierce the soul, threats of murder and wanting to die, and "forgetting" (dissociating) the intolerable or going insane. This is all standard fare. The horrible truth is that most ritual abuse is even more severe. I hope that most people reading this have been fortunate enough, cared for enough, to not be able to conceive of abuse worse than Lois's "Typical Abuse Day." I was that lucky.

I grew up in a beautiful town in New York State, in the 1950s. My parents could not have children, so they adopted my brother and me. When I was three years old, and my brother was still wiggling in his crib, my mother read me a story she had written about a couple who loved each other very much, but were lonely. So, they adopted a bird on page 3, and a dog on page 4, and adorable me in a room full of toys on page 5 (my brother was on page 6 of course). You get the picture. Like many

162

parents in the 1950s, especially of Eastern European Jewish heritage, they were a bit strict, especially when it came to academics, and they had some personal problems of their own. But, I was loved and safe and encouraged and very sheltered.

Three years ago, a psychologist from New York contacted me through my website on ritual abuse asking me for suggestions on treating his client, a victim of ritual abuse. His being from New York, my curiosity was piqued, so I asked, "Where did your client live when she was abused?" He named the county I grew up in. I expressed surprise and asked for the town. He named my town.

I had often wondered, having come to understand the prevalence of ritual abuse, who in my high school might have been abused in this way. Could my town have been miraculously spared? A comforting thought. Oops! So, having tread this far, I asked, "What year was she born?" The psychologist named my year of birth. Lois and I were five months apart. I knew the street where she lived until her family relocated. My mother often took me to the park near her house to feed the ducks. I was happily feeding ducks while Lois was a block away being tortured. And her family was Jewish. More harsh realities, more darkness. Lois and I happened to have attended different elementary schools. Had I known Lois as a child, it would have hurt even more.

Lois asks the tough questions that all ritual abuse survivors struggle with. Am I responsible, at least in part, for the acts of abuse I was forced to perpetrate? What if the rage I felt toward my abusers was partially released onto the victims I was forced to hurt? Is this human and forgivable? Or is it evil at any age? Am I just like my abusers? Or are they more like me?

Knowing that ritual abuse is passed down through generations within families, how much chance or choice did my parents have to act otherwise? Why did I reject sadism, while others seemed to embrace it? Were they more abused? Were they more effectively programmed? Or did I experience something that allowed me to cling to hope and the capacity for love? Was it that first grade teacher who pled with me to tell her what was wrong? Did my parents have personalities who genuinely loved me? (Ritual abuse usually splinters the psyche into multiple dissociated identities.) When I could bear no more, did a higher source come to my side?

Or does free will exist beyond life experience? Did my abusers freely choose evil? Should there not be some form of justice? Or is justice simply revenge? Do people learn from punishment or does it only engender more hatred? If it is destructive to hate, what do I do with my anger?

Is forgiveness the answer? What is forgiveness? Is it compassion for my abusers? Does it mean that I try to understand why they made the choices they made? Do I choose to believe that they must have been too psychologically broken to do otherwise? Is it telling them that I forgive them and harbor no ill will toward them? I know ritual abuse survivors who have done just that.

Or is forgiveness about me? Is it a process of grieving? Is it bourn of deep acceptance that my abuse happened and cannot be undone? Is it divesting myself emotionally of the outcome for my abusers, on earth, and after death? Is it the choice to shed toxic anger and to embrace love and joy? If I cannot forgive my abusers, is this because I will not forgive myself?

What is self-forgiveness? Is it self-analysis, gaining insight into the forces influencing me at the time? Is it acknowledging that I was truly helpless as a child? Is it the acceptance of human frailty? Or is it a process of honestly facing the times I violated my conscience, without minimization or global self-condemnation, and working to become the best person I can be.

Before I address these complex issues, it is critical to place them in proper perspective. As abhorrent an exercise as this may be, ritual abuse is best understood if one attempts to adopt the mind-set of a perpetrator. Ritual abusers seek absolute control over the actions and thoughts of their victims. Every foundation of self must be destroyed: self-worth, self-agency, volition, all bonds of love (except with the abuser), and all hope. This is aimed as deeply as possible within the psyche, to "break the spirit" and "wound the soul".

This is probably most effectively accomplished by forcing victims to abuse or kill others. Margaret Smith, in her book, *Ritual Abuse: What It Is, Why It Happens, How to Help* (San Francisco: HarperCollins, 1993) in a study of 52 ritual abuse survivors found that 75% were forced to torture others. (Most experts in ritual abuse would hypothesize that the remaining 25% had not yet penetrated the dissociative barriers concealing their forced abuse of others.)

Interrogators know that prisoners will more quickly yield if a compatriot is being tortured rather than the self. One of the miracles within this darkness is that most children would rather be abused themselves than to witness someone else being hurt, to wit, Lois pleads to her father, "Do whatever you want to me. Just don't hurt my sister."

164

The psychological and spiritual cost of this Machiavellian manipulation is palpable in her following description: "My father hits my sister 100 more times because, he says, my sister did not hit me hard enough. For trying to be nice, my sister is getting hurt more. When my sister faints from the pain, I want to die. I have nothing left to fight for. My insides are empty. I feel worse than worthless; I feel repulsive and despicable."

Forcing children to harm others, particularly loved ones, is the ultimate weapon. And the more the child clings to love, the more the abusers seek to exploit and destroy it, by threatening harm to loved ones and forcing the child to harm and kill others. This typically begins as soon as the child has the physical capacity to execute a brutal act, beginning with killing small animals as a toddler. This is a set-up for which full responsibility lies with the abusers, not the child victims.

Victims are programmed to never remember how their abusers orchestrated their abuse of others. Great lengths are taken to make victims define themselves as deeply evil, irredeemable, unworthy of love, and forever trapped in the underworld of the group. As dissociative barriers are shed, survivors usually gain insight into the traps that were set for them and their helplessness to have acted otherwise. Being armed with these insights helps. But it does not eliminate the devastation of having inflicted harm on others. A 3-year-old victim once told me, "They broke my heart". The child was too young to have the words: "self-worth", "capacity for attachment", "conscience", "soul", or "spirit". What did this child grasp that transcends the limitations language later places on thought?

Working with ritual abuse survivors has challenged me to walk an unfamiliar terrain where psychology and spirituality co-mingle, with different languages, different models of the mind, and different methods of study. Survivors have taught me lessons about spiritual good and evil that I must now incorporate into the psychological constructs I have long used to understand people.

A guiding principle in my current understanding of people is that there is something within all of us that experiences profound and irreversible pain when we inflict pain on another person. I believe there are no exceptions to this (unless the brain is severely organically compromised). Those who attempt to fully embrace evil cannot extinguish this. Their drive to destroy it may fuel greater wickedness, but their efforts are doomed to fail. I know of ritual abusers who apologized to their children on their deathbeds. I know of ritual abusers who committed suicide because they could no longer live with the heartache of the harm they were doing to others. I believe that if people do not begin to come to terms with this heartache in life, it will remain inescapable in death.

This principle greatly impacts my beliefs about forgiveness. It is a process of facing truth that we can only do for ourselves. I deeply respect survivors who have gone to their parents and spoken words of forgiveness. I believe it demonstrates to the abuser the capacity to move from hatred to love, from self-deceit to self-reckoning. It teaches that it is possible to walk another path. It is an act of mercy for someone who feels inexorably evil. It reduces the deep, often unconscious, dread of the harm one has caused, and the rage one has engendered, both which help sustain barriers to facing painful truths. To that degree, it can lessen the abuser's burden. The rest is a solitary path.

Similarly, anger cannot help people face truth. It only breeds more fear and defensiveness in those already dominated by fear, as most abusers are, though their fear is often unconscious.

Intense anger and longings for talion-style revenge are natural, unavoidable consequences of having been severely abused. Contending with these urges cannot be short-circuited. In play therapy, abused children almost always exact revenge against figures representing their abusers. Their dramas are replete with themes of turning the tables on their abusers, sometimes in disguised form, and often quite directly. Adult survivors must find ways to reckon with these same urges, whether that takes the form of talking, writing, art, music, dance, body work, etc.

Owning one's sadistic fantasies of revenge is often the key to "unlocking" oneself from a position of helpless paralysis to one of mobilized empowerment.

Reconciling one's desire for revenge is an essential step. But clinging to a wish for actual revenge is fraught with peril, spiritually physically, and psychologically.

Spiritually, the personal cost of fixating on anger or revenge is that there is no room for serenity or joy, little space for love to flourish, and little ability to open to future possibilities. But, the greatest spiritual danger may be that a stance of hatred permits a spiritual opening that abusers exploit. Practitioners of abusive witchcraft devote themselves to harnessing evil in rituals to wield power in the astral realm. Great efforts are made to maintain bonds to their victims to curse and control them; and they believe bonds of hatred are more powerful than bonds of love.

The cost of chronic anger to the immune and cardiovascular system is well known. (There is also significant evidence that overly constricted emotional expression has important negative health consequences). Psychologically, I believe that harboring a need for revenge or punishment, or even justice, derails the process of acceptance and grief. Just as endless self-punishment can never undo the acts of abuse one was forced to commit, retaliation, even justice, can never reverse the losses that ritually abused children sustain. Not having been tenderly gazed at and held, the loss of personal efficacy (psychological and physical), the absence of all sanctuary, the absence of joy, the loss of hope, the eradication of self-worth - nothing can undo that these happened. Nothing can right these violations.

But, grieving requires sorrow and compassion for the self. And many survivors of ritual abuse feel undeserving of any compassion; anger is worthy of them, but sorrow and love are not.

This brings me back to the difficult task of self-forgiveness. I would like to take one last trip back to the town where Lois and I grew up, one mile, yet worlds apart. While Lois is deciding whether to resist abusing her sister, knowing that this will only spawn greater wrath in her father, which will be directed to either her sister or herself, I am playing in the front of my house with the little girl from down the street. I am shy and the subject of ridicule by the local bullies, but my friend is even more of a target. The bullies approach on their bicycles, and I tell my friend to stand behind the tree so they do not harass me for playing with her. I know I am doing wrong.

I am 53 years old and have finally settled on not excusing myself for what I did. I know I violated my sense of right and wrong. I abused my power for personal gain. For years, I tried to blame this act on my own victimization by the bullies. Their cruelty was a source of great pain.

I even tried to engage a few friends in absolving me of my guilt. But that "something within" would not buy it! I finally learned to accept my violation of myself. I do not let it go. I also do not dwell in it. I am finally able to condemn myself for this act, to tolerate the knowledge that I stepped into something dark, without fear that this transgression negates all of the good within me. This has finally diffused the anxiety that was associated with this event.

Survivors of ritual abuse live their childhoods in a world of people behaving like monsters. Hatred, rivalry, and danger exist at every turn. In the depths of this depravity, they discover darkness within themselves. They had moments in which they violated their own self. Perhaps they embraced power over another to be spared greater torture. Maybe they vented some of their rage on the innocent. They may have considered

167

aligning with their abusers to be spared. Maybe they yearned to be at the top of the heap. Perhaps there was a period when they tried to make that climb. They may have even discovered that when pain or starvation or suffocation.... cross a certain line, an animalistic survival instinct takes over, at the expense of everything else.

These are the self-violations that ritual abuse survivors have to mediate. I want them to know that I honor them. I want them to know that they are my spiritual teachers. I want them to do for themselves what I have done for myself in my own small way.

Healing in Truth

Judge thyself through a filter of truth
That beats as one with your heart
Beyond the influence of others,
Beyond the passing comfort of self-deception,
Beyond easy answers.
A filter free of self-punishment,
For such is only a game of magic
That can undo no wrongs.

Fear not pain,
For no human can escape the pain of having hurt another,
And it is human to have chosen one's want over another's need,
More than once.
Neither the career criminal,
Nor the sadistic abuser of children,
Nor the so-called sociopath,
Can build a wall thick enough to dull this pain.
Face the darkness.
Where your heart says, "I did wrong",
Leave off "because..."

Fear not rage,
For it is human to wish to inflict pain on your assailant,
And until this rage is known and owned,
It is human to release it on the innocent.
Grapple with this human frailty,
And your gift will be true freedom

168

To make the sublimely human choice
To rise above the wish for revenge.

Fear not submission, helplessness, or frozen defeat.
In the face of terror, these are also deeply human.
To condemn oneself for being overpowered will set a trap of rage,
An endless childish game of seeking to undo the done.

Fear not deep grief for the wounds to thy heart.
As you embrace others in sorrow,
Embrace sorrow for thyself.

And if you are the victim of evil,
Fear not the truths
That others cannot bear to know within themselves.
There is a breaking point in all of us,
Where animal instinct for survival overrides one's humanity.
Torturers exploit this.
You have been taken to that point.
Human beings are most wounded by the suffering of another.
Torturers manipulate this.
You have been forced to hurt others.
Perhaps you have been forced to kill.
Forgive yourself, because only you can.

And if you lost your connection to your heart along the way
And the casing grew hard and thick,
And you felt cold through and through,
Reach in toward your heart,
with an offering of solace.
And ask what it needs to heal.

©2022 Ellen Lacter, Ph.D.
Addendum to My Contribution to:
Forgiveness and Child Abuse: Would You Forgive?
By Lois Einhorn

Sixteen years have flown by since I first responded to Dr. Einhorn's story of her child abuse and her questions about whether she should forgive herself for the harm that her abusers coerced her to do to other victims and whether she should forgive her abusers for the abuse they inflicted on her and others.

I have been working as a psychologist with victims of extreme and sadistic child abuse, including ritual abuse, torture-based mind control, and production of sadistic child abuse materials, for more than 25 years. In the last ten years, my understanding of coercion of victims to harm and kill other victims, including victims' pets and other animals, has considerably deepened, and I am happy for the opportunity to share what I have learned.

Understanding Coerced Perpetration

I now understand that coercion of children to harm other victims through torture and terrorization is a mainstay of extreme and sadistic abuse; it is the rule, not the exception. Sadistic abusers take deep satisfaction in coercing victims to harm others as it inflicts two forms of abuse simultaneously – psychological devastation to one victim and physical and sexual abuse or torture to the other.

Coerced perpetration is also a highly effective form of psychological control. The effects are immediate and long-term psychological devastation, heartbreak, moral injury, self-hatred, and self-recrimination. By design, victims generally feel like accomplices, and unworthy of affiliating with anyone outside of the abuser group. They are effectively silenced and rarely disclose their abuse or seek help.

This trauma is calculatingly inflicted on countless numbers of children, often in abuse that continues into adulthood, by perpetrators who have completely shut down their humanity and who embrace this form of unthinkable cruelty as a means of coping with whatever trauma they have themselves endured.

Lois and the victims abused alongside her are among tens of thousands of other victims, or more.

I am convinced that to be able to help survivors of extreme and sadistic abuse, those of us who support victims – therapists, clergy, friends, loved ones, fellow survivors, etc., must develop a deep understanding of how torture-coerced harm works, that torture can force anyone do anything, and quite quickly, and the kinds of "breaks" in self-agency that happen under torture. We need to understand all of this well enough to put it into words, as many times as it takes, to help victims of this soul-crushing abuse to begin to understand and forgive themselves for things that they could not escape and for which they hold no responsibility.

The calculated evil that underlies coerced perpetration is unthinkable and unspeakable, painful beyond words to acknowledge, to most everyone, but especially to the victims who have lived through it. Therefore, those who love and support survivors must be prepared to talk about it for them and with them. I will now explain why this is so critical.

1. Survivors need the knowledge and support of people outside of themselves to be able to make sense of coerced perpetration and to process these horrors, to grasp that this form of abuse exists, and to understand that it is a common tactic of sadistic perpetrators, even though the world, the media, even most trauma professionals, do not usually speak about it.

2. Survivors need to be able to share their experiences of this victimization with others, to release their devastating grief, and to receive love and compassion in response.

171

3. Survivors need to hear others explain that victims of torture-coerced perpetration are completely entrapped, terrorized, and stripped of all self-agency and free will, in order to begin to replace their self-condemnation with self-compassion – to begin to heal their moral injury.

What Words Can Supporters Use to Help Victims Heal their Devastating Moral Injury?

As I sit with victims, my heart breaks as I witness the torment and devastating moral injury of having been coerced to harm another person, usually a very young child, sometimes an older child, sometimes an adult, and sometimes an animal. The magnitude of the abusers' cruelty is absolutely terrifying. Simply listening to these accounts is almost too much to take. I sometimes feel that I am losing my mind. But I write down every word. I type it up later. I will not let these horrors vanish into thin air, be forgotten, trivialized, or dismissed.

I work to mentally put myself in the victim's position. When I do, I am clear that I could not hold out any longer than they did, that I too would "break" and submit to the will of torturers. Always knowing that my words are inadequate, I tell them words to the effect of:

"I too, under torture, would harm and kill another person."

"I know that they would have been able to make me do that too, even though I am a grown adult, not a child. There is no way that anybody would not submit to abusers' demands under torture conditions. Anyone who says they would not have complied is lucky enough to have never been tortured and to never have had to find out how these horrors work."

I believe that the guilt, shame, and moral responsibility for these acts are borne entirely by the perpetrators who executed the torture, not by the victims who were being coerced. I say:

"The abusers reduced you to a hammer, a tool that they wielded. You had that little control over your actions. The one who holds the hammer holds the responsibility."

172

"You don't have to ask forgiveness. You have done nothing that needs to be forgiven."

"Intention is everything. It was never your intention to harm anyone else. You wanted no part of any of it. The intention was that of the abusers. They forced you. The blood is on their hands, not yours."

I sit with how bad the torture was and try to put the intensity of the coercion into words. I say:

"You were trapped, stripped of all control. You had no choice to do anything different."

"Torture is completely intolerable. Anybody can be coerced to do anything under torture and they are not to blame for what they are forced to do."

I tell them that I know that they would never have committed any of these acts of their own will:

"I know that you would never have done any of these things if you had any choice. You were completely stripped of your free will. There was no escape. I know you were completely trapped."

I let them know that by the time of the episode of coerced perpetration, they had already learned that any resistance, no less any defiance of their abusers, would be immediately met with an escalation of torture:

"You had learned a long time ago, by the time they forced you to do this, that you don't cross these people."

"I know that you learned early on in the torture that any resistance resulted in an escalation of torture."

I remind them of their true wishes and that they had no option to act on them:

"I know you would have rescued the victims if there was any way for you to do that, but there was none."

When I see despondent shame in their eyes that betrays that they believe themselves monsters, I say:

"You are innocent. You are as worthy of love and compassion as anyone else. In fact, any person with a heart would feel even more love for you because of what you have suffered."

These words are never enough and I believe it helps to express this as well:

"I know if I were made to do these things, I would also unjustifiably hate myself. How could anyone not feel that way? But it is unfair. It is unfair."

"I know that no matter how many times I say you were not to blame, it will not take away the pain of what you were forced to do, and the memory of looking into the eyes of the other victim(s), but I will keep saying it anyway because it is the truth."

When I try to explain torture-coerced perpetration to people who know nothing about it, they often reflexively say: "I would have died before I tortured or killed another person."

These people do not understand torture. The objective of torture is not murder. Torture is inflicted to coerce a behavior, to extract information, to instill a belief, or in the case of sadism, to take pleasure in inflicting pain, terror, helplessness, heartbreak, and self-hatred on one's victims. A victim of General Augusto Pinochet's regime of torture on the country of Chile explains:

> [Torture] kills people's spirits but keeps their bodies alive, transforming all those who escape it into zombies in the service of another despicable torturer: fear. It is a gruesomely effective tool, for it knows just how to manipulate imagination and paralyze instincts for rebellion or resistance.
>
> – Rafael Gumucio, My Tortured Inheritance, New York Times, December 13, 2004, at A27. Link: https://www.nytimes.com/2004/12/13/opinion/my-tortured-inheritance.html

Perpetrators of extreme and sadistic child abuse do not give victims the option of death while they are torturing them. Many victims report being brought close to death, but that perpetrators skilled in resuscitation revived them. In a relatively small portion of cases, perpetrators kill their victims when they are done with them, when they have met their objectives in torturing them.

I work to help victims to remember that their torturers did not give them the option of suicide:

"The objective of torture is not murder. You were not given the option to die."

"I know that you probably wanted to die many times while you were being tortured. Most torture victims do. But, they are not given that option."

"I know you would have chosen to die rather than torture or kill someone else. You were not given that choice."

"It is essential that you not allow yourself to judge yourself by what you imagine people who do not understand torture may think or say. This can only be fully understood by having lived it."

Breaks in Self-Agency

It is important to help survivors understand the kinds of "breaks" in self-agency occur in victims while being torture-coerced and terrorized to harm to others. I will describe five kinds of breaks.

1. First there may be subjective resistance and observable hesitation, which is reliably met with an escalation in torture, and also often mockery and ridicule.

2. The next adaption is outer compliance, while still maintaining some awareness of inner resistance.

As the torture continues or intensifies and the pain, helplessness, and heartbreak of being tortured, terrorized, and entrapped into harming another human being or animal become even more painful to bear, the next psychological responses to coerced perpetration are involuntary.

Victims describe the mind instantly "snapping" into an altered mental state, often taking the form of the spontaneous formation of an alter identity generally dissociated from the rest of conscious awareness, who can submit to the behavior being demanded while experiencing less emotional anguish. Victims have described to me these two kinds of "snaps" into altered mental states, the first usually preceding the second:

3. The victim's mind snaps to form a robotic self-state who obeys the commands to harm or kill like a machine, an automaton, like a hammer in the perpetrator's hand, with no conscious experience of resistance, grief, or remorse.

4. In response to further unrelenting, unthinkable, and unbearable torture to coerce a victim to harm to another victim, the mind involuntarily, reflexively, snaps again, this time, in a burst of violence against the second victim. My best understanding of this response is that it is a release of pent-up terror, tension, and rage that is unconsciously felt toward one's torturers, but cannot be safely directed toward them. Even though this response is involuntary, this self-state is aware of the power and size differential between itself and the abusers. The victim knows who holds the reins. I have never heard of a child releasing rage on an adult perpetrator while being abused. So it explodes in the only direction possible. This is a "kill-or-be-killed" response to torture and terrorization. It is a primitive sympathetic nervous system response, a physiological reaction to threat to life and limb based in the survival instinct. In response to acute stress, we react with "fight or flight." Since "flight" is clearly not an option while being tortured, "fight" kicks in.

This fourth psychological response emotionally devastates victims. Victims feel like they became non-human, like an animal, a monster. It makes them feel that they are inherently evil, not as good as other people. But, they are no different from the rest of us and we are no different than them. They were simply trapped in a situation in which they were forced to discover this potential within themselves, a potential that exists in all humans, in most mammals, and in many other animals. This response is the basis for the devastating "moral injury" that so many combat veterans struggle with in response to killing others. It is a large part of what drives their posttraumatic stress disorders (PTSD).

Most people are never placed in situations that force them to discover this response within themselves. Most people would like to believe they do not have this capacity, that they could inhibit such reactions. Torture and combat veterans know better. I often say:

"This thing you think is unforgivable is in all of us. It is in me."

"This is a primitive animalistic response. It is not who you are, but it is an involuntary psychological state that all of us can be pushed to."

"You were inside a pressure cooker that finally exploded. It would happen to anyone within these kinds of entrapment and torture."

"Discovering this response within oneself is why so many combat veterans live isolated on some mountaintop."

Many victims also describe a fifth psychological response, one that is even harder for victims and other people to acknowledge, understand, and accept.

5. When the physical pain and psychological torment become even more severe and unrelenting, the victim's mind "breaks" again to form a dissociated self-state (or more than one) who adopts violence or sadism as its identity, i.e., not limited to reflexive responses to unbearable torture. This violent identity believes itself an abuser and often nothing else. It does not have access to the memory of the events that caused it to form, until the survivor works to make this conscious.

Victims of the most extreme forms of abuse describe abusers going to great lengths to coerce this fifth response, this fifth "break." Reported tactics include extensive coerced harm of other victims; manipulations to cause victims to believe that they harmed others of their own free will; torture-conditioning to force them to pronounce themselves and believe themselves to be evil; group ceremonies in which they are condemned, pronounced as evil, and/or elevated in status in the group; set-ups, tricks, illusions (often through film or virtual reality technology), mind-altering drugs, etc., to cause them to believe themselves possessed by demonic entities; and caging, starving, and otherwise terrorizing them until they behave like predatory animals.

Victims explain that abusers exploit these identities to do violence for their networks. Each act of violence causes these identities to experience themselves as even more entrenched in evil and less human. Being forced to commit repeated violent acts paradoxically helps them escape the self-loathing of having harmed and killed others, as explained in the two sections that follow.

Note: I have learned of a sixth response to sadistic torture and coerced perpetration that is even more challenging to understand. I know of a case in which a victim made his abuse more than okay – he made it pleasing. For the first seven years of his life, his abusers imprisoned him and subjected him exclusively to sensory deprivation, torture, and coerced harm of others. The victim's mind, or particular identities, somehow managed to make all of this acceptable. My best understanding is that the only sensory stimulation and human contact that this victim experienced occurred while being tortured, so he learned to focus on particular aspects within the torture that could be experienced as enjoyable – a color, a sensation, a human touch even though it hurt. Alternatively, or perhaps in combination, this victim may have done this with some degree of intentionality to get the upper hand on his abusers by depriving them of the sadistic pleasure that they took in causing pain, terror, and heartbreak.

Identification with the Aggressor

In addition to the calculated tactics described above to induce violent identities to form and similar tactics to maintain them, a "position" of violence as a trait is caused and maintained by well-known psychological mechanisms understood within psychoanalytic theory that addresses the psychological defense of "identification with the aggressor." Aggressor identities need not feel repeatedly and horribly defeated, helpless, and terrorized. By identifying with their abusers and becoming aggressors, they preserve some sense of self-agency, some rudimentary sense of self.

"Identification with the aggressor" is a well-established psychological defense against feelings of helplessness and fears of annihilation. It preserves the relationship with the adult on whom the child depends for survival, and it permits the victim to discharge tension and rage toward one's abusers, now displaced onto oneself or onto less threatening others.

Identification with the aggressor was first described by Sandor Ferenczi in a paper entitled, *The Passions of Adults and Their Influence on the Sexual and Character Development of Children* in 1932, which he read at the Twelfth International Psycho-Analytic Conference in Vienna. It was first published in print in 1933 in German (in the Int. Z.f. Psa. 19, 5–15). It is now best known by the title, *Confusion of Tongues*, published in 1949 in the International Journal of Psycho-Analysis.

(See: 30:225-230: https://www.sas.upenn.edu/~cavitch/pdf-library/Ferenczi_Confusion.pdf).

This passage well-captures the dilemma of the abused child:

The real rape of girls who have hardly grown out of the age of infants, similar sexual acts of mature women with boys, and also enforced homosexual acts, are more frequent occurrences than has hitherto been assumed.

It is difficult to imagine the behavior and the emotions of children after such violence. One would expect the first impulse to be that of reaction, hatred, disgust and energetic refusal. "No, no, I do not want it, it is much too violent for me, it hurts, leave me alone," this or something similar would be the immediate reaction if it had not been paralyzed by enormous anxiety. These children feel physically and morally helpless, their personalities are not sufficiently consolidated in order to be able to protest, even if only in thought, for the overpowering force and authority of the adult makes them dumb and can rob them of their senses. *The same anxiety, however, if it reaches a certain maximum, compels them to subordinate themselves like automata to the will of the aggressor, to divine each one of his desires and to gratify these; completely oblivious of themselves they identify themselves with the aggressor.* Through the identification, or let us say, introjection of the aggressor, he [the aggressor] disappears as part of the external reality, and becomes intra- instead of extra-psychic; the intra-psychic is then subjected, in a dream-like state as is the traumatic trance, to the primary process, i.e. according to the pleasure principle it can be modified or changed by the use of positive or negative hallucinations. In any case the attack as a rigid external reality ceases to exist and in the traumatic trance the child succeeds in maintaining the previous situation of tenderness.

I would add that identification with the aggressor is also a defense against the psychological devastation and heartbreak of being subjected to extreme cruelty at the hands of another human being. Being in close proximity to evil is a terrifying form of trauma in itself. Children do not expect people to harm them intentionally. This is even true in adulthood. The unfathomable cruelty of torture and being coerced through torture and terrorization to harm others cause intense heartbreak and cognitive dissonance. The events seem unreal. The perpetrators seem non-human, like monsters. Monsters are not real, so how could this be real? Victims, their therapists, and others struggle to understand how another human being can be so heartless. Being in the presence of such complete perversion of everything that it is to be human is completely intolerable to the child and I believe it is likely a large factor in causing victims to dissociate such horrific events.

Hardening oneself by identifying with one's abusers defends against being further emotionally devastated by them. It shuts down vulnerability, dependency needs, and longing for human connection. It chooses hate over hurt. And it blocks empathy for others.

Once identification with the aggressor develops as a defensive response, it has a tendency to become more fixed. Carl Goldberg (1996), in *Speaking with the Devil: A Dialogue with Evil*, (New York: Viking), explains that identification with the aggressor leads to repetition compulsion of cruel, aggressive, and antisocial acts. For example, the victimized child acts out aggression with a weaker or younger child, then feels guilty and hates the self, then is again confronted with the weaker child and defends against the guilt-ridden memory by viewing the weak child as worthy of being hurt and thus repeats the act. Others see the aggressive child as bad, which causes the child to give up on any hope of being seen as good. If the cycle is not interrupted, the downward spiral will continue.

Identification with the aggressor is also likely to become increasingly fixed in dissociated identities who have identified with their abusers within torture-coerced perpetration. In addition to abuser machinations to entrap these identities in this stance, these identities likely "turn off" their empathy because their victims' pain and terror and their own guilt become completely intolerable. They often identify themselves as vicious killers, as one of their abusers, sometimes even as serial killers. They can stay locked in this mind-set because to soften it, to allow for a crack in this defensive posture, would cause them to be consumed with unbearable guilt and force them to re-connect to their own terror, helplessness, pain, and heartbreak. Their options are essentially to remain addicted to violence or to become terminally terrified and guilt-ridden.

Child Soldiers

A window into these psychological mechanisms is afforded us through the study of soldiers and

For example, Roland Weierstall, Susanne Schaal, Inga Schalinski, Jean-Pierre Dusingizemungu, and Thomas Elbert (2011), studied Rwandese genocide perpetrators and found that, "appetitive aggression can inhibit PTSD and trauma-related symptoms in perpetrators and prevent perpetrators from getting traumatized by their own atrocities." These authors state that their research suggests that "humans may enjoy cruelty, when moral restrictions do not prevent or even command organized violence." (See: "The thrill of being violent as an antidote to posttraumatic stress disorder in Rwandese genocide perpetrators," in the *European Journal of Psychotraumatology*, 2:1. Link:

https://doi.org/10.3402/ejpt.v2i0.6345). Clearly, in torture-coerced perpetration, violence is organized and commanded.

The study of child soldiers offers similar findings. From 1991 to 2002, approximately 10,000 children were forced to be child soldiers in the Sierra Leone Civil War by both the Sierra Leone Army and the Revolutionary United Front (the RUF, aka, "the rebels").

(See: https://borgenproject.org/10-facts-about-child-soldiers-in-sierra-leone/).

Ishmael Beah, in his book, "A Long Way Gone: Memoirs of a Boy Soldier" (2007), describes how the Sierra Leone Army recruited him and other young adolescent boys and systematically cultivated in them a hatred for the rebels and a deeply entrenched addiction to violence. They did this by manipulating their emotions, with stimulant drugs, with war films, by forging familial-like relationships with the boys, and by exploiting their rage about their families and villagers having been massacred by the rebels.

A short video of Beah being interviewed by CBS Early Show co-anchor, Harry Smith, is available here:

https://alchetron.com/Ishmael-Beah.

It includes a segment at minute 5:10 to 5:25 that shows the young age of the boy soldiers. It also explains that "kill or be killed" were the only options available to him and his friends, the phrase I use above to explain coerced perpetration.

Beah and the other child soldiers did not experience terrifying flashbacks, posttraumatic nightmares, etc., during their more than two years of fighting. These symptoms began only once UNICEF forces removed the boys from the army and placed them in a residential rehabilitation program in Freetown, Sierra Leone, where they could no longer kill, were detoxed from drugs, and "deprogrammed" (see Early Show clip above).

I will cite some of Beah's descriptions of these events from his book.

Here, Beah provides an example of the language his commanders used to motivate the boy soldiers to hate and kill the rebels and how the boys reacted:

"They have lost everything that makes them human. They do not deserve to live. That is why we must kill every single one of them. Think of it as destroying a great evil. It is the highest service you can perform for your country." The lieutenant pulled out his pistol and fired two shots into the air. People began shouting, "We must kill them all. We must make sure they never walk this earth again." (p.108)

Here, Beah explains how the commanders manipulated them to see guns as the solution to their losses and fears:

I had my gun now, and as the corporal always said, "This gun is your source of power in these times. It will protect you and provide you all you need, if you know how to use it well." (p. 124)

The commanders sent the armed boys into battle. Beah describes how he was initially consumed with anguish upon hearing people dying in pain and could not shoot his gun:

We walked into the arms of the forest, holding our guns as if they were the only thing that gave us strength... I lay there with my gun pointed in front of me, unable to shoot. My index finger had become numb. The forest had begun to spin. I felt as if the ground had turned upside down and I was going to fall off, so I clutched the base of a tree with one hand. I couldn't think, but I could hear the sounds of the guns far away in the distance and the cries of people dying in pain. I had begun to fall into some sort of nightmare. (p. 117)

However, in this nightmare of kill-or-be-killed combat, Beah's innately human survival-driven capacity to kill kicked in, much like the fourth and fifth breaks in self-agency described above:

My face, my hands, my shirt and gun were covered with blood. I raised my gun and pulled the trigger, and I killed a man. Suddenly, as if someone was shooting inside my mind, all the massacres I had seen since the day I was touched by war began flashing in my head. Every time I stopped shooting to change magazines and saw my two young lifeless friends, I angrily pointed my gun into the swamp and killed more people. I shot everything that moved, until we were ordered to retreat because we needed another strategy. (p. 119)

Beah describes the numb, robotic state of mind that followed that night, much like the third break in self-agency described above:

After that first day of fighting: —I went for supper that night, but was unable to eat. I only drank water and felt nothing. As I walked back to my tent, I stumbled into a cement wall. My knee bled, but I didn't feel a thing. . . . Nothing happened in my head. It was void, and I stared at the roof of the tent until I was miraculously able to doze off. (p. 120).

Here, Beah describes his commanders' use of violent war movies to incite the boys to violence:

War movies, Rambo: First Blood, Rambo II, Commando, and so on, with the aid of a generator or sometimes a car battery. We all wanted to be like Rambo; we couldn't wait to implement his techniques. (p. 121)
 Sometimes we were asked to leave for war in the middle of a movie. We would come back hours later after killing many people and continue the movie as if we had

184

just returned from intermission. We were always either at the front lines, watching a war movie, or doing drugs. There was no time to be alone or to think. (p. 124)

Here, he describes the use of stimulant drugs to further facilitate an addiction to killing in the boys and the above-described the third or fourth breaks in self-agency, that is, the ability to kill without the conscious experience of resistance, grief, or remorse.

We walked for long hours and stopped only to eat sardines and corned beef with gari, sniff cocaine, brown brown [a drug cocktail of cocaine and gun powder] and take some white capsules. The combination of these drugs gave us a lot of energy and made us fierce. The idea of death didn't cross my mind at all and killing had become as easy as drinking water. My mind had not only snapped during the first killing, it had also stopped making remorseful records, or so it seemed. (p. 122)

Once the boy soldiers were taken from the army and placed in the UNICEF-supported rehabilitation facility, the boys could not stop their engineered addiction to killing. He explains:

We needed the violence to cheer us after a whole day of boring traveling and contemplation about why our superiors had let us go. The jubilation was stopped by a group of MPs who walked into the kitchen and asked us to follow them. They had their guns pointed at us, but we laughed at them. (p. 136)

It was only once the boys could no longer kill that they became consumed with the horrors of their experience:

But we were still traumatized, and now that we had time to think, the fastened mantle of our war memories slowly began to open. Whenever I turned on the tap water, all I could see was blood gushing out. I would stare at it until it looked like water before drinking or taking a shower. (p. 145)

I would try desperately to think about my childhood, but I couldn't. The war memories had formed a barrier that I had to break in order to think about any moment in my life before the war (p. 149)

I tried to think about my childhood days, but it was impossible as I began getting flashbacks of the first time I slit a man's throat. The scene kept surfacing in my memory like lightning on a dark rainy night, and each time it happened, I heard a sharp cry in my head that made my spine hurt. (p. 160)

Here, Beah describes his horrifying posttraumatic nightmares, violent outbursts, and episodes of dissociative amnesia:

But at night some of us would wake up from nightmares, sweating, screaming and punching our own heads to drive out the images that continued to torment us even when we were no longer asleep. Other boys would wake up and start choking whoever was in the bed next to theirs; they would then go running into the night after they had been restrained. The staff members were always on guard to control these sporadic outbursts. Nonetheless, every morning several of us were found hiding in the grasses by the soccer field. We didn't remember how we had gotten there. (p. 148)

Finally, Beah describes the agonizing guilt that consumed him while in the rehabilitation facility. His empathy was so profound that he vicariously experienced the assaults he inflicted on others:

I held my ears to stop hearing them, but I began to feel their pain. Each time a person was stabbed, I felt it worse; I saw the blood dripping from the same part of my body as that of the victim. (p. 164)

On February 14, 2007, Ishmael appeared on The Daily Show and talked about the difficulties of returning to civilized society. He said: "Dehumanizing children is a relatively easy task" (see: Ishmael Beah's website: https://aalv2001.wixsite.com/aalvaj).https://aalv2001.wixsite.com/aalvaj). For Beah and the other child soldiers, facing the reality of the violence they were forced to commit was the greater challenge.

I believe that the documented psychological responses of child soldiers teach us the following:

1. In metaphorical pressure cookers of many kinds, we can all be forced into "kill-or-be-killed."

2. Once this entrapment is accomplished in the person as a whole or in specific dissociated identities, it is likely to become increasingly fixed.

3. Violence is not the whole of such persons or identities, even when this is the individual's subjective experience.

4. The process of re-connecting with one's inner humanity is grueling – full of horror, guilt, and severe posttraumatic stress.

Survivors of extreme abuse benefit greatly from learning about the psychological responses of child soldiers. They were both subjected to hell on earth. Understanding child soldiers can build a foundation for self-compassion in survivors of extreme child abuse and coerced perpetration. It can help identities who were made to believe by their abusers that they were evil to realize that they are not unidimensional – they were victims of extreme torture and sophisticated psychological manipulations.

An advanced treatise on dissociative responses to extreme abuse, including comparisons to the experience of child soldiers, and the role of identification with one's perpetrators, is Harvey Schwartz's 2013 book, The Alchemy of Wolves and Sheep: a

Relational Approach to Internalized Perpetration for Complex Trauma Survivors (published by Routledge).

Sitting with Survivor's Emotional Devastation about Having Harmed or Killed Others

In addition to expressing words to help survivors understand their inability to defy the abusers who were torturing them, we also need to be able to sit with them in the pain of having harmed another human being, no matter what the reason, no matter what the level of torture.

Victims of coerced perpetration had to look in the face of another victim, perhaps a child who trusted them, who previously relied on them, who hoped they might be rescued by them, maybe a sibling or best friend, maybe their own child or parent, and had to see the absolute terror and utter anguish. Perhaps the victim begged for them to stop. Perhaps they watched the victim's heart break right in front of their eyes. Perhaps they killed the intended victim robotically and without feeling. Or maybe they had been pushed to the point of "kill-or-be-killed" rage. Perhaps they killed while in a dissociated identity who had finally embraced sadism as his/her own, who had aligned him/herself with the abusers as one of them in an underground where they had no real options. They may live in fear and grief that this last experience may haunt the victim forever.

Listening to this, allowing survivors to express the pain and horror associated with this, is very, very hard. Our natural impulse is to try to relieve their unjust self-hatred before they can tell us how bad it was. But, if they cannot tell us, who can they tell? Very few people have the capacity to hear this and sit with it. We have to figure out how deep to let them go in expressing this pain before we offer them the lifeline of solace, words of compassion, understanding, and realistic rather than abuser-engineered self-judgment.

We Need to Cry with the Victims

I let myself cry, with victims and survivors, with colleagues, and by myself.

I cry for Lois. I cry for the children she had to hurt and for the children who had to hurt her.

Survivors deserve our tears, our outrage, an admission of our own feelings of helplessness in response to these forms of ferocious and calculated cruelty, and our willingness to travel into the nightmarish hell-holes of these memories with them, in order to extend a hand that they can grasp to begin to climb up and out, and to feel worthy of the love of people who will rally with them against this evil.

Some Closing Thoughts and Words to Help Victims

I rage at the injustice of extreme abuse. I am often left with tears and rage that has little place to go except to unite with survivors and supporters to bring truth to light. Although I cannot stop these unacceptable horrors, I can work to help victims and survivors to have compassion for themselves as I have deep compassion for them. Here are some more thoughts that I share:

"I know that when I was born, I was born no better than you. We are the same, both born innocent babies who only wanted to experience reciprocal love and who had no innate sadistic instincts. But under sadistic and brutal torture as children, anyone and everyone will form parts who will release rage, who can commit violence. Most people get to live their lives never knowing this response. They do not want to believe it. They cannot withstand the possibility that they too would have "broken" under torture. No one wants to know this capacity exists within them. But, it exists within all of us."

"I get that it feels like only the other victims could ever truly understand all of this, forgive you completely, and love you anyway – actually love you more because of it. But I believe that everyone owes you to understand all of this as deeply as we can, to

189

forgive you completely as there is nothing to forgive as there was never any choice, and to love you, have deep compassion for you, respect you for what you have endured, and to want to do everything in our power to help you to feel loved and to love yourself. That is the only way to begin to bring any justice at all to any of this."

Below is something I wrote to a survivor who was subjected to extreme torture and coerced perpetration and who believes "themselves" stupid, evil, weak, selfish, and unworthy of love:

"You and the other victims abused beside you understand things that are almost impossible for other people to understand in terms of the ferocity of the evil and how it comes very close to destroying the mind and soul of its victims. The cruelty perpetrated against you went very deep and almost accomplished what the sadists intended, to make you purely evil like them. But, you are here sitting with me because your heart is broken and that tells me that they did not win, that you did not succumb to becoming like them, even if you sometimes 'snapped' within the worst moments of hell inflicted upon you."

"I do not believe you did anything out of weakness. I think it is simply easier to condemn yourself as weak than to remember what it was like in your mind, in your body, and in your soul to be relentlessly tortured with no conceivable means of escape. States of entrapment, of complete helplessness, while being assaulted, raped, etc., are intolerable to human beings. If you have trouble functioning, if you condemn yourself because you do not have the internal resources to "contribute to society," try to be kind to yourself, to have compassion for yourself, to remember that the abuse you suffered devastated you psychologically. Please do not punish yourself to try to force yourself to function better. It will not work. It will only increase your already intolerable "trauma load." Do not condemn yourself as selfish or a burden because you need help to live your life. This does not make you selfish or ungrateful."

"You believe yourself evil, but I believe that the word "evil' does not apply to you. Yes, you have parts who could not stand being victims anymore, who were completely alone in the depths of hell and unbearable, unrelenting torture, and who may, at a point of horrific torture, have taken all of their inevitable and justified rage and vented it on others. I know I would have done the same and I do not believe I am evil. To "break" in this way is inevitable when one is tortured, terrorized, and humiliated and coerced to harm others for unending hours and days. I feel angry at anyone who would like to pretend that they could do better and I feel no anger at you at all."

"Truly, deep in my heart, I believe you are wonderful."

I will now share the words that one victim, who I will call "Victim C," spoke as she tried to soothe the heartbreak of Victim A who was forced to harm Victim B while Victim C was forced to watch. When Victim A and Victim C were alone again, Victim A explains what happened:

"...When I saw [Victim C] again, she hugged me for a long time and finally said, 'It's okay. Only thing you could do, no choice. You never have a choice. I love you. She [Victim B] wasn't mad, just scared. But so were you. Dog-eat-dog place here. You're not bad; you're an angel in a nightmare. It's not your fault, please don't feel sad'."

Although moral injury runs deep and although it may take years for survivors to overcome their unjust self-condemnation, our insight into the power of torture and our words of compassion for the heartbreak of coerced perpetration mean the world to survivors. The more we bring this truth out into the open in the world of working with extreme abuse, on websites, etc., the more momentum we gain in helping survivors out of the psychological traps that the abusers sought to lock them in forever.

191

30. Sammy Lee, M.D.

Dr. Sammy Lee (1920 to present) was the first Asian-American to win an Olympic gold medal for the United States, capturing the gold in ten-meter platform diving at the 1948 Olympics in London. Four years later at the Helsinki Olympics, he again won the gold medal in ten-meter diving and also the bronze in the three-meter springboard. He became an M.D. in 1947 and currently is a retired otologist. In 1990, Dr. Lee was inducted into the U.S. Olympic Hall of Fame.

* * * * * * *

After reading and re-reading your story, I cannot comprehend having endured such abnormal, unbelievably parental psychopaths and being strong and courageous enough to be a compassionate adult. You are like great athletes who when they fail to win get up and keep trying until they do win.

My diving coach used to enjoy having whoever did a better dive that day swat the loser with a knotted towel. When he thought we did not hit hard enough, he would put his 6'4" and 275 pound frame into hitting the winner and loser as hard as he could! He enjoyed verbally abusing me (and other divers) in front of anyone around by cursing and making bigoted remarks. But I took his abuse because I was paying him for his diving knowledge that allowed me to win the Olympic gold medal twice. All those days and years of tirades made me stronger. Your abuse seems to have made you stronger too.

Both your parents must have been pedophiles and sadists. It is too bad that they were not seen by a team of psychiatrists to see if they could explain their make-up!

After finally becoming a grandpa, I understand the instinct to protect offspring. Almost all animals will kill to protect their children. With children and grandchildren, the medals fade, but loving each child gets brighter every moment.

Now the revelation of the Catholic church's cover up of sexual abuse by priests makes the church no better than the "common," sick pedophiles. How many of the abused have forgiven?

I am with you, Dr. Lois. If I had sick parents as you had, I could not and would not forgive them as long as I lived.

As Franklin Delano Roosevelt said (but did not practice when he signed the bill interning Americans of Japanese descent after Pearl Harbor), "If we teach our children that one religion is better than another, then we seek to destroy all religions. If we teach that one nationality is better than another, then we seek to degrade all nationalities. If we teach that one race is superior, then we teach everyone to enslave all races."

31. Eric Loeb, Ed. D.

Dr. Eric Loeb (1930–2011) was a licensed psychologist in Binghamton, New York beginning in 1975, having earned his doctorate in psychology at Columbia University in 1974. While he dealt with a wide variety of issues, he specialized in the problems of survivors of traumatic incidents and circumstances, such as, accidents, rape, or assaults, and including child abuse, incest, and other sexual abuse (male and female), and people with chronic illness, physical challenges, dissociative disorders, anxiety and depression. He believed strongly that all people are capable of healing from even the most traumatic experiences, and that all people are capable of and deserve happy and fulfilling lives.

It was easy, according to Dr. Loeb, to produce clients who could talk extensively about their dynamics, but hadn't changed a bit. Therefore, he liked to use experiential approaches, such as Gestalt and Psychodrama.

His willingness to try new approaches led to his dealing with Lois Einhorn's abusive past. He was the therapist during the time she recovered most of her memories.

* * * * * * *

Precious Daughter, Lois,

It's twenty-five years since you walked into my office for help with depression, which we decided was secondary to chronic pain brought on by multiple abdominal surgeries. You told me your birth family was "close". Little did I know just how "close" your family was! Nine years passed, during which you saw me off and on. I didn't seem to be able to make much of a dent in your depression. Then again, other people and approaches to dealing with pain and depression didn't seem to help either. There were some indications that your parents weren't quite as nice as you claimed. For example, they blamed you when a blizzard made you late in getting home, and they seemed to see their own illnesses as more important than yours, but nothing foreshadowed the horror you have described here. Were someone like you to walk into my office today, I would suspect severe abuse, but then, it didn't cross my mind.

Two events closely preceded the onset of your recovered memories. Like many depressed people, you could not access any feelings of anger. I began suggesting things that would make almost anyone angry, saying for example in the first person, "You can rob me and I won't get angry." Nothing worked until I said, "You can tell me to spread my legs and I won't get angry." At that, you did get angry. On another occasion, you told me the following story about your family: Your sister wanted some money. Your father agreed to play a board game with her. If she won the game, she got the money. I asked what happened if she lost the game. You told me that, if she lost the game, your father got to spank her. Little did I know what "spanking" meant in your family, but I did suggest that getting pleasure out of spanking had sexual implications. (Note: I did NOT say that it indicated sexual or physical abuse.) I'm not sure which of these two events precipitated your recalling between sessions that your father had molested you. After that, the memories came thick and fast, getting ever more sadistic and bizarre. You've told me many times that your parents said, "The more bizarre the abuse, the less likely anyone would believe you."

Though the False Memory Foundation alleges that recovered memories result from suggestion by the therapist, I did not and could not have suggested your memories. Never in my wildest nightmares did I imagine such scenes. Occasionally, when you had trouble remembering something, you asked me what I thought happened next. Invariably, if I ventured a guess, the missing part then came to you, but it was never what I had guessed. Often it was less severe than I had imagined. For example, they might hit you only once, telling you "how lucky you are; they're the kindest parents in the world, any other parents would have 'spanked' you within an inch of your life!"

Both your physical and psychological symptoms are consistent with your memories to a degree that could not possibly be just coincidence. For example, your lack of motility of the colon, which provided the rationale for your seven abdominal surgeries, and which continues to be a problem for you despite the surgeries, is consistent with being made to eat your own feces. If you knew you might have to eat it, you would make Herculean efforts not to produce it! Having been made to remain on your hands and knees for hours, in "tushi-up position", waiting to be tortured, or while being hit to "make your little tushi red", it is hardly surprising that you still react with panic to seeing a teddy bear or other stuffed animal face down. Accidentally touching your right ear causes spasms of terror. The same is not true of the left ear. It was the right ear they threatened to cut off if you didn't kill a cat or dog at their command. When you regressed in therapy, it was always to age five or age two. Later we realized that age five was when you were first made to kill an animal. Much later we realized that age two was when your sister was five and you witnessed her kill an animal! We traveled together to the place you lived from age three to age eight. Everything you had told me about it was just as you had described, including the way the house was isolated so that abuse could more easily take place without discovery. There is also other corroboration, e.g., a childhood friend who remembers that your bedroom was repeatedly filled with teddy bears one week, and bereft of them the next week. Other consistencies are too numerous to mention.

My training had been largely to break through defenses, not to unearth memories, but to get in touch with the feelings associated with them, and the messages learned from them that might still be operative in the present. When we breached your defenses and you became a five or two-year-old, we often couldn't put the adult back in charge for hours! You can't tell a five-year-old to drive home, so we were sometimes in my office until the wee hours of the morning! We sought consultation. Dale McCulley (see his response) was most helpful, instructing us over the phone how to keep the adult present while allowing the child to come out. It was important to address the adult directly as the session began, asking her to stay present. During the session, while working with the child part, I frequently called on the adult part for comment and advice. When we followed these steps, the adult was able to function when it was time to go home.

While you are clearly dissociative, you do not qualify as a multiple personality. Both the adult and the child parts are clearly Lois. Furthermore, each is aware of the activities and thoughts of the other.

Over some time, I'd been reading about "reparenting" in the writings of Eric Berne and others. I was also impressed by an M.A. thesis on "Gentle Reparenting" by Jeanne Alvin (Goddard College, 1987). You seemed the ideal candidate. After some discussion, we mutually decided to try. It started as an office procedure, but it became more and more real. Many common interests and values, as well as the overwhelming struggle we were engaged in, drew us to each other. This is to say nothing of the enormous number of hours we spent together. Gradually, I became "Daddy" both inside and outside the office. In the office, you

196

were able to regress to being a toddler, sitting on my lap (mighty big baby!) and drinking a bottle. Outside, we went to the zoo and did other "age appropriate" activities.

However, as you "grew up", it became clear that we had to choose between our two relationships, therapy and parenting. We chose the latter. You went on to a series of other therapists, but we continued the father-daughter relationship we still have today. Several years ago, we formalized our father-daughter relationship in a Native American "Hunka" ceremony (the making of relatives by love not blood).

It is often said that those who are abused become abusers. That is a misinterpretation of the statistics. While abusers usually have a history of having been abused, it is not true that most of those who have been abused become abusers. Nevertheless, most of those who have been abused as severely and sadistically as you continue the cycle, according to experts we have consulted. Furthermore, few of those who are not abusers are self-sustaining, contributing members of society. They are addicted, in prisons or mental hospitals, or, at best, on disability. You have never felt revengeful, even in your imagination. After your memories returned, you were never able to visualize your father in any activity such as hitting a punching balloon. You said then (and still say) you don't want to dehumanize people as your parents did to you. Indeed, you are a miracle!

Should you forgive your parents? How can you forgive yourself? A lot depends on what you mean by "forgive". Of course, you cannot and do not condone what your parents did. However, anyone who has been abused has an enormous well of unexpressed feelings that are controlled by muscle tension. These cause a myriad of symptoms including headaches, arthritis, digestive problems, depression, and anxiety. The list goes on and on. You had permission to express the rage and anguish they produced in you (we screamed, threw playdoh, pushed pillows, and broke garage-sale china. We also had a ritual mourning ceremony for all the animals, real and stuffed, that you were made to kill with your present teddy bears as witnesses. Eventually and gradually you worked through many difficult feelings and are able to go on with your life with fewer periods of haunting flashbacks. "Eventually" is a key word here. A rapid or superficial decision to forgive puts premature closure on a situation, denies your own feelings, and interferes with forgiving yourself.

As a child of abusive parents, you are faced with a terrible dilemma. If you disown your abusive family, you become an orphan. If you belong to your abusive family, you implicitly condone the abuse. By not forgiving yourself, you are choosing to be part of the family. You are also seeing yourself as deserving of the abuse they meted out, and denying that you are worthy of the love of others. (You used to tell me I was crazy for loving you!) As you gradually became ready to accept love from others and forgive yourself, you also became ready to let go of your birth family by forgiving them.

You ask if all criminals and abusers are, emotionally, young children, if any of them have real choices. Certainly, it is true that criminals and abusers are emotionally young children. However, while we do not condemn children for destructive acts, neither do we allow them to continue doing them. We try to help them find better ways to get their needs met. We need to do our utmost to prevent abuse even while we have empathy for the abusers.

Lois, you have worked harder and grown more in therapy than anyone I know. Almost every therapist who has worked with you has commented on how hard you work. Many, many people love you. I am proud of you, and proud of the work I did with you. Once I had a client who said she was my work of art. When I told you this, you said that, if she was my work of art, you were my magnum opus! Indeed, you are!

I love you,

Daddy

* * * * * * *

(PUBLISHER'S NOTE: Lois's precious "Daddy" died in her home in the spring of 2011. Eric Loeb will always remain a part of her soul; and we are with her in her grief, and all others who held Eric so dear in their hearts. – Cleone Lyvonne Reed, Editor)

32. Rev. Dr. Richard P. Lord

Richard P. Lord has been a pastor at Rush Creek Christian Church since 1978. He has trained clergy regarding victim issues in several states and has first-hand experience working with victims of school bus crashes, plant explosions, courthouse shootings, and terrorist bombings. He received his Doctorate of Ministry Degree from Texas Christian University. He has published articles in *Christian Century* and *Disciple Magazine* and has presented papers at national conventions regarding victims and religious issues.

* * * * * * *

You honor me by sharing your story. My immediate reaction is similar to that of Job's three friends when they first saw him: "They sat on the ground seven days and seven nights, and no one spoke a word to him, for they saw that his suffering was very great." (Job 2:13) But you ask me to speak and so I will, though with a clear awareness that I can never fully understand what you have experienced.

I have worked with crime victims and know something of their anguish over the issue of forgiveness. My ideas on forgiveness come from my listening to crime victims and my study of theology.

I, too, have been influenced by *The Sunflower* and think it is a great model for your book. While Wiesenthal asks the question, "What would you do in my place?" I found it easier to deal with his other question, "Did I do the right thing in not forgiving?" since this invites discussion from various traditions of thought. I find it not only difficult, but inappropriate to deal with what would I do in a similar situation (either holocaust or child abuse) since either situation is horrible beyond anything I have remotely experienced.

Therefore, I think it better to respond to the more academic question that Betty Jane Spencer, a congregant who watched her four sons be murdered, asked me: "Preacher, as a Christian, am I obligated to forgive the men who murdered my four sons?" My final word is "No."

One of the points of confusion in the issue of forgiveness is thinking that forgiveness is "letting go." There is a necessity at some point, if a person is to regain a measure of healing, to let go of the anger and rage one feels about the trauma. But letting go of anger is not the same as the forgiveness of sins. I think you, as well as my friend, Betty Jane, understand that. You are not consumed by anger toward the past, but you are aware that forgiving your parents is different from letting go of your anger toward them.

My main point is that forgiveness of sin is not forgetting or excusing, but restoring a relationship. Forgiveness is between, not within. To say you must forgive is to say you must be open to a relationship with your parents, and I do not think you have any moral or psychological obligation to do so.

Involved in the understanding of forgiveness in the Bible is that of remorse, restitution and regeneration. If there is not genuine sorrow over the offense, if there is no attempt at restitution, if there are no signs of renewal so the offense will not be repeated, then it is shameful to talk about forgiveness.

Jesus did pray for forgiveness for those who crucified him because they did not know what they were doing; your parents knew exactly what they were doing when they tortured you and your sister. Jesus also condemned people to hell when they persisted in harming people: "But if anyone causes one of these little ones who believe in me to sin, it would be better for him to have a large millstone hung around his neck and to be drowned in the depths of the sea." (Matthew 18:6 NIV) "He will reply, 'I tell you the truth, whatever you did not do for one of the least of these you did not do for me.' Then they will go away to eternal punishment, but the righteous to eternal life" (Matthew 25:45, 46).

I understand when I say, "God forgives me and my sin" that God is saying, "What you have done will not come between us." It's a matter of opening oneself to relationship, to becoming vulnerable to the offender. When one is doing one's best not to be vulnerable again, where there is no desire to restore a relationship, which has only been pain, there is no reason to talk about forgiveness.

I have found the reason victims like you and my friend, Betty Jane Spencer, are so reluctant to entertain the possibility of forgiveness is that you are aware it does involve a relationship with the offender. It is not just an inward attitude within yourself, but a turning toward and opening yourself up to the perpetrator, and that is just what you don't want, need or are obligated to do. I strongly support your "gut" feeling that forgiveness is not an obligation you have to your parents.

Now as far as forgiveness for yourself, I am not as clear on how to respond. I want to say all the things that you have heard how, of course, you may forgive yourself since you were the victim. But I understand it is not a simple "of course."

200

Let me share the story of three people I have known who have had somewhat the same thoughts about themselves. One woman was raised in a satanic cult, one woman was raped, and the third person was my son, a Marine in Desert Storm who killed a number of Iraqis. The feeling they had was not so much guilt as being dirty. Their focus was not on being forgiven, but of being cleansed. The two women were baptized and found the religious use of water to be very powerful in gaining a sense of being clean. My son went through the formal sacrament of penance in his church and found that helpful. Obviously, the scars are still there for all three, but they do have a sense of openness to the future. The two women have married and have children; my son is preparing for the priesthood. Because of their experiences, the only suggestion I have is for you to explore religious ceremonies in your Native American or Jewish tradition, which provide cleansing, either through water or formal religious ceremony.

I will pray for your continued healing.

33. Cleone Lyvonne, M.S.E.

Cleone Lyvonne Reed (she married Bob Reed in 2008, hence the name change, and he died July 24, 2021) earned her Master's Degree in Education with an emphasis in Community Counseling from the University of Wisconsin in 1986. She worked for ten years as an outpatient mental health therapist; her specializations included helping adult survivors of sexual abuse. When Cleone was four months old, her mother was brutally raped, knifed, and left for dead. This incident and an abusive marriage led her to deal with issues of forgiveness. She works as an Editor and Graphic Artist for Robert D. Reed Publishers (publishers of this book). After just ten days of working on this book in 2006, she felt as if she had to write a response.

* * * * * * *

Working on this book for you, the contents lurk in my consciousness throughout the days and nights, and I feel compelled to write a response. I suspect many readers will want to write their stories. That is the implicit invitation that I feel, and sleep escapes me as my fingertips yearn to fly over the keyboard in these wee hours of the morning.

When I was fourteen and visiting my friend's house for the first time, my friend's mother asked me if I was the daughter of the woman who was attacked when I was a baby. I had no clue what she was talking about. I went home and asked, and even though my mother would hardly talk about it, over the years I learned progressively more details about the story.

When I was four months old and in the bassinet beside my mother's bed, a young man came into the bedroom and raped my twenty-two-year-old mother at knifepoint, then stabbed her seven times with a butcher knife in the stomach, back, and neck, severing her jugular vein. When my mother gave up the fight and pretended to be dead, he grabbed the car keys off the dresser, stole the car, and fled. My mother got up to go to the phone, tied her apron firmly around her neck (which was an instinctive move that saved her), called out my name, and then passed out on the living room floor. My father came home from an errand and found her unconscious in a pool of blood. She was in the hospital for over two months and nearly died on at least two other occasions in her process of healing.

This assault didn't happen directly to me, but it did happen to me. It was part of my journey in therapy for decades. I went on what I called a "forgiveness marathon" once and tried everything to forgive the assailant. In response to the Bible's quote about forgiving seven times seventy, I wrote out "I forgive...." 490 times! What a futile and exhausting attempt at forcing forgiveness! I lived with a "should" mentality and worked so hard at forgiving. Finally, in exasperation, I exclaimed, "I give up. If the spirit of forgiveness wants to find me, it can just find me, but I am not going to look for it anymore!"

It wasn't long after that when an epiphany experience swept into my consciousness like a feather duster clearing away all the particles of dust in my mind, and I felt a peace unlike any up until that time. I felt compassion for the assailant's soul. It was a major turning point in my life.

I was not abused as a child, but I was sexually abused at age thirty-two and physically abused twenty-one times during the first year of my second marriage when I was forty. The hardest part of the forgiveness process in this scenario was forgiving myself for staying in the marriage for eleven years. When questioned, "How could such an intelligent woman stay with that man for so long?" I was ashamed. Here I was, a woman with a Master's Degree working as a therapist specializing in counseling people with abuse issues and living this incongruent life— happy and confident in my work yet not wanting to go home and face the facts of my own "craziness" and unhappiness. Who would believe the dynamics in my own home?

Denial, repression, and rationalization are powerful survival tools. Had I not kept a detailed journal for five years (which I started a year or two before I got married), I probably would have not recovered the memory of many of the abuses. I got him to stop the physical abuse after one year; and not wanting anyone to know what kind of situation I was in, I pushed the memories out of my mind, too.

After my divorce, the turning point in my healing process came in response to this story: "If you put a snake down your shirt and it bites you on the belly, are you mad at the snake for biting you? Or are you mad at yourself for putting the snake down your shirt? The snake was just being a snake." I knew the most arduous task was to forgive myself.

Sitting at my typewriter, I imagined myself high above my body looking down at myself with the utmost of compassion and unconditional love, understanding why I stayed. I cried and I wrote and I cried some more. I rocked myself like a little child. When there were no more tears and no more words, I felt cleansed and a wave of peace swept through me.

After I forgave myself, forgiving my ex-husband was easy, but first I needed to let my feelings flow freely. No way could I NOT experience anger while married to such a critical alcoholic man. I stopped being such a "nice" person and got real. I got in touch with my own anger, my wounds, and my own tendency towards violence (I sometimes got so angry I had to hold my hands behind my back so I wouldn't hit him). I got to the point I didn't want to be angry anymore. That was the beginning of the end of the marriage. Once out of the marriage, I realized my ex-husband was one of my greatest teachers in life—even though the hardest and most profound.

When I left and moved 2000 miles away, I left my career, my marriage, and my family. Determined to create a whole new life, I vowed to enter only relationships based on love, mutuality, and respect.

My views on forgiveness have changed over the last few years. I took the Avatar® Courses (Avatar, Masters, and Wizards) created by Harry Palmer. These courses impacted me in the most powerful life-changing experiences of my life.

To surrender all judgment, to see the perfection in the imperfections, to be observers of all our experiences, and to know we create our experiences by our beliefs—that all is a tall order! How can we not judge the atrocities that happened to you as a child or all the horrific things that go on in our world? On one level of thinking, that seems preposterous! How could our individual souls or soul groups come into existence and attract horribly painful things to learn our lessons? Isn't that going a bit too far? Do our souls really reincarnate repeatedly until we have become enlightened?

As a result of the Avatar Course, I have adopted the viewpoint that forgiveness is necessary only when we judge. If we see the perfection in everything, even things that seem to be glaring imperfections, and we surrender all judgment, then forgiveness is a moot point. We only need forgiveness when we have made a judgment.

I hope to be in a place of non-judgment, but I know it would be a spiritual bypass to get there without going through all the other states of consciousness first. We must feel all our feelings to the fullest, recognizing that they are all okay, before we can let them go and let the spirit of forgiveness find us. We live in a state of spiritual maturity when we become compassionate observers of humanity living in a judgment-free plane.

It appears to me that the reason you feel the need to forgive yourself is because you have been judging yourself so harshly. It appears you adopted the belief early on that you were powerless over your situation and that you had no choice but to comply with your parents' abusive demands. Fearing being killed seems like a pretty natural belief to have created in response to your circumstances. I believe that when you get to the point of loving yourself unconditionally, viewing yourself and your experiences with the utmost of compassion, and surrendering all judgment on yourself, then forgiveness will not even be necessary—or it will be just a natural by-product of your healing process.

Once you surrender all judgment on yourself and forgive yourself, then it will be easier to release your parents from any grips of judgment, resentment, anger, and blame.

I believe what is most important for individuals and for our relationships—intimate, family, friends, community, national, international—is to surrender all judgments and come from a place of unconditional love and acceptance. That is the goal of enlightenment. Peace comes when we unhook ourselves from the clutches of the dramas and let go of all the recriminations, resentments and regrets, criticism and judgments.

And live in the present moment.

What you have done with your life is nothing short of amazing. Maybe your long list of achievements and awards are a compensation for your harshness on yourself. It is understandable and even natural to want to prove your worth given what you went through and how you have felt about yourself. Your pain has been a fuel to create a most beautiful path, one of tremendous impact on our world. Your pain and your courage to share your story are real gifts to all those who have issues of forgiveness.

You were told if you told anyone (communicated), you would be killed. Here you are, a professor of communication… telling the world! I certainly am not happy with what happened to you, but I am delighted with what you are doing with your past.

YOU are a GIFT to the world!

NOTE: Here is a poem that I wrote and included in the book, *Domestic Violence: Tragedy and Hope* by Frances T. Pilch (ed) and contributors, © 2021:

Abuse Is NOT an Option

I got remarried when I was thirty-nine
And expected life to be really fine.
Who would have guessed it would be hell?
Domestic violence, I could not foretell.

Twenty-one episodes in that first year.
Every day I was full of fear.
I didn't dare go to work
For fear he would again go berserk.

The worst was when he tried to choke me.
Sensitive thereafter my neck would be.
A kick in the stomach landed me on the ground.
Scared stiff to the neighbors I'd be found.

Grabbing me by the wrist
Leaving me bruises with his fist.
His rampages were all about control
And on my mental health they took a toll.

I didn't want another divorce
But just to get on a better course.
I told him henceforth every time he touched me
Lovingly it absolutely had to be.

He changed and was no longer rough,
But the marriage was still not good enough.
His temper and language were full of anger
And life still had an element of danger.

I told 32 people I was getting a divorce before I told him.
I knew I couldn't blurt it out in a whim.
The fear was he could kill me with his gun
And then kill himself when he was done.

So out of the marriage and on my own
At age fifty, two thousand miles were flown.
I wanted to heal and create a better life
And be a healthy, loving man's wife.

Forgiveness of him became a goal.
He had stolen a big piece of my soul.
After some work, I labeled myself a survivor.
Was this doing my consciousness a favor?

It was at least beyond the victim state
But I wanted to thrive and move beyond that fate.
So I went on an intensive healing journey
That took me deeper than I wanted to be.

Painful, it was like a wild roller coaster ride.
One minute happy, the next wanting to hide.
Some would say I set my sights too high,
But I didn't think they were pie in the sky.

More than getting a Master's Degree,
The Avatar Course was what really set me free.
What I integrated can never be taken away.
My soul transformed; the changes are here to stay.

Then meeting Bob when I was fifty-seven
Felt like I had maybe gone to heaven!
Later, when I was sixty-two, I married Bob.
It wasn't too late to land my heart-throb.

We are viewed as compatible by everyone.
He is supportive, loving, generous, caring, and fun.
Gratitude fills my whole being every day and night.
He is truly a star in my eyes, shining ever so bright.

PS
Cleone Lyvonne Reed ©2022

Here I am, a widow, feeling so sad at seventy six.
He is gone, and I feel like I am in a terrible fix.
I miss him more than words can ever convey.
I loved him in each and every way.

I bask in the many thousand photos I took
Knowing now that is the only way at him I can look.
Yes, I am grateful for eighteen years of memories galore,
All so happy – can you blame me for wanting more?

34. Dale McCulley

Dale McCulley has been involved in the issue of childhood trauma since 1975. During his long tenure as a writer/producer at his family production firm, Cavalcade Productions, he oversaw more than a dozen projects dealing with child abuse and its manifold sequelae. He has written *Multiple Exposure*, a book-length memoir of his adopted daughter, Robin Hall, herself a multiple personality as the result of satanic cult abuse.

He also is the author of "Satanic Ritual Abuse: A Question of Memory" (*Journal of Psychology & Theology*, 1994).

* * * * * * *

Highest praise certainly is due the author for her honesty and courage in sharing such searingly painful episodes from her abusive past, incidents that are, in the words of psychiatrist Roland Summit, "Too terrible to Hear" (Summit, unpublished, 1985). In examining the scorched detritus of her own life with such candor, Lois Einhorn is demanding that we listen, no matter the cost in terms of personal comfort. To be sure, for those of us who have heard such tales of horror a hundred times over, acceptance is automatic. Things that to an outsider sound preposterous—eating of feces, electric shocks, constant Sophie's Choices—are standard operating procedure for sadistic, ritualistic, and satanic abusers. It is questionable, however, that repetition makes the hearing any less distressful.

In attempting to respond to the central issue of self-forgiveness raised by the author, I hope to reflect a Christian perspective. Such a viewpoint, I believe, challenges Dr. Einhorn's repeated characterization of her acts as "unforgivable." While there is in the *New Testament* some fleeting reference (Mt. 12:31; Mk. 3:28-30; Lk. 12.10; I Jn. 5:16) to a sin that is beyond the reach of divine mercy, it clearly does not apply to the situations here described. In short, in Christian theology the atonement seems to make forgiveness broadly available.

If so, what about the perpetrators; would repentance secure forgiveness even for them? In this connection it may be significant that the harshest words spoken by Jesus, statements about deep waters and heavy millstones, refer to just such crimes as coercing co-perpetration by innocent children: "But if anyone causes one of these little ones who believe in me to sin…" (Mt. 18:6 NIV).

Let's be precise about the choices confronting a child in the hands of the kind of sadistic abusers the author describes: "Comply or die!" usually is the ultimatum.

Who is to say which choice is morally more acceptable? More than one survivor has wistfully commented that those who died—because they were non-compliant, or because they cried at the wrong time, or because the perpetrator had a sudden sadistic rush—those were the lucky ones. How are we to weigh an early departure from this life against the lifetime of agony described by the author?

I recall speaking with an alternate personality of a survivor of satanic cult abuse. The particular alter was continuously afflicted with the terrible sounds of a cult ritual; screams of tortured victims, chants, and animals "making sounds no one ever heard an animal make." When I suggested that there was a way we could remove these audio horrors, she was hesitant. If she no longer heard the sounds, she wondered, would she forget how terrible the rituals were? Such was the tender conscience of a survivor who had been involved in all of the atrocities detailed by the author, and others too hideous to mention. Would our world have been better served if such a person had chosen to die rather than to comply?

Lois Einhorn does not have multiple personality disorder, but the fact that many victims of childhood trauma do adds another dimension to the questions before us. We may then have a situation where the host personality is completely unaware that compliant alternate personalities are committing heinous acts. While most clinicians would maintain that the executive personality is completely responsible for all the actions of the body, such a position seems highly irrational. Someone who is completely dissociated from actions can hardly be responsible for them, and even our criminal courts have sometimes so ruled. Should our position be any less lenient?

With extreme reluctance, I now address the questions the author has posed: "What should I have done?" My first thought is that God only knows. My second is that I do not have to go nearly that far. The author has made much of the fact that she sometimes abused others with no feelings of empathy for her victims. Nevertheless, I would not wish my own acts of deliberate cruelty, committed without duress, to be placed in a moral balance against the coerced offenses of a tormented child. If the author is unable to forgive herself, how then can I dare to claim such a benison for myself?

The key questions, after all, seem to me this: What did the author do? What choices did she make, when she was free of coercion; when there was no more torture, no more double binds, and no more devils' dilemmas? Her own life history provides an eloquent answer.

Finally if God freely offers us forgiveness, as I believe the Christian religion affirms, who are we to refuse to forgive ourselves? Are we holier than God? I say "we" because I cannot accept that the dark seeds detailed by the author are under the circumstances in any way more reprehensible than my own moral lapses.

While I have attempted to speak from a Christian perspective, I suspect that other spiritual disciplines, although by somewhat different routes, would arrive at similar conclusions.

35. Robert Muller

Robert Muller (1923–2010) was co-founder of the United Nations' University for Peace in Costa Rica, where he serves as Chancellor Emeritus. He is considered one of the New Millennium's greatest minds for peace. Muller served as the Assistant Secretary-General to three Secretary-Generals of the United Nations. While growing up, Muller witnessed first-hand the atrocities of war, and knew that a peaceful philosophy of living was essential to the longevity of our species.

In 2003, Douglas Gilles wrote a biography of Robert Muller: *Prophet, The Hatmaker's Son: The Life of Robert Muller*. Muller's own book, *Most of All They Taught Me Happiness* has just been re-released.

Anthropologist Margaret Mead called Robert Muller "the most brilliant person in the world," and visionary Jean Houston says, "When the true history of the Twentieth Century is told, Robert Muller's name will stand out."

* * * * * * *

With my warmest wishes, I send to you a poem I have written about forgiveness. You will see here that I urge you to forgive your parents.

Decide to Forgive

Decide to forgive
For resentment is negative
Resentment is poisonous
Resentment diminishes
And devours the self

Be the first to forgive
To smile and take the first step
And you will see happiness bloom
On the face of your human
Brother or sister

Be always the first
Do not wait for others to forgive
For by forgiving

You become the master of fate
The fashioner of life
A doer of miracles

To forgive is the highest
Most beautiful form of love
In return you will receive
Untold peace and happiness

Decide to be peaceful
Render others peaceful
Be a model of peace
Radiate your peace
Love passionately the peace
Of our beautiful planet

Do not listen to the warmongers,
Hate-seeders and power-seekers
Dream always of a peaceful,
Warless, disarmed world
Think always of a peaceful world
Work always for a peaceful world

Switch on and keep on, in yourself,
The peaceful buttons,
Those marked love,
Security, happiness, truth,
Kindness, friendliness,
Understanding and tolerance

Pray and thank God every day for peace
Pray for the United Nations
And all peacemakers
Pray for the leaders of nations
Who hold the peace of the world
In their hands

Pray to God to let our planet at long last
Become the Planet of Peace
And sing in unison with all humanity:
"Let here be peace on Earth
And let it begin with me."

36. Bill Pelke

Bill Pelke recently wrote a book, *Journey of Hope... From Violence to Healing*, which details the murder of his grandmother by four teenage girls. Paula Cooper, the fifteen-year-old ringleader, was sentenced to die in the electric chair.

Pelke, who originally supported the death penalty, went through a spiritual transformation, becoming involved in an international crusade on Paula's behalf and working to abolish the death penalty for all. He has traveled to over forty states and ten countries with the *Journey of Hope* and has told his story over 5000 times. "Love those who hate you," he says, "love those who persecute you, and love those who do all manner of evil against you."

* * * * * * *

Should I forgive? My answer for many years would have been, "It depends on what that person did to you and whether you want to forgive."

I learned the most important lesson of my life on the night of November 2, 1986. I was at work at Bethlehem Steel where I had been employed as an overhead crane operator for twenty years. As I sat in my crane cab fifty feet above the steel mill floor, I had a period of free time, and I began to contemplate the murder of my grandmother.

Nana had a reputation in her neighborhood of being a Bible Teacher. On the afternoon of May 14, 1985, four ninth grade students from the local high school in Gary, Indiana, knocked on her door and told her they would like to take her Bible lessons. Nana invited them into her living room and turned to go to her desk and get the girls some information.

One of the girls hit Nana over the head with a vase, and as Nana fell to the floor, another girl pulled a knife out of her purse and began to stab Nana. After ransacking the house, the girls managed to come up with $10 and the keys to her old car. They took her car and returned to school to see if any of their friends wanted to go joy riding.

Nana died on the dining room floor.

My father found Nana's body the next day. Our family was almost in a state of shock upon receiving the news. We could not believe it. Who would do such a terrible thing to such a wonderful person?

The girls were arrested the next day.

The state of Indiana said justice for the Pelke family was that they were going to sentence all four of these girls to death.

By the time the trials took place over a year later, only one girl, Paula Cooper, who was deemed to be the ringleader, received the sentence of death. The other girls were given varying periods of time in prison. I was in the courtroom on July 11, 1986 when Paula Cooper was sentenced to die in the electric chair. I was surprised the judge gave her that sentence because she was only fifteen years old at the time of the crime.

Although surprised, I still thought it was the right sentence. I felt that if they didn't give the death sentence, then the court would have been telling me that you had to be someone important for your killer to be sentenced to death, and I felt Nana was a very important person.

As I walked out of the courtroom I was asked by a TV newsman what my opinion was. I said, "I felt the judge did what he had to do," and barely holding back tears I added, "but it will not bring my grandmother back." I withheld from saying that Paula Cooper would regret the day she met the Pelke family.

Fast forward to a few months later – the night at work that changed my life. As I sat in the crane thinking about my grandmother's life and her death, I began to think about the trial that had taken place. I recalled an old man beginning to wail out very loudly, "They are going to kill my baby; they are going to kill my baby" as the judge began to deliver his verdict. The judge ordered the man out from the courtroom because he was disrupting the proceedings. I watched as a bailiff led the old man out of the courtroom. I noticed tears streaming down his face. I found out later that the old man was Paula Cooper's grandfather.

Then I recalled when Paula Cooper was led off to death row. When I had first seen Paula Cooper that day, she was smiling and laughing with the jail matron who escorted her into the courtroom. I thought to myself, "You won't be smiling when this day is over with." And sure enough, she wasn't. There were tears streaming down her face; in fact, the tears were running onto her dress and making dark blotches on her light blue dress.

It was at that point where I began to picture an image of my grandmother. There was a very beautiful picture taken of Nana shortly before her death, and whenever the newspapers did a story about her murder, the various trials, and the news of the death sentence, they always showed that beautiful picture. I began to picture that image of

Nana but with one distinct difference. There were tears streaming down Nana's face. At first I thought they were tears of pain, but quickly realized they were tears of love and compassion for Paula Cooper and her family.

I immediately began to think of Nana's faith, the Christian faith and what it taught about forgiveness. I recalled Jesus preaching the "Sermon on the Mountain." Jesus said that if we wanted our father in heaven to forgive us that we needed to forgive others.

Then I thought about when Jesus was talking with some of the disciples and Peter asked him how many times should we forgive. Peter asked if seven times were proper. Jesus responded by saying seventy times seven. As I sat in the crane that night, I knew Jesus was not saying to forgive four hundred and ninety times and then stop forgiving, but He was saying that forgiveness is a habit, a way of life.

As I sat in my crane cab, I thought about when Jesus was crucified. I envisioned Him on the cross and looking up to heaven saying, "Father, forgive them for they know not what they do."

It was at that point that I felt Paula Cooper did not know what she was doing. I felt that someone in their right mind would not take a twelve-inch butcher knife and stab someone thirty-three times. What happened that night was a crazy, senseless act. I felt that Jesus was telling me I should forgive, and I said to myself that I should try to forgive.

Immediately I began to picture that image of Nana again with tears streaming down her face, and I knew they were tears of love and compassion for Paula Cooper and her family. I felt Nana wanted someone in our family to have that same love and compassion, and the responsibility fell on my shoulders. At that point I knew forgiveness was the right thing and that I should try to forgive, but the love and compassion thing was another story. I had absolutely no love and compassion for Paula Cooper. Nana had been brutally murdered. And yet I felt that if I didn't at least try to generate some love and compassion, I would feel guilty whenever I thought of Nana again. The tears I pictured in her eyes had a great impact on me.

Not knowing what else to do, with tears streaming down my own cheeks, I began to say a prayer. It was a short prayer, but I will never forget the words I said that night in the crane. I begged God to please, please, please, give me love and compassion for Paula Cooper and her family and to do it on behalf of Nana. I ended the prayer, "In Jesus' name, Amen." It was a very short prayer.

I begin to think about writing Paula a letter and telling her about Nana and sharing Nana's faith with her. I could tell her about a God that loves and forgives.

I immediately realized two things. The first was that I knew I no longer wanted Paula to die in the electric chair, and the second was that without trying, I had forgiven Paula. And with that forgiveness came a tremendous and immediate healing.

It had been a year and a half since Nana's death, and whenever I thought about Nana, I pictured how she died. It was terrible to think about it. At the trial they pointed out that not only was she stabbed 33 times, but also they had the section of the carpet that had been under Nana's body and showed how the carpet had been slashed with the knife. They also had a picture of the hardwood floor underneath the carpet, and it showed how the floor had been bruised and splintered by the knife. When I thought about Nana, I pictured someone I loved dearly, butchered to death on the dining room floor – the same dining room where our family gathered every year for Christmas, Thanksgiving, Easter, birthdays and other happy joyous occasions. To think about Nana was very, very painful.

But I knew right away that from that moment on that whenever I thought about Nana again, I would no longer picture how she died, but rather picture how she lived, what she stood for, what she believed in, the beautiful wonderful person that she was. And I knew that something wonderful had happened inside of me, and it was not something that happened so I would feel good for a while but it was something to be shared with other people.

37. Robert W. Plath, J.D.

Robert W. Plath is an attorney who has practiced law in the San Francisco Bay Area for forty years. He is Founder and Director of the non-profit Worldwide Forgiveness Alliance. The Worldwide Forgiveness Alliance is trying to make International Forgiveness Day the first international holiday. Presently, it is celebrated in nine countries and twenty cities in the United States. The Alliance honors outstanding Heroes and Champions of Forgiveness, Reconciliation and Peace worldwide.

* * * * * * *

"You are born into a family that sadistically abuses. You are forced to torture and destroy. As an adult, do you forgive your parents? HOW do you forgive yourself?" These were the questions you posed to me asking for answers.

Lois, I was born to a father and a mother who abused me, although to a much lesser level than what you described your parents as having done.

In my opinion, whether to forgive my parents is simple—I *have* to forgive them if I am committed to my own wholeness and well-being. The studies done by Dr. Fredric Luskin and others prove that forgiveness heals, and that lack of forgiveness causes stress and all sorts of major health problems.

The real problem lies in your second question: "HOW do I forgive myself?"

I believe that forgiveness of our parents and of ourselves is interchangeable, i.e., it is like a mirror. When we forgive our parents on some level we forgive ourselves of those same faults, sadistic acts, etc. (This could be on a much lesser level.) And when we forgive ourselves we are in effect forgiving our parents.

The most difficult question is: "HOW do we forgive ourselves?" I take a rather spiritual approach to this question, i.e., "enjoy the journey" and "trust the process"—both of which, in the midst of lacking forgiveness, are very difficult to do.

I believe that God, the Higher Power, Life—whatever you want to call it—is endlessly seeking to heal us to total wholeness or self-realization. Our main function in this process is to commit totally to fully face and deal with every situation that is drawn to us (or that we draw to us) along the way.

It means being committed to facing every fear or illness or predicament or sadistic torture and processing it through meditation, psychiatry, catharsis – literally going into the hurt or pain inflicted, as different aspects of it are brought inevitably to you by God or Life.

I've been working with forgiveness particularly since I was 13 years of age wherein I had often wished my father dead after he struck me heavily across the face, and all of a sudden on a cold pre-Christmas evening I was told, "Bobbie, Daddy's dead." My religious background was full of sin and guilt, and I punished myself severely out of fear of Hellfire and Damnation, to some degree to this date.

Just this last week a friend who has assumed a father's role with me turned against me and fired me from work I was doing in an abrupt, brutal manner. The effect on me was somewhat the same as I felt at the death of my dad – a devastating and overwhelming feeling of anger, loss of confidence, hopelessness, helplessness, blame, etc. I felt like a victim.

I feel now that whatever occurred "is coming up for healing" (a new age quote often used).

And I feel that by processing (I wrote out fully my feelings of anger, sadness and fear and took responsibility for my past and came back as much as I could to forgive and love.) I feel that by processing the pall, the fear, the loss of belief in the protection of God, the isolation and desperate loneliness, and the finality of death, that they have lifted today. And this lifting came about from everything—all events and happenings—i.e., the death of a dear friend, firing by my other friend— all combined to work a magical healing – when I could see it that way!!

So, the HOW involves a journey of great commitment and some understanding (be it ever so little at first) that *forgiveness works.*

It's like my process frees me to be the Hero of my story rather than the goat or victim. And maybe that process involves, if only in my imagination, striking back at them, i.e. "How does it feel, you bastard?"—blasting a pillow. It symbolizes taking back our power— setting limitations, and then finally being willing to release and let go— for *our* sake!

First, open up to a *little willingness to forgive.* Then let go and let God. Trust—flow—process—go into it—and when the freedom, the sunshine, the new day arrives—thank you God, Allah, Buddha, Life. Thank you, Thank you.

218

38. Daniel Quinn

Daniel Quinn (1935–2018) is an internationally acclaimed author. His books include *Ishmael, The Story of B, My Ishmael: A Sequel, After Dachau*, and *The Holy*.

His book, *Ishmael* (1991), won the Turner Tomorrow Fellowship, an award encouraging authors to find "creative, positive solutions to global problems." The prize was the largest ever awarded for a fictional work. Ishmael has sold over 800,000 copies and has been translated into over twenty languages.

In his critique for the *Whole Earth Review*, Jim Brittel wrote, "From now on I will divide books into two categories—the ones I read before Ishmael and those read after."

* * * * * * *

When *Ishmael* came out, I was surprised by the number of readers who wanted to know the origin of the strange ideas embodied in this book. Some imagined the ideas could not have come to me in an ordinary way, simply by reflection. They wondered if I was "channeling" them from some departed spirit. They wondered if the ideas came to me from some **other** teacher (not stopping to wonder how they might have come to this other teacher—perhaps from yet another teacher?). The story seemed to me worth telling, and so I wrote a sort of autobiography called *Providence: The Story of a Fifty-Year Vision Quest*. In that book, among other things, I had to address the questions that you, Lois, ask (as perhaps most people must eventually do, whether they suffer deliberate and systematic abuse at the hands of their parents or merely the casual and unplanned abuse that is endemic in the families of our culture).

Though I've never seen an actual citation of it, Sigmund Freud is alleged to have said, "To understand is to forgive." Taking my own liberties with these words, it's my belief that (if he said them at all), he was merely stating a tautology: to understand is to understand; I'm sure he would agree that forgiveness is another matter entirely and not at all an automatic consequence of understanding.

Through their own surely unintended behavior, my parents instilled in me a profound belief that I was utterly worthless and unlovable. I call this unintended because I really feel they could not have thought me worth the trouble of deliberately deforming me in this way. To them, I was like household dust, an ever-present but insignificant nuisance. I entered adult life without the slightest inkling that I was in fact an emotional cripple, and it took me ten years of misery and two disastrous marriages to realize that, without help, this was going to be the pattern of my whole life. The help I needed was, first, to see how thoroughly I had come to accept my parents' valuation of myself as worthless and unlovable; and second, to accept the possibility that they were simply mistaken in that valuation.

In fact, they were mistaken. Why? I haven't the slightest idea. I don't understand them—and have no need to understand them. The reasons for their rejection of me are of no interest or importance to me.

Have I forgiven them? To my mind, this would be like forgiving someone for being a philistine (who is, almost by definition, someone who doesn't even know what philistinism is). Forgiving them would accomplish nothing for them or for me; to be made whole, all I needed to know was that they were wrong about me.

Parents who deliberately torture their children are, of course, an entirely different matter, making issues of understanding and forgiveness vitally important. If we don't understand such people, then we can only think of them as monsters, as embodiments of evil in some abstract sense (which is, in effect, to deny that their behavior is comprehensible, to deny even their humanity). Your parents got something out of the appalling torment they inflicted on you and your sister. To say that what they got out of it was sadistic pleasure simply puts the question at a further remove. Why did they need sadistic pleasure—and this particular sadistic pleasure? Obviously I haven't the slightest clue, though I would like to have, because I'm not at all satisfied to think of them as merely evil. It's likely, as you suppose, that they were themselves abused as children, but this provides no light; it just pushes the question back a generation: what did your parents' parents get out of abusing their children?

Although I want to understand them, this has nothing to do with forgiving them. And if for some reason they deserve forgiveness, then they deserve it not only from you but from all humanity, for their crimes were crimes against humanity as surely as were the crimes of Josef Mengele or Adolf Eichmann. Even if I were to understand them (and here I speak only personally, of course), I would not forgive them. On the other hand, if I'd been the direct object of their extraordinary cruelty, forgiving them might give me some beneficial release; since I wasn't, I can't say whether it would or not.

220

You tell the story of a dying Nazi soldier, Karl, who expressed remorse for his crimes and asked Simon Wiesenthal for his forgiveness, which was withheld. My interest in this exchange is not in Wiesenthal's refusal but in Karl's request. I wonder what he really wanted. In my dictionary, the two relevant meanings of the word forgive are:

"1. To excuse for a fault or an offense; pardon.

2. To renounce anger or resentment against."

To excuse Karl for his offense was, of course, not in Wiesenthal's power. To renounce his anger against Karl for his offense was in Wiesenthal's power and might have benefited Wiesenthal, but he preferred to forego that benefit (as I would have done). But since it would not have benefited Karl in any way that I can see, I conclude that what Karl actually wanted was to be excused for his crimes, presumably on the grounds that he now regretted having committed them. A sentimentalist would perhaps feel that genuine remorse must unfailingly be rewarded by forgiveness.

It seems to me relevant to discuss an accusation of abuse laid against me by one of my own children. The tale, told to me by my son some thirty years after its supposed occurrence is this: during an Easter egg hunt, a single egg remained to be found, and he alleges that I told him that if he didn't find it, he was a worthless person, doomed to a life of failure. Even though I might conceivably be wicked enough to say such a thing to a four-year-old, I couldn't possibly be silly enough to say such a thing, and so I knew the story was false (as anyone would who knows me). He later admitted to a sibling that he had no actual memory of the incident; it had been told to him many years later by his mother, who, as he well knows, made a career of blackening me in my children's eyes and who (strangely enough) admitted that she hadn't even been there at the time of the alleged crime. Yet he believes it without doubt and credits it with ruining his entire life. He has made it clear that in some sense his salvation depends on my asking forgiveness for this imaginary and absurd slight; presumably, granting me forgiveness would enable him to "renounce anger or resentment" against me that is poisoning his life. Forgiveness can evidently (or at least notionally) confer an important benefit on the person granting it without conferring any benefit on the recipient.

The torture devised by your parents for you and your sister was specifically designed to destroy your humanity by forcing you to become torturers yourselves. And forced you were; there can be no doubt of that.

It would be the very rare adult who could have held out against your parents' diabolical system and chosen to accept limitless pain rather than inflict pain on someone else. To expect this of a child would be grotesque. But the physical pain inflicted on the two of you was only an ephemeral gratification for them; the scar they wanted you to bear forever was a guilt that must seem unforgivable no matter how clearly it's shown to be undeserved.

In your questions, you ask what I would do now, as an adult, if I'd been a victim of such abuse. Would I forgive my parents? I give two answers to this question, because forgiveness comes in two senses. First, I wouldn't forgive them in the sense of excusing them for their crimes; Jesus is reported to have asked his heavenly father to forgive his tormentors in this sense, precisely because they had an excuse: they didn't know what they were doing. (I can forgive my actual parents in this sense, because they had the same excuse: they didn't know what they were doing.) Your parents have no such excuse; they knew perfectly well what they were doing. Second, I might forgive them in the sense of renouncing anger or resentment against them, but only if the renunciation served the purpose of healing me. (In the case of my actual parents, I feel no deep anger or resentment against them, and so have no need to forgive them in this sense; simply understanding what they did to me was wrong was enough to heal me).

Would I forgive myself? Absolutely, to the fullest possible extent—in both senses of the word. No mere human could be expected to behave differently under the circumstances you faced, and anyone who says they would have behaved differently is either lying or deluded. The same can be said of child abuse in general. It is the abuser's art to contrive a situation in which the child believes s/he cannot behave differently than to collaborate in the abuse. As adults, we can look at the situation and imagine all sorts of things the child might have done—if only the child had an adult's experience and physical strength. It is precisely the child's inexperience and physical weakness that abusers are exploiting, fully aware that they can count on the passive collaboration of the society around them.

The statistics tell us that every elementary and secondary classroom in America harbors five or more children who are being abused at home, but the schools prefer not to know this, prefer not to get involved in providing a secure escape structure for them. It's "not their job." Indeed, it's not anyone's job—and the abuser counts on this.

In the matter of child abuse, there is plenty of guilt to go around: to those monsters who perpetrate it and to a society that abets it by looking the other way. There should be no guilt whatsoever left over for the victims. They are guilty only of being defenseless—and undefended.

39. Billy Ray Riggs

Billy Ray Riggs is a Black/Cherokee Indian/German man on death row in San Quentin, California. An ex-ghetto king and drug dealer, he was convicted in 1994 of robbery and murder. In prison, he is representing himself while appealing his conviction, writing poetry, and studying the Bible. He has also dedicated his life to saving others. He's known at the prison as "Pops" because he advises new inmates in a fatherly way to get off drugs and to read instead and educate themselves. Riggs' motto is, "Reach one! Teach one! Help one!"

* * * * * * *

Your question of forgiveness required some thoughtful consideration on my part. I read your story about child abuse. It had me in tears for two days. I finally came up with an answer for you. It might not be the one that you are searching for, but it is the one that God gave me to share with you.

I will begin by telling you two stories. The first is about a child and some ice cream.

A mother took her family to a restaurant. Before the meal, her 6-year-old son prayed, "Thank you for the food, and I would thank you even more if Mom got us ice cream. Amen!"

Amid the laughter, a woman nearby said indignantly, "That's what's wrong with this country. Kids today don't even know how to pray. Asking God for ice cream!" Just then an elderly gentleman came by, winked at the boy, and whispered to him, "Too bad she never asked God for ice cream. A little ice cream is good for the soul sometimes."

When dessert came, the boy picked up his sundae, walked to the lady's table, and set it before her. With a big smile he said, "This is for you. Ice cream is good for the soul sometimes, and my soul is good already!"

We must all become more childlike in all our relationships with others in order to deal with a sin someone has done to us. Then we can deal with it in a Godly fashion.

Now my last story deals with what we all have had problems with in our lives – that is the grip of guilt.

Can you think of anything too hard for God to do? Put yourself in the shoes of a fellow Christian who has committed a sin so awful that the person simply cannot imagine that God would forgive it. Think about what he or she considers to be impossible for God.

I remember a teenager who was having a hard time believing that God could forgive her sexual sins. She told me she was a Christian and had asked Jesus many times to forgive her. Even though she knew the Bible says God had forgiven her, she still felt dirty in her heart.

This teenager thought she had found something that was too hard to do—be forgiven. When we tell ourselves that our sin is so bad God won't forgive us, we are doubting His power. We are robbing ourselves of the great gifts of a clear conscience and of fellowship with God (1 John 1:5-10).

Does guilt for sin have its icy hands around your heart? Is it strangling your joy and making you forget that God's forgiveness is not based on what you do but on what Christ has done? Ask for His forgiveness. Then thank Him for it, and moment by moment remind yourself of the wonder of God's grace.

I conclude with a poem I wrote.

Compassion

How compassion touches your heart
Though it be hard as tempered steel.
For in there lies the saving grace
To leave all wounds healed
As we walk this revolving rock
Held prisoners in fate's ticking clock.
What would cause you and me to stop?
And reach to stir the ashes
That burned so long ago
To start an inner fire
That illuminates the soul?
Release the best of vengeance
Feeling the freedom that this brings
And show the love of God
For we all are spiritual beings.
Chance moments must not slip away,
As if we've never lived,
For we become immortalized
With the goodness that we give.

40. Robert C. Scaer, M.D.

Dr. Robert Scaer a board certified neurologist, is currently the Medical Director of Rehabilitation Services at the Mapleton Center in Boulder, Colorado. He is also the Medical Director of the Pain and Trauma Recovery Center at Mapleton. He has had extensive experience in traumatic brain injury and chronic pain rehabilitation during his thirty years of practice. This has included management of the recovery of thousands of patients injured in motor vehicle accidents. Based on his experiences with these patients, Dr. Scaer has concluded that in many cases not only the emotional, but also the physical symptoms experienced by them are related more to the exposure to a traumatic event than to the physical injuries suffered. He has written and lectured extensively on this topic.

* * * * * * *

I was so moved by your letter and story that I felt compelled to respond immediately. I have also recently begun to think about the role of forgiveness in the process of healing from trauma, prompted by a colleague who has become interested in the concept of forgiveness in healing from physical illness. To really respond to your questions, I must, at least in brief, tell you my story also.

I was not abused as a child, but I can remember very little of my childhood. My mother was a sweet, passive but tortured woman who never punished my sister or me in any way. Nevertheless, she was childlike in many ways, cyclically depressed, requiring hospitalizations and shock treatment. Unfortunately, she was also terribly emotionally labile, and never slept a night without terror. All of her life she required sleeping pills to sleep, and I frequently could hear her sobbing uncontrollably after I had gone to bed. I grew up terrified of her next emotional eruption. My mother's pain finally was eased at age 70 when she took an overdose of sleeping pills, suffered from anoxic brain damage, and lived the last seven years of her life mildly demented, but blessedly without affect. When she died, I told my wife how much I hated her. After I entered the field of trauma six years ago, my sister off-handedly commented that the family secret was that my mother's father supposedly was thought to have done something bad to my mother. I suddenly realized that she had behaved throughout her life like many of my patients who had been victims of incest. I was overcome with remorse, sadness and understanding. I have now come to forgive her and remember the love I actually felt for her as a child.

I firmly believe that children are born quite pure, free from any vestige of evil, and infinitely malleable by their life experiences. Far from "resilient," they are exquisitely sensitive to every nuance of their early life experiences from a time long before they are born. Although they do not acquire conscious memory until age three or four, they store the meanings of their life experiences in procedural memory, especially those events pertaining to survival. Their brains and therefore their behavior are shaped by their caregiver's behavior from before their birth. They do not possess the abilities to protect themselves, and so they can only freeze or dissociate when threatened.

When traumatized, as you were repeatedly, the only defense is to "leave the scene" and achieve a state of numbing. A child in that state will do anything that is demanded of them. An interesting analogy is the phenomenon in some cultures of "induced startling". Members of the culture will be chosen to startle, and the community will then constantly attempt to startle them unexpectedly. After a while, they will startle at the slightest stimuli, and will curiously then be subject to perform any act requested by any member of the community, almost as an automaton. Often they are ordered to dance, and will do so until told that they may stop. In essence, they have been induced to a state of perpetual dissociation, and in fact are thereafter revered as special members of the tribe or community. This behavior is really quite analogous to that of the abused child.

When children are traumatized by their caregivers, they have nowhere to go, and no one to blame but themselves for being abused. How can the parent be at fault when she/he is their only resource for safety? Where can you run if the abuse is in your own home, from your only source of nurturing? Every abused child therefore feels existential guilt for having been so bad that their parent would need to do such terrible things to them. They will continue to blame themselves for being deserving of the abuse they received, and for any other behavior associated with it.

Finally, as you know, there is a powerful drive the traumatized individual has to repeat the trauma. Most prostitutes are victims of childhood sexual abuse. Most male murderers are victims of terrible childhood physical abuse or sodomy. Most serial murderers are victims of violent childhood abuse. Most pedophiles are victims of sodomy or other forms of childhood sexual abuse. We often tend to recreate the behavior of our abusers, or for that matter seek to re-experience the abuse in real or symbolic form, probably in an attempt to complete the aborted escape, and allow our survival brain to realize that the trauma is indeed over. The psychologist, Harville Hendrix, even related this phenomenon, probably unwittingly, to the unconscious tendency of a person to seek out and attach to someone in courtship who possesses the most painful and negative aspects of their caregivers. And so abusive parents usually replicate the behavior to which they were subjected as children in their own child-rearing practices. I was largely able to avoid this through a helpful wife, and some instinct that told me how I had been raised was wrong. You clearly have found the power to heal though intelligence, determination and a healing and loving social network, the most critical element in healing from trauma.

How does this apply to your dilemma? How can you forgive yourself for the horrible things that you have done? How can you forgive your parents for their depraved, cruel, and evil behavior? Was Wiesenthal right or wrong in his not forgiving a person who perpetrated unspeakable evil but now repented?

First, how can you not forgive a child? You were innocent and without guile or intent in all of the terrible things that you did. Children, or adults for that matter (example, my mother), acting in a state of dissociation are acting in a state of "brainlessness". The cerebral cortex is "shut down" during dissociation. Scans of the brain show essentially no energy utilization in the cortex, the area of planning and intent. The brain is operating on brainstem survival reflexes under those circumstances, and will follow survival instincts, which is basically what you were doing as a "perpetrator". The abused child is quite analogous to the curious cultural victims of induced startle, and their subsequent puppet-like societal compliance. The guilt that you now feel is that of an adult passing judgment on a child who was for all intents and purposes unconscious while doing bad things.

How can you forgive your parents? Of course, what they did was evil. There's no way to excuse what they did. There's no way one can forgive any evil done in the world – or is there? The German nation is a product of a child-rearing system of "poisonous pedagogy" (read the German psychoanalyst, Alice Miller, *For Your Own Good*). Its ability to perpetuate the Holocaust is in part a product of a mass catastrophe of child upbringing, which goes back many generations. We all are subject to trauma of one sort or another throughout our lives, and the personality of individuals, of cultures and of nations is shaped by those collective experiences. Unfortunately, the greatest predictor of trauma is trauma in the prior generation. The terrible rate of depression and suicide in children of victims of the Holocaust is testament to that. And so, evil is relative, and given the critical mixture of life experiences, culture and perhaps genes, any one of us has the capacity to do evil things. Your parents undoubtedly were a product of terrible experiences in their own childhoods, as you implied.

This argument is not necessarily sufficient for one to forgive evil, but I do feel the act of forgiveness releases one, at least in part, from the terrible bond that the victim of evil shares forever with the perpetrator(s). That bond remains forever painful, a stricture around the heart that is only painful for the victim. So I do believe that it is in fact part of the healing process for the victim to forgive, not only herself, but also her abuser. Rage is inevitably a product of healing from trauma, and held rage is not good for the brain, the body or the soul. It's hard to feel rage if forgiveness has occurred.

Is it wrong not to forgive the abuser/perpetrator? There is nothing right or wrong about forgiveness. It is a personal choice, and I believe entirely a choice within the right and privilege of victims to exercise or not. They at least possess that power over their abuser, and should have the right to do whatever they choose, without being subject to bias or criticism. No one should ever stand in judgment of the emotions or opinions of the victim of personal trauma. Simon Wiesenthal had every right not to forgive Karl.

I hope that this very spontaneous response to your inquiry is helpful. I am touched and a bit awed to be included in the list of responders to your letter. I think that you bring up a critical issue in the field of trauma, one that is in my experience often neglected. As you continue your healing, I sincerely hope that you find answers to your questions, most importantly answers that contribute to your healing process, and to your book. I look forward to reading it.

41. Pete Seeger

Pete Seeger (1919–2014) is one of the world's most beloved folksingers. He has dedicated his music to raising awareness, bringing social justice to all, cleaning the environment, and other social and political causes. He was a key singer in The Weavers, a group dedicated to combining folk music with political commentary.

Seeger has dealt with the issue of forgiveness after being blacklisted when in 1955 he refused to speak to the House of Un-American Activities. He served a short jail term and was banned from American radio and television for seventeen years.

Seeger has won several awards including the Presidential Medal of the Arts (1994), Kennedy Center Award (1994), induction into the Rock and Roll Hall of Fame (1996), Grammy for Best Traditional Folk Album (1997), and Felix Varela Medal (1999), Cuba's highest honor for his "humanistic and artistic work in defense of the environment and against racism."

* * * * * * *

I believe in change, and hence I believe in forgiveness as a possibility. I've done lots of stupid things in my life and hope for forgiveness. Part of this belief comes from helping some good people I knew who were in prison. I still sing the song below when I sing in prisons.

Walking Down Death Row

Walking down death row,
I sang for three men, destined for the chair;
Walking down death row,
I sang of lives and loves in other years.
Walking down death row, I sang of hopes that used to be.
Through the bars, into each sep'rate cell,
Yes, I sang to one and two and three.
If you'd only stuck together you'd not be here!
If you could love other's lives you'd not be sitting here.

And if only this you could believe,
You still might, you might still be reprieved!

Walking down death row,
I turned a corner and found to my surprise;
There were women there as well,
With babies in their arms, before my eyes.
Walking down death row,
I tried again to sing of hopes that used to be.
But the thought of that contraption,
Down the hall,
Waiting for whole fam'lies, one dozen, two or three.
If you could've loved another's child as well as your own,
You'd not be sitting here!
And if only this you could believe,
You still might, you might still be reprieved.

Walking down death row,
I concentrated singing to you.
I sang of hopes that flickered still,
I tried to mouth each sep'rate human tongue
Walking down death row,
I sang of hopes that still might be.
Singing, singing, singing down death row.
To each sep'rate human cell,
One billion, two, or three (or four or five or six!)
If we'd only stick together, we'd not be here!
If we could love each other's lives,
We'd not be sitting here!
And if only this we could believe,
We still might, we might still be reprieved.

42. Bernard S. Siegel, M.D.

Dr. Bernard S. Siegel, who prefers to be called Bernie, is a physician, healer, counselor, teacher, author, speaker, and advocate. His published works include *Love, Medicine, & Miracles, Peace, Love, & Healing, How to Live between Office Visits,* and *Prescriptions for Living.* His goals are to humanize medical care and to empower patients, making everyone aware of their healing potential and their choice to live fully and die peacefully. He stands at the forefront of the medical ethics and spiritual issues that confront society, breaking new ground in the field of healing. He has touched innumerable lives directly and indirectly with his loving presence and generous energy that transcends time and place.

* * * * * * *

Yes, I would forgive your parents and be free of them. Some of what you are doing is projecting your shit onto your parents. Their energy from the past is a flame melting your prison walls. Also continue to say "no" to hurting others. As the marines say, "Don't whine or make excuses." Seek to love and see goodness and change in your life. This book may be a part of that journey.

You have to understand to forgive, and when you learn to forgive, you can love. There is justice and mercy, compassion, too. I said love, not as in love is a weapon. Kill with kindness. Torment with tenderness. We need to become one family again. As Helen Keller said, "Deafness is darker by far than blindness. Listen to each other."

I re-parent people and inspire people, not just inform; that doesn't change them. One woman, who like yourself had a Chosen Dad (me), taught me, "The opposite of love is not hate or fear. It is indifference. Keep loving."

I know. I was born an ugly duckling, and we have raised five children. My parents hid me, but I had what the ugly duckling didn't have—grandparents who loved me unconditionally and changed me. Read what I write below, and then rest.

Many years ago my great grandfather told me of the persecution he experienced in Russia that led him to come to this country. He said the Cossacks would pursue him at night, when he was out teaching, and slash him with their sabers. One night he was on the hill above his village with his rabbi, The Baal Shem Tov. As they looked down they could see the Cossacks riding down and killing their Jewish brethren. My grandfather and the rabbi might have felt the same way had they seen their loved ones being taken away to become slaves in a foreign land.

My great grandfather heard the rabbi say, "I wish I were God."

He asked, "Do you want to be God so you can change the bad into the good?"

"No, I wouldn't change anything. I want to be God so I can understand."

Remember our present problems are not new to humankind. Ninety percent of the natives of North and South America died when the explorers brought infectious diseases, which they had no immunity for, to their continents. Forty percent of Europeans died during plagues of the past. Human-made wars and holocausts have taken millions of lives. With today's destructive weapons, we are more of a threat to each other than are infectious diseases, which we can learn to resist. The question is not, "Will there be difficulties and threats to our existence?" Instead, the questions are, "How will we deal with the threats to our existence? What can we learn from them? How can they become blessings to society by teaching us about the meaning of our life?"

When I was a young boy, several of my friends became seriously ill, and one was hit by a car while bicycling to my house. When he and others died, I asked my father, "Why did God make a world where terrible things happen? Why didn't God make a world free of diseases, accidents, and problems?"

My father answered, "To learn lessons." I didn't like that answer and asked my rabbi, teachers, and others. They said things like, "God knows." "Why not?" "Who knows?" "That's life." "To bring you closer to God." Some were honest enough to just say, "I don't know." This didn't leave me feeling satisfied or enlightened. When I told my mother, she answered, "Nature contains the wisdom you seek. Perhaps a walk in the woods would help you to find out why. Go and ask the old lady on the hill whom some call a witch. She is wise in the ways of the world."

As I walked up the hill, I saw a holly tree had fallen onto the path. As I tried to pull it aside, the sharp leaves cut my hands. So, I put on gloves and was able to move it and clear the path. A little further along the path, I heard a noise in the bushes and saw a duck caught in the plastic from a six-pack. I went over and freed the duck and watched him fly off. None of this seemed enlightening.

Further up the hill, I saw five boys lying in a tangled heap in the snow. I asked them if they were playing a game and warned them that the cold weather could lead to frostbite if they didn't move. They said they were not playing but were so tangled they didn't know which part belonged to whom and were afraid they'd break something if they moved. I removed one of the boy's shoes, took a stick, and jabbed it into his foot.

He yelled, "Ow."

I said, "That's your foot. Now move it." I continued to jab until all the boys were separated, but still no enlightenment.

"As I reached the top of the hill I saw, in front of the old woman's cabin, a deer sprawled on the ice of a frozen pond. She kept slipping and sliding and couldn't stand up. I went out, calmed her, and then helped her off the ice by holding her up and guiding her to the shore. I expected her to run away, but instead of running away, she and other deer followed me so I ran towards the house. When I reached the porch and felt safe I turned, and the deer and I looked into each other's eyes before I went into the house.

I told the women why I had come. She said, "I have been watching you walk up the hill, and I think you have the answer."

"What answer," I asked.

"Many things happened on your walk to teach you the lessons you needed to learn. One is that emotional and physical pain are necessary or we cannot protect ourselves and our bodies. Think of why you put on your gloves and how you helped those boys. Pain helps us to know and define ourselves and respond to our needs and the needs of our loved ones. You did what made sense. You helped those in front of you by doing what they needed when they needed it."

"The deer followed you to thank you for being compassionate in time of trouble; the deer's eyes said it all. What you have learned is that we are here to continue God's work. If God had made a perfect world, it would be a magic trick, not Creation, with no meaning or place for us to learn and create. Creation is work. We are the ones who will have to create the world you are hoping for—a world where evil does not respond to the person with disease or physical or emotional pain. God has given us work to do. We still grieve when we experience losses, but we will also use our pain to help us know ourselves and respond to the needs of others. That is our work as our Creator intended it to be. God wants us to know that life is a series of beginnings not endings just as graduations are not terminations but commencements.

Let me tell you about a few other people who have been my teachers. The first, a teenager who was abused by his parents and was

234

HIV+ was about to commit suicide by jumping in front of a subway train. I asked him why he didn't kill his parents instead. He said, "I never want to be like them." Love has sustained him, and he is still alive today.

Another young man with a life-threatening illness told me, "What is evil is not the disease. Many great creative works will come from individual suffering. What is evil is not to respond with compassion to the person with the illness."

An example are parents I know who, because they had a young child die, are improving the lives of other children and raising funds to find a cure for the disease that took their child.

How do we turn our afflictions into blessings? How do we use them to help us complete our work and ourselves and understand the place for love, tolerance, and kindness? Justice and mercy must both be a part of how we treat those who terrorize us because when we understand we can forgive; and when we forgive, we do not hate. When we do not hate, we are capable of loving, and love is the most powerful weapon known to humankind. It is not an accident that we say, "Kill with kindness, love thine enemies, and torment with tenderness."

As Golda Meir said, "The only way to eliminate war is to love our children more than we hate our enemies." When we raise a generation of children with compassion, and when parents let their children know they are loved, teachers truly educate, and the clergy let children know they are children of God, we will have a planet made up of the family of people where our differences are used for recognition and not persecution.

In closing, let me say that as a surgeon, I know something you may not know: We are all the same color inside. To paraphrase Rabbi Carlebach, let us hope that someday all the Cains will realize what they have done and ask for forgiveness of the Abels they killed. In that moment we all rise and become one family accepting that we are here to love and be loved. Until that moment, may you accept and learn from your mortality, rather than from future disasters, what is truly important in this time of your life.

43. Tamarack Song

Tamarack Song is a personal counselor and founder of the Teaching Drum Outdoor School in Wisconsin, which offers wilderness-based instruction in primitive living skills and guidance in reawakening the native person within. As a child and young adult, he lived with a pack of wolves and apprenticed to elders from traditional native cultures. Currently, he also is a storyteller. He has published the groundbreaking books, *Journey to the Ancestral Self, Remembering: Native Teaching and Healing Stories for Our Time,* and *Sacred Speech: The Way of Truthspeaking.*

* * * * * * *

Lois Einhorn's tragic and private story, most courageously revealed, tells of a sequestered time in a nameless place, and yet it exploded before me into a metaphor for my culture and myself. It was me, forced to the floor, whipped and raped. I became an indentured peasant, given only enough to keep me alive and working. And then I was a horse, forced to haul so much, and for so long, that I went blind and dumb from hemorrhaging. Finally, I found myself huddled with my beaten tribe, being pillaged in every imaginable way by soulless conquerors.

These stories—our stories—of abuse, are customarily either whitewashed away or given face lifts, so they pass as acts of patriotism in time of war, or as the cost of progress in times of peace. Our foul stories are never-ending, because the disguisers, opiated with greed and given the sanction of forgiveness, have perpetuated an unbroken chain of abuse throughout the ages.

No one will tell Lois's story at a family gathering, nor will our culture's real stories be found in our history books, because pretense is more palatable than truth, and because history is, after all, written by the victors. The people in the news media often choose not to see or report the real story, because they are controlled and paid for by the victors. For the same reasons, questions like Lois's are seldom asked in our political and economic forums. And sadly, they are not often or loudly enough raised in religious and academic circles. They must, therefore, be addressed by you, and me, and anyone courageous enough to face them. I stress the *must* because these questions take us to the pith of our species' paradoxical ability to maltreat its own kind. They are the hard, underlying questions that we as individuals, and as a culture, need to ask of ourselves if we are ever to know peace.

This book is first our opportunity to serve Lois in her healing, and then it is Lois's gift to other abuse victims, our demoralized culture, and our plundered Mother Planet. And lastly, it is Lois's gift to us – our forum, our catalyst, our work, and I am honored to be a part of it.

A Cornerstone of Our Culture

I have had the privilege of knowing Lois for a number of years, so her self-searching question, "Do I forgive, and if so – how?" is not new to me. Even though I had the wisdom of my Native-American elders to draw upon, the guidance of other traditions, and the teachings that living in the wilds have given me, only recently was I able to take Lois's question fully into the arena of human experience. I heard a poem at a wedding in which one line was helpful to me. "The Art of a Good Marriage," by Wilferd Arlan Peterson, in part said: "It is having the capacity to forgive and forget." From this, I went into a reflective journey into the dynamics of relationship: If I accept my mate for who and how she is, what is there then to forgive? What is there then to forget? If I am my spouse's soul mate and equal, who am I to presume the position to forgive?

There were no easy answers. All I heard was the echo of my culture's voice, "To err is human, to forgive, divine." "Forgive and forget." "You are richer today if you have laughed, given or forgiven." Norman Cousins summed it up when he said, "Life is an adventure in forgiveness."

Some research quickly confirmed my hunch that forgiveness is a cherished value in most cultures. The French say the confessed mistake is already half forgiven; the Albanians have a saying, "To forgive the letting of blood, even a killing, is to be a man."

"How deep do the roots of forgiveness go?" I asked myself. I found it at nearly every turn when I explored the Jewish tradition. "Thou givest a hand to offenders, and thy right hand is stretched out to receive the penitent," states the *Hebrew Prayer Book*. The same was true of Christianity, with their most popular prayer containing the line, "Forgive us our trespasses, as we forgive them that trespass against us" (from *The Book of Common Prayer*). Every other major faith offered the same message: "Forgive me, O Lord. Forgive my sinful past deeds," is a Hindu example from the *Stotra Mala*. "The Buddha resides in a place of forgiveness," says the contemporary Buddhist monk. Beopjeong; the *Koran* of Islam states, "With kindness Allah forgives and invites to Paradise." And from *A Book of Pagan Prayer:* "If I have done anything to offend you [Ancestors]... I ask for forgiveness."

Is Forgiveness Natural?

My research shows that forgiveness is a common practice; however, that was not good enough reason for me to accept it. The saying, "Choose to be forgiven," hints that forgiveness might be a matter of belief or preference rather than a natural human trait. If so, what are my other choices?

In my Ojibwe tradition we have a practice called *Chi Debwewin,* which means Greater Truth. When a person wants to know if his or her knowledge or beliefs will hold up outside his own realm of experience, he will test them by applying them to a variety of people and situations. I did this with forgiveness, in order to determine whether or not it is a natural human trait. Reasoning that hunter-gatherer peoples would represent the essential human, I applied Chi Debwewin to a number of native groups from around the world.

Again, I had no trouble finding references to forgiveness. Southeast Australian Awabakal Aborigines have a term, *Wa-re-kul-li-ko*, which means *to forgive. Antaa* is reported to mean the same in the Saami (northern Scandinavian Laplanders) language. "Strange," I thought, "I have personal friends who are Saami and Aborigine, and they are not forgiving. I know that the word *booni* in the Ojibwe language, which some linguists translate as *forgive*, merely means to leave alone or not think about." That, coupled with my own awareness that people generally view an alien culture through the tint of their own culture's lens, inspired me to keep looking.

"Wait a minute," I realized, "forgiveness is not a word; it is a practice! More than that, it is a state of being, a way of life; how can one word in a dictionary begin to convey that?" With the inspiration that must have gripped Einstein when he discovered a new law of physics, I hurriedly jotted down notes from my own body of knowledge and tradition: "**Ho'oponopono** is known to most as the old Hawaiian practice of forgiveness. The literal translation of Ho'oponopono is *make good-good,* or simply *correct*. That is taking responsibility for actions—a matter of honor, whereas forgiveness is a pardoning—a matter of perspective."

My notes continued: "My clan does a Smudging Ceremony (an invocation and cleansing done with incensing herbs) before building a new lodge, which some see as asking forgiveness for disturbing the land and killing the plants. The elders explain that they do this to ask if it was okay to be there, to give thanks for the privilege, and to voice their intent to live in harmony and disturb as little as possible."

Why then Forgiveness?

"If, as it appears, forgiveness was not commonly practiced by hunter-gatherers (which include all of our ancestors), where then did it originate? And why is it now not only found worldwide, but also held as a virtue?" I realized that I already had part of the answer, because I live it every day in the wilderness, and watch others find it themselves as they learn primitive living skills.

Hunter-gatherers live what is called the Beauty Way – dwelling in the bliss of the moment, with little regret for the past and little care for the future. Earth Mother provides for virtually all necessities and desires, so there is no need to work, form governments, or accumulate wealth and possessions. With little to cause regret, tension or strife, there is little need for forgiveness.

When humans became agriculturists, they had to deal with feast and famine, wealth and poverty, bureaucracy and plague, and work, work, work. Their lives turned into routines of endless toil in the fields. With little contentment in the present, and much to cause the aforementioned regret, tension, and strife, people began looking to the future. Religions were founded to support people throughout life, promising that their long-suffering would be rewarded after death. Buddhists saw life as pain and suffering: if people suffered well, they gained enlightenment. Christians were rewarded with heavenly afterlives if they fared well through lives of suffering, temptation and sin. Karma, the legacy of a previous life, dictated the degree of misery for Hindus. If people's karma was worked out before death, they could expect to re-incarnate to higher states, eventually reaching Nirvana.

Reward upon death was usually not enough. The misery of daily life forced people, often through religious auspices, to come up with coping mechanisms for the here-and-now. Enter sin, karma, meditation, tolerance, justice, and forgiveness.

When people return to the Beauty Way, they gradually abandon these coping mechanisms, because they are no longer needed.

The Paradox of Forgiveness

Mark Twain once said that forgiveness is the fragrance a violet sheds on the heel that has crushed it. Was he implying that forgiveness is a costly virtue? The Portuguese have a saying, "The noblest vengeance is to forgive." Noble perhaps, and yet it is vengeance. "Forgiveness is the attribute of the strong," said Mahatma Gandhi. But, what about the weak? And what does this say about the strong?

I have found forgiveness to be a trap, for both the forgiver and the forgiven. There is a saying, "To forgive is to set the prisoner free and then discover the prisoner was you." Trapped! Maintaining a prisoner also imprisons yourself. Prison is the metaphor for a life of misery, and freeing the prisoner is the metaphoric coping mechanism; however, the freeing creates only the illusion of freedom, because then you realize that you are the prisoner. Or perhaps the coping mechanism simply numbs the pain, and as soon as it is abandoned, one finds that he is still a prisoner – trapped in a life of misery. As the saying goes, "He has forgiven all but himself."

It is commonly believed that forgiveness is healing. In my experience, however, the healing is an illusion, and a short-term one at that. In the long run, forgiveness usually proves to be an impediment to healing. It is a diversion from the real work that has to be done – it can mask the truths that need to be spoken, and often leaves unresolved issues and raw feelings.

Perhaps its greatest disservice to healing is that in order to forgive, there must be both a victim and a perpetrator. This pigeonholing creates a distance between the two, which limits the healing and the manifestation of love that may still be possible.

Forgiveness Is Judgmental

The *American Heritage Dictionary* defines *forgiveness* as the act of "excusing for a fault or offense; a pardon." I wish to stress that a fault or offense was committed only if someone is judged as having done so. The mere fact that I have taken a bushel of apples from my neighbor's tree does not mean that I have committed an offense. It is up to my neighbor to determine. She might condone the act, and perhaps even offer more apples, knowing my need. Another neighbor might overlook the circumstance and judge me as guilty of stealing.

Even though the second neighbor may yet forgive, he first judged me as guilty. If he had not, there would have been no reason to forgive in the first place. There is no forgiveness, therefore, without judgment. Judgment contributes to the distance created when we label victim and perpetrator. This distance is vertical rather than horizontal – the victim assumes the moral high ground and the perpetrator is relegated to the moral cesspool. In simple terms, the victim is right and the perpetrator is wrong. From this righteous position the victim bestows forgiveness.

Apology, defined by the *American Heritage Dictionary* as "expressing regret or asking pardon for a fault or offense," is judgmental in reverse – this time from the moral cesspool. The perpetrator judges himself wrong and the victim, right, and acknowledges this to the victim.

Several years ago a friend wrote me a letter of apology because she thought she had offended me. In my reply I stated, "An apology is not something you have to express to me. I feel that most people are doing the best they can at any particular time, so to be sorry for what you've done is to be sorry for doing your best."

Apology also doesn't take into account that how someone reacts has more to do with what they perceived was done to them, rather than what actually did occur. And apology does not acknowledge the control we each have over our lives. Many of us choose, consciously or unconsciously, to place ourselves in situations where we get hurt.

The bottom line is that forgiveness and apology – seemingly innocuous and supposedly virtuous acts – are both candy-coated judgments.

If Not Forgiveness, then What?

Robert Browning said it is good to forgive, better to forget. And yet forgetting closes the door to healing. "Sin is that which once had a place, but now has no place," stated Oribundo. Sin, karma, punishment, hell, and perhaps even heaven, are all the results of judgments. If we ceased to judge, sin and its allies would cease to exist. There would be no need to forgive, or apologize. Guilt and blame would become things of the past.

This may sound utopian, and like many utopian envisionments, it ignores a stark reality or two, in this case, woundedness. Oftentimes it is so severe that the lives of those involved will never again be normal. Usually it does not stop with the incident, and severe woundedness goes on tormenting throughout life, and then is passed on from generation to generation. No – forgive and forget is not good enough. We need answers. We need to be proactive in healing the woundedness and healing the behavioral patterns that cause it.

I do not claim to have all the answers; however, I have learned the first step – acceptance. With acceptance we acknowledge the event and all parties involved, without the judgment. We provide the groundwork for dialogue and understanding.

What does this give us? Acceptance is healing in and of itself, both for the individual and the relationships involved. Anger and judgment bleed the body and warp the soul. Acceptance is also a doorway to further healing – it opens a range of possibilities that forgiveness precludes. Notable is what acceptance does *not* give us – the distancing between perpetrator and victim that results from the standard judgment-based approaches. Without distancing we are less likely to demonize and deify. The line between victim and perpetrator fades, which encourages new perspectives. For example, some discover that the "perpetrator" has been, or still is, an abuse victim, or that the "victim" has become a perpetrator. I have witnessed miracles that I would previously never have imagined, such as both "victim" and "perpetrator" expressing thankfulness for an abuse incident, because it proved pivotal in their awakening and subsequent healing.

Acceptance is not a virtue, nor is it a religious ideal. It is a simple matter of practicality. Without acceptance, we are right back to judgment in its various guises. With acceptance we can gain perspective on the situation and take charge of our lives by:

- Acknowledging the relationship of all people involved

- Identifying the behavioral patterns that trigger the abuse

- Recognizing the generational history of the abuse

- Contributing to the self-esteem of both perpetrator and victim

- Encouraging trust

- Inviting others to help and support

- Opening to emotional honesty and the potential for love.

As insidious as child abuse is, and as sickening as it might strike us, we must recognize that acceptance is the first critical step to any real healing. It may help to remember that acceptance does not mean agreement: it is merely recognizing and honoring another person's

242

reality, even though it may differ from our own. This includes past realities of our own that may not resonate with our present reality. In that case, acceptance of the incident can provide a giant step toward self-acceptance.

What is the cost of this acceptance? Few people, whether abused or abuser, come by acceptance easily, especially when first introduced to the option. Shame and anger cloud their perspectives, and fears of vulnerability and accountability loom. This can make them suspicious of any outside involvement, so rather than seeing acceptance as a doorway to healing, they fear it is being dangled before them as bait to lure them into the usual blame-shame scenario. For these reasons it is important to spell out, along with the benefits, exactly what they have to let go of:

- Expectations of forgiveness or being forgiven

- Desires for retribution or restitution

- Anonymity—their story will be known to others

- Being right—there are no sides

- Remaining victim/perpetrator—acceptance is an opening to change.

With this approach we are honoring the relationship of the people involved. In the overwhelming majority of cases, childhood sexual abuse occurs within the context of established relationships. Focusing on the abuse itself is simply treating the symptom of an out-of-balance relationship, and it is seldom the only symptom. The core of the imbalance lies in the relationship, so healing focus ought to be on the relationship rather than on a particular individual.

Barriers to Acceptance

Healing is energy, and the healing process requires the uninhibited flow of energy. Blockages often manifest when people feel threatened or overwhelmed. Even those who see the benefits of acceptance might still struggle with engaging in the process. Attachment to outcome and resistance to change are the primary reasons. Acceptance can be frightening because it is open-ended; no clue exists as to what course it might take, and there are no defined goals.

"Forgive your enemies, but never forget their names," said John F. Kennedy. Many of us find it easier to forgive when we take a silent oath not to forget. This is conditional forgiveness – we force the forgiven to bear the cross of being remembered as "the one who did such-and-such," and of being under continual scrutiny.

In contrast to attachment's subtle, often hidden, protest to acceptance, resistance is a blatant statement that is easily recognized. Perhaps the best argument against resistance is its paradox – the more one resists involvement, the more he involves himself. Initiating the process of acceptance requires little energy, and the process itself usually develops its own rhythm and direction, whereas resistance can require great effort, reinforce entrenched patterns, and further erode trust and damage already-fragile relationships. The very act of resisting is creating a bond—a relationship—with that which one is attempting to avoid.

To help individuals overcome their initial skepticism of acceptance, I find it helpful to remind them that the event is history, and that they are not being asked to go back and change anything. "Acceptance," I tell them, "is merely an acknowledgment of the relationships and individual truths involved."

Acceptance Is Empowerment

With acceptance we can acknowledge and allow the existence of something hurtful, even insidious, without needing to embrace or condemn it, or even to be directly involved with it. This allows us to be involved in the relationships around the issue, and to learn from the experience in a personally safe and mutually supportive way.

Fortunately, acceptance is not a simple answer. It involves a shift in perception, a transformation of the way we live. It will change the way we vote, the way we make love, the way we greet a stranger. Acceptance is the recognition that everything is energy. All things, all people, are energy taken form; and in time they will return to energy. This energy, whether or not it has taken form, is continually flowing through and around all that is, without prejudice or boundary. In this sense, everything is relationship. We are related; we are one. This puts new perspective on any judgments regarding the good or bad of a relationship or the individuals involved. That awareness alone can encourage and empower individuals to find and speak their truths. In this way acceptance takes us beyond forgiveness and becomes a doorway to sharing our truths—a doorway to healing.

44. Oswaldo Soriano

Oswaldo R. Soriano (b. June 26, 1975) is on death row in Texas. Born in Mexico, he was convicted of murder and given the death sentence on May 6, 1994 for a murder he committed when he was seventeen years old. He draws, writes poetry and reads, especially books that give him "some type of wisdom and knowledge."

* * * * * * *

Many times I think about what you write, and at times I ask myself, "Who really cares about those who were abused?" How many times do you think that much of what you describe goes through my own thoughts?

The truth is people don't care about children who were abused any more than they care about those of us who are behind bars for one crime or another. It's difficult for somebody to even think of forgiving, much less to forgive. Because of the negative influence of those who control others through manipulation, today people are too quick to judge.

Even, Ms. Lois, if I spoke about my life and what took place to be the person I was and am, how many people would stop to think, read, and try to understand with an open and sincere heart?

Throughout the years I've been here, I've tried and tried and have never been given a chance to speak to others of what can take place if you choose to forgive or not to forgive? I've never had a voice to help people understand the value of life given to us from above.

Many people believe that no matter how much people change, no matter how much they suffer, there will never be anything that could change their mind, but, Ms. Lois, I believe differently. We do suffer deep down for what took place, and it is pain that only you and God can comprehend together, because He changes us. Society and men don't change us; only God does.

I thank you for what you are writing and for extending your help to those in need by bringing light to the stuff that society doesn't want to look at. I hope your life becomes full of love and joy. For all of our sakes, continue!

45. Gerry Spence

Gerry Spence, nationally known lawyer, has dedicated the past half century to fighting for justice, freedom, and truth. His clients have included Karen Silkwood, Imelda Marcos, and Randy Weaver. In addition, he has successfully defended countless people generally ignored, injured, and considered invisible. He has never lost a criminal case, and he has not lost a civil suit since 1969. Spence founded Trial Lawyers College. Here lawyers learn Spence's unorthodox ideas about how to fight with integrity in the courtroom and in life.

Spence has written over a dozen books including the bestseller, *How to Argue and Win Every Time*; *Seven Steps to Personal Freedom*; The *Making of a Country Lawyer From Freedom to Slavery, the Rebirth of Tyranny in America*; and *O.J.: The Last Word*.

* * * * * * *

I cannot imagine the pain, the horror, the scars, the anger, the guilt. I can only imagine the opportunity.

You suffered an introduction to hell and somewhere along the road you came to a fork—a struggle there. The struggle was between age-old forces of good and evil. You could have as easily become a sadist of the first order. That you should have seen it, the light, the possibility—there was a magic that touched you at the fork.

Today you are dealing with the issue—that's the opportunity. I'm always touched by how horrors become blessings, how pain becomes the stuff of growth. The power of it. The gift of your parents created something beautiful. That's part of the magic.

What would I do? We have all suffered our own brand of pain. I could not imagine any as great as yours. But my own pain has been a profound gift to me. I would not wish to endure it again. But I would not be who I am without having suffered it.

My mother killed herself when I was twenty. I thought I had been the cause of it. In fact, one of her friends confirmed it when she would not see me after my mother's death. She let it be known that she believed my mother had killed herself over the sorrow she suffered because I'd "failed to follow the way of the Lord." I lived for over thirty years with that torment until one day I realized that my mother had her own problems. They were not mine, nor was I the cause of them. I learned over the years that forgiveness of the self is the first virtue. One should forgive and forgive and then begin to forgive all over again. The forgiveness must begin with the self. Otherwise there is no fund from which to forgive another.

Would I forgive your parents? They were sick. They were doubtlessly the product of hate, not love. They suffered from a sort of scurvy of the soul. The curing vitamin is always love.

46. Walter Starcke

Walter Starcke began a career on Broadway after ending his career as a naval officer in World War II. Starcke collaborated with playwright and director, John van Druten, on his play "Bell Book and Candle," and became Van Druten's assistant director on the original production of Rogers and Hammerstein's musical, "The King and I." Tennessee Williams, a friend of Starcke's, wrote of him, "With simple and deeply personal eloquence, Walter Starcke explores for us a way out of and above the finally fatal world of materialism"

* * * * * * *

Lois, you are right. The battlefield is not in Afghanistan but in the mind of man. Until we stop being terrorists ourselves, terrorism will not end. As long as our government keeps terrorizing us with threats of terrorism, and as long as our media fans the fire, we project that into the collective consciousness and terrorism becomes a self-fulfilling prophecy.

As for saying what we who have not been through what you went through would do in a like situation – that is impossible. We might fantasize about what we would do, but I believe such would be more harmful than helpful. It isn't in our consciousness to encounter such an experience, and we can only answer in terms of our consciousness. On the other hand, as I said, each of us has made threatening statements; so we must become aware of doing this and begin to practice finding solutions that do not include "or else."

It just came to me that in this context most people turn the Ten Commandments into a terrorist document. They think, "Thou shall not or else." Ever since, people have perhaps been scared into practicing the laws of social conduct rather than becoming lovers who do not need to conform to man-made laws.

What I am really saying is that, without ignoring the need to end suffering, we must first and foremost turn within and come from a place of love rather than fear before taking whatever intuitive and objective action we come up with.

In my eighty-two years, I have at least touched upon all major religions and philosophies of the world. That has led me to realize that today we have to do something that has never been done before. We have to close the gap between the human and the divine, between what you call "the personal and the planetary." That will only be done when we go beyond either/or thinking and realize that cause and effect are one.

47. Mike Thaler

Mike Thaler is a children's book writer, illustrator of humor, and cartoonist. His first book, "The Magic Boy," was published in 1961. Since then, he has written over 210 published books. Recently he created the "Heaven and Mirth" series of humorous retellings of Bible stories, like "Moses Take Two Tablets and Call Me in the Morning," and "David and Bubblebath Sheba." He is best known as "America's Riddle King" and the "Court Jester of Children's Literature."

* * * * * * *

Forgiveness is not only important – it's essential to wholeness. We don't forgive to free those who hurt us; we forgive to free ourselves. Forgiveness is the heart of love, and love is the heart of happiness. It is the message of life. It is the message of Christ. We don't need to forgive ourselves – God has already forgiven us. We just need to accept His forgiveness to free our hearts and allow His love to come in.

48. Susan Thornton, Ph.D.

Dr. Susan Thornton (1949–present) is a writer, editor, and university professor. Her memoir, *On Broken Glass: Loving and Losing John Gardner* (2000) tells the story of her love affair with American author John Gardner, who died in a motorcycle accident on September 14, 1982, four days before she and he were to be married. In her book, Thornton tells the story of her own coming to terms with the disease of alcoholism and of her recovery. She also writes about her abusive relationship with Gardner: while telling her he loved her, Gardner denigrated her intelligence, pursued other women, and on one drunken evening, struck her with his fist. The *New York Times* wrote: "Thornton's book is a moving account of one woman's struggle to make sense of a relationship that at once felt intensely satisfying and full of pain, endowed with creative energy yet characterized by a terrible abuse of power… Toward the end of his life, Gardner had become for Thornton 'a moral monster, confused, compelling, and grandly manipulative.'"

* * * * * * *

I have known Lois Einhorn for more than twenty years. But how deeply have I known her? Twenty-two years ago, I was a Ph.D. candidate at the University where Lois teaches. I never took classes from her, because she did not teach in my area of specialization. We are about the same age, but were separated by status: she a professor, I a student. Yet we were drawn together by some bonds: we were both women, we were both academically inclined, she had reached a professional level I aspired to.

In addition to being a graduate student, I was involved in an amateur theatre group that put on original plays. I invited Lois to a summer time performance and to the cast party afterwards. She surprised me by attending both the play and the cast party, a noisy, happy affair held at a remote weekend cottage on the banks of the Susquehanna River. She wore a yellow blouse. She seemed pleased to be asked, but also shy.

I was pleased that she honored my invitation and came to the party.

We saw each other in the corridors of the university and smiled at each other.

I completed my graduate work, received the Ph.D., married, and began to teach at a local college. One summer day I ran into Lois at a local arts festival. She was selling beautiful earrings, necklaces and bracelets that she had created from brightly colored glass beads. I was surprised that she would make time in the middle of her academic career for such a pursuit, and even more surprised that she would participate in the community by selling these items at a local craft fair. Here was a new dimension of Lois.

We each continued the path of our lives.

My teaching job ended, my daughter was born, and I wrote and published a book. After my book was published, Lois approached me. She too was working on a book. Would I be kind enough to read her manuscript? I agreed.

To say I was horrified by her story would be to understate the case. I read and read and became physically ill. I stared at the photo of Lois as a child that accompanied the manuscript. How could this happen to Lois? Could I believe this narrative? Yet Lois was a person, a person I "knew." But how well did I know her? How well did I know anyone? I could not lightly dismiss this. Lois was passionate about her book. I was appalled and sickened by the material. Yet I wanted to honor Lois as a person. Once she telephoned me. "Susan, can I read you a new passage? I have been revising my book." Quickly I responded. "Please send me the typed manuscript." I asked this because I knew I could not listen to any part of her story over the telephone. The telephone is intimate. It is the voice of the person directly into the ear of the listener. I could not listen to the words she had to say. I could only consider her story if it was safely written on paper. In a few days her envelope came in the mail. I did not want to open it. Again I struggled with myself. I wanted to honor Lois. But here was this awful story.

In order to be helpful, I sent her manuscript to my literary agent. I warned my agent that the material was "difficult." My agent rejected the material and sent it directly back to Lois.

Lois thanked me for my help.

I should add here that I was raised in a loving home. My parents had problems to be sure: financial, emotional, medical. But they loved me, nurtured me, provided for me, and protected me. I was so naive that I thought the words "child abuse" meant a parent who spanked, or perhaps beat a child. I had no knowledge of experiences like Lois's. No knowledge at all. Gradually I became aware that all families were not like mine. I learned mostly by reading. I read *The Three Faces of Eve,* a nonfiction book about personality disorder brought about by childhood torture. I read parts of *A Boy Called It.* I spoke with friends in the social work field who had seen and heard terrible things. I read stories in the newspapers, stories that horrified and sickened me.

I also had one personal experience. A close friend was Jewish. In the early 1970s we were shopping together at a local market. She grasped my elbow and pointed to the wrist of the older man who waited on us. I saw the blue marks on his skin. Outside the store she said: "That's a tattoo. That's a number. He was in one of the Nazi camps in the war." She meant World War Two. She was so horrified she was almost physically ill.

Sometimes people confided in me. A friend was sexually abused by her uncle. She struggles with obesity in her body and despair in her soul. A widow in her sixties told me that her son had been molested by their Roman Catholic parish priest. He sought escape from his feelings in drug addiction. He has spent his entire adult life in prison on charges for drug-related crimes. A female friend was victimized in her teen years by her dentist: he abused her sexually at the same time that he over-tightened the braces on her teeth. I heard these stories. I realized evil and violence existed in the world.

But I had never met anyone like Lois. She was herself. She was about my age. She was professionally accomplished. She got up every day and dressed herself in lovely outfits and taught really well at a major university. I did notice her voice. It is hoarse, urgent, and whispery. She sounds like she is always recovering from laryngitis.

Why does her voice sound like someone tried to strangle her? Tried to silence her?

Lois has persisted. She has created this book. She has found a publisher. She has written her story and asked for my response. When I first heard this news, I readily agreed to write a response, and then I put it off, pretended to forget about it. I didn't want to have to think about Lois's past. I had read her story once. I didn't want to read it again. Yet I told myself I want to honor her and to support her in her efforts to write and share her story. I felt like a hypocrite. At the last possible moment before her publisher's deadline, I opened the computer file and reread her story. Now I see the parts I didn't read carefully the first time. I also see how I struggle to distance myself from her. Why is it so difficult for me to consider Lois's experience? Surely it is not that unlikely that I would one day meet some who had survived satanic, sadistic, continual abuse. Evil exists in the world. The sex industry in Melbourne, Australia is a one-million-dollar-a-day business. In certain communities in Southeast Asia, the family that does not sell its eight-year-old daughter to a brothel is considered unusual, perhaps slightly mad. Women and girls right here in the United States are caught in nets of international sex traffickers who openly defy the law. And certain parents torture their children. Because I do not want to reread Lois' story does not mean it didn't happen. If I do not look at evil does not mean that it goes away.

What would I have done as a child? I would have done as Lois did. I would have participated. I would have obeyed my parents. Perhaps this is what frightens me about Lois and her story.

What would I have done as an adult? Would I have been as strong as Lois? Knowing myself as I do, I wonder if I would have destroyed myself by alcoholism, drug addiction, or suicide. I might have become an abuser. I hope that I would not have. Is the human spirit strong or weak? Perhaps this is what frightens me about Lois.

Now she asks me, if I were her, would I forgive?

I was raised in a Christian home. I am a member of a Christian church. In scripture I find, "hate the sin, but love the sinner." Faced with Lois's story, I do not know what to say or do. I would like to say that I could come to a spiritual place in myself where I would be able to forgive, be able to hand this over to a Higher Being, but I do not know if I would be able to.

One day last year Lois telephoned me. In her voice was a new strength, a new joy, a new tone. She did not sound strangled. She sounded happy. She invited me to attend a solo dance performance she was giving. I was glad to attend. I went to the dance studio on the south side of town and saw many friends and colleagues. I was astonished at Lois' good humor and bravery. She announced that she had taken up dance about one year before, and she had worked with a teacher, had created all the choreography, and was offering this performance of her dances for us, for her friends. At the age of 51 she appeared before us in a leotard and tights, with a colorful, feminine skirt, and to music, shared with us wonderful and unique dances. All were graceful, some were funny, and some were more serious, more thoughtful, and spiritual. In one piece I saw a glancing reference to abuse she had suffered. On her face I saw that she had overcome this history, had learned to honor and to love herself, and had created from her pain an experience of beauty to share with her friends. Here was another dimension of Lois.

Lois is very brave to publish her story. She wishes to help others who have suffered; she offers her experience to us for us to think about and learn from. Is the human spirit strong or weak? Lois's spirit is strong. She is an extraordinary teacher. I feel privileged to be her friend.

49. Richard Vatz, Ph.D.

Dr. Richard E. Vatz is a Distinguished Professor of Rhetoric and Communication at Towson University where he has taught for over 30 years. In 2004, he won Towson University's "President's Award for Distinguished Service," the university's highest honor. In that same year he won the Maryland "Governor's Citation for Achievements in Higher Education and Service" and also the Teaching Fellow Award from the Eastern Communication Association, an award recognizing a lifetime of distinguished teaching.

Vatz was the 1994 winner of the Thomas Szasz Award, and he has written a book on Szasz. His countless articles and reviews have appeared *in The Wall Street Journal, The Washington Post, The Los Angeles Times, Philosophy and Rhetoric, Quarterly Journal of Speech, The New England Journal of Medicine, Psychotherapy*, and elsewhere. He has discussed issues on CNN (including "Crossfire"), "The Phil Donahue Show," and "Larry King Live." He had done extensive national and local media political commentary for over twenty years, and he speaks often to national groups.

* * * * * * *

Dr. Einhorn, I was stunned by your article, but it did not affect my reaction to your questions. You should be so proud of how you turned your life around. One of my stereotypes was that Jewish people were incapable of such torture.

I would like to respond to your questions: "You are a child in a family that sadistically abuses. You are forced to torture and destroy. Should you forgive your parents? HOW do you forgive yourself?"

My response would be that I would have no difficulty, intellectually at least, forgiving myself, but it would be impossible for me to forgive those who affected the sadistic abuse. Both responses owe to my concept of responsibility. The law does not apply criminal responsibility to minors and particularly to minors who are coerced into the behaviors in which they engage. Put simply, the sadistic sociology has been created, and children have no way of contextualizing it accurately, so they surely cannot be held responsible when their primary authority figures promote the dastardly perspective. Thus, I would have no trouble arguing for my own self-forgiveness.

With regard to your parents, the perpetrators, I would be merciless in my appraisal of their unforgivable actions, and I would not, I hope and believe, forgive them because there's been no contrition on their part. I can understand forgiving for the exclusive goal of what it may do for the victim – allowing the situation to be put behind him/her and move on. As a genuine act of "forgive and forget," however, in the absence of the abusers' articulating profound and sincere regret, I would not forgive. Finally, should the abusers manifest regret of the apparent profundity to which I allude, I would demand some sort of measurable actions, such as a public confession, that would make the abusers suffer and would demonstrate their sincerity. I would also demand some sort of recompense.

In sum, I believe that forgiveness can only come when it is asked for and when there is real or symbolic sincerity in the abusers' request, unless, again, there is overwhelming psychological benefit or necessity for the victim to grant it. The victim's needs are paramount in this situation.

50. Kurt Waldheim

Kurt Waldheim (1918–2007) has spent most of life as an Austrian diplomat. He served as President of Austria (1986 to1992) and Secretary-General of the United Nations (1972 to 1982). He helped peace negotiations in the Middle East and between India and Pakistan. He also traveled extensively in Africa and Latin America.

Waldheim wrote a book on Austria's foreign policy entitled *The Austrian Example*. The book has been published in German, English, and French.

* * * * * * *

Lois, I understand your concern about the problem of forgiveness and have read with compassion your personal story.

Child abuse is an abominable aberration of human behavior. The victims of such acts merit our sincere sympathy, and we should try to help them overcome their tragic experience.

As far as forgiveness is concerned, I can only tell you that that the question of whether or not to forgive is a deeply personal question. There can be no general rule. It is a problem that can only be solved by oneself on the basis of moral, philosophical, and religious reflections.

I sincerely hope and wish for you that you will be able to come to the right decision.

With warm regards.

51. Ken Wapnick

Kenneth Wapnick, Ph.D., (1942–2013) was involved with *A Course in Miracles* since 1973 and was considered by many to be its preeminent teacher and writer. He integrated the principles of the Course with a practice in psychotherapy. With his wife, Gloria, he established the Foundation for *A Course in Miracles* and the Institute for Teaching Inner Peace through *A Course in Miracles*.

Wapnick authored over thirty books, including: *The Message of A Course in Miracles, The Most Commonly Asked Questions about A Course in Miracles* (co-authored with Gloria), and *The Fifty Miracle Principles of A Course in Miracles*.

On a website about him, Joe Jesseph, a colleague, writes, Kenneth Wapnick "is now clearly the world's leading authority on *the Course,* the most widely published author of books about *ACIM,* and in my opinion at least, a wonderful teacher of God by example as well as by the agency of words."

* * * * * * *

Living in this world, it is difficult to ignore the brutal acts of what Robert Burns referred to as "man's inhumanity to man." The signs have always been with us, from the brutality of ancient Rome to the modern day holocausts of Nazi Germany, Southeast Asia, Rwanda and Bosnia; from the tortures committed in the name of political or religious ideals to the all-too-common tales of child abuse and torture, such as we have in Lois Einhorn's graphic portrayal of life in her psychological death camp. How to make sense of this is one of the greatest challenges to any observer of the human condition. And it does appear to be a particular *human* condition. Animals kill, but almost always out of physical need, not the psychological need of a cruel sadist, *intending* to bring harm, often brutally, to another. It is a *biological* fact that *all* living things must feed off external sources to meet their survival needs, including food, water, oxygen, carbon dioxide, light, etc. It is a *psychological* fact that human beings have a strong need to project the unconscious darkness of their self-hatred onto others. This crucial dynamic results in a condition where people believe and then experience that they are able magically to escape the pain of this guilt or hatred by attacking others – verbally, behaviorally, in their thoughts or a combination thereof.

These *dark forces* of hate, buried within all of us, can be reduced to our need to survive – physically *and* psychologically – a guilt-laden need which ultimately is the expression of the principle that "someone must lose if I am to gain." It is this all-too-human tendency to find pleasure, satisfaction, and personal gain at the expense of others that runs like a blood-drenched thread throughout our history, both as societies and as individuals. The clear fact that a vicious minority blatantly lives this out does not obviate the presence of those same tendencies in all of us. Freud's systematic study of the dynamic of projection – wherein we see outside what we find unacceptable inside – helps us to understand how this phenomenon of projected hate operates in everyone's unconscious. *A Course in Miracles*, a contemporary spiritual thought system that builds upon Freud's psychodynamic insights, offers us a spiritual perspective that does full justice to our physical/psychological experience in the world, at the same time affirming our Identity as spirit, the true Self, that transcends this material world entirely, as does, of course, our Creator, transcending the dualistic and illusory world of good and evil, victim and victimizer, life and death.

A Course in Miracles teaches that "projection makes perception," that the world is "the outside picture of an inward condition" (*A Course in Miracles,* Text, p. 445). Therefore, our *perceptions* of an external situation reveal the thoughts in our minds that we wish to deny. It goes without saying that, for example, accusing someone of being a sinner because of rape does not mean that I am accusing myself of the specific *form* of rape. However, the *meaning* of such an aggressive act is surely in me as well – the need at times to dominate another through sheer force of will or physical strength in order to have my desires fulfilled; not caring about the other person, but only about myself. Again, that tendency may not be nearly as extreme or violent in expression as sexual rape, but it exists in all of us. And it is our guilt over such a wish that finds its projected scapegoat in actual rapists. Their blatant "sin" nicely serves this need of finding a suitable object for projection, obscuring the fact of our common unity both as children of the flesh and of the spirit. In the words of Harry Stack Sullivan, the founder of the School of Interpersonal Psychiatry: "We are all much more simply human than otherwise..." Unfortunately, being "simply human" carries with it not only the capacity for fulfilling our highest aspirations of life and unity, but also our lowest. As Sullivan's statement continues: "...be we happy and successful...miserable and mentally disordered, or whatever." The challenge to us is that our common humanity – for good and evil – is not always so readily apparent.

While in her middle teens, Anna Freud took a walk with her famous father, and as they passed by some beautiful Viennese homes, Freud said to his daughter: "You see those lovely houses with their lovely facades? Things are not necessarily so lovely behind the facades. And so it is with human beings, too." One might well add "*all* human beings" to Freud's reference, an addition of which the father of psychoanalysis would almost certainly have approved, being so aware of the *dark forces* lurking within *all* members of our species.

If we are to fully realize our inherent wholeness as a spiritual creation of God, we must be willing to forgive, in the sense of looking first at the outer hatred – the projection of the hatred within ourselves – and then beyond it to the love that truly unites us all as one Self. Without this final step, we are condemned to what Freud calls the *repetition compulsion*; in this case, being compelled as a species to repeat endlessly the cycle of guilt and hate, self-loathing and abuse, fear and attack: the cruelty that has so characterized our history, both on the collective and personal levels. All clinicians are familiar with the cyclical pattern of many abused children growing up to be abusing adults. And the vicious victim-victimizer cycle that is lived out by individuals sadly recapitulates itself in the lives of groups, large and small.

As a psychologist, I am aware of the destructive consequences of denial, and I am certainly *not* advocating pushing down memories and thoughts, feelings of hurt, humiliation, and rage, or attempting to overlook them in the so-called spirit of forgiveness. Indeed, in so many instances some form of therapy is necessary as a means whereby people can first come to accept the pain of what has been denied for so long. This is an essential step in the process of forgiveness, if one is going to eventually move beyond the painful, scar-filled memories of the past to an integrated sense of self that alone can bring fulfillment and happiness. Once again, we must not deny what has been done to us, but we all have the capability to grow beyond a victimized self-concept to realize our true potential as whole human beings. Thus, we demonstrate to our abusers that regardless of their actions, they ultimately were not damaging to us, for we were able to use the experience as a means for personal growth. Importantly, this does not mean allowing others, unchecked, to abuse others or us, the point here being our *attitude* towards the attacker. One can certainly act in a firm, strong manner to prevent attack and abuse *without* concomitant feelings of hate or revenge.

A Course in Miracles empathizes that our perceptions are inherently interpretative. In other words, while our sensory organs report back to us scenes of hate, abuse, and suffering, these need not be instruments with the power to deprive us of our ability to grow, mature, and finally to attain inner peace, not only psychologically but spiritually as well. If these forms of darkness are accorded such power, then the responsibility lies *not* with the events themselves, but with our having made the event more powerful than the love of God, our Source and constant guide for growth and inspiration for change. This recognition becomes the basis of true forgiveness: Nothing in the world – however reprehensible, repulsive, and vicious – has the power to take from us inner peace and a sense of wholeness. Indeed, the only power that can accomplish this rests within our own minds, which alone can choose peace or war, forgiveness or attack, love or hate. Such a principle presents an overriding challenge to us all, but it is a challenge we know can be met, as in the inspiration of the Dutch Ten Boom sisters and the Viennese Victor Frankl during the Nazi Holocaust. Thus, we need not give the events of our individual lives the power to deprive us of attaining the highest spiritual goal to which we can aspire: knowing, *truly knowing,* our Identity as spirit, part of the living and loving oneness of God. Extreme examples of brutality can afford us the opportunity of overcoming the easy temptation to hate, calling instead on the Love within to teach us how to forgive – others and thus ourselves.

A medieval legend provides us with a beautiful example of this vision of true forgiveness, an ideal that we all should hope to achieve one day: Jesus and his disciples had gathered to re-enact the Last Supper. They waited around the table while one place remained vacant. Then Judas walked in. Jesus went over to him and greeted him warmly. "Welcome my brother. We have been waiting for you." In the same vein, the third-century Christian philosopher Origen taught in words that did not endear him to the Church authorities that even the devil would in the end be saved. In other words, every seemingly separated fragment of the spiritual creation of God would and will return Home, as God's love can only embrace totality. Thus our forgiveness here in the world reflects the totality and oneness we all share as spirit.

In summary, Lois Einhorn's disturbing example of an extreme form of brutal victimization affords us all still another opportunity to project our *interpretation* of events, giving them the power to destroy our vision

261

of a common humanity. However, another way of looking at the situation is that we all are calling out for help, especially the sadistic victimizers, which reflects our common Identity as spirit. If God is truly love, then the wholeness of that love can have no exceptions. Thus it is that even the most heinous act demonstrates, if looked at kindly, the desperate call for help and love that lies just beneath its vicious form. It is the same call that cries out in all of us. Learning to give that call a voice is alone what gives this world meaning. Leaving that call unheard carries the terrible risk of perpetuating a life of justified hate that continually seeks to punish others rather than mercifully acknowledge our own need for mercy and forgiveness. In these days of world crises, we are all witnessing the horrific implications of *not* heeding that call. Our only hope – personally and collectively – lies in looking *within* at the hatred that joins us all in madness, which is at the same time the defense against the love that joins us all in sanity. In such hope is found the true Kingdom of God: a God of all-inclusive love, a God of perfect oneness, a God whose wholeness embraces totality, *without exception.*

52. Gloria Wendroff

Gloria Wendroff is a receiver of messages from God, teacher, founder of *HeavenLetters™, Love Letters from God*, and the Godwriting™ International Society of Heaven Ministries, an international spiritual movement. Subscribers of HeavenLetters range from a hard-working father in Iran to a yogi in an ashram in Nepal; from a fourteen-year old school girl to Dr. Bernie Siegel, author and early pioneer in the field of mind, body, and spirit medicine; from clergy of all religions to atheists; from truck drivers to college professors.

Heavenletters™ are presently translated into Italian and Dutch. In whatever language, God's words stir what is already in your heart. She believes that there truly is no one out there in the world who, deep in their hearts, doesn't yearn to come closer to God.

There are currently over two thousand *Heavenletters™*. Wendroff has published ninety-one of them in *Heavenletters, Love Letters from God, Book One;* and she is the winner of the Chelson Inspiration award. At present, she is writing other books about death and dying, how to Godwrite, and God's words about Christ. She teaches workshops wherever she is asked, all in the Name of God with the one desire to bring Earth closer to Heaven.

* * * * * * *

Dear Lois, I am so sorry for the hurt and suffering you went through. I want to apologize to you for it. I want to pick your child self up and your stuffed toys and hug you and make you all better and keep you safe. I am humbled by the miracle of who you are now.

I wept for the crimes against you. Here I was, a mere reader of your story, and I found myself incapable of forgiving your parents. They were not my parents; they were yours. This inhumanity didn't happen to me. I was not there. I didn't have to live through it nor observe it, and still I could not forgive them. I cannot imagine anything harder to forgive.

Later I asked God to help me undo my hard feelings and God said:

This is where her parents were. This was their vision. For you, there is no excuse for it. For them, this was their right. Were they ill? Certainly. Did they perpetuate enormous cruelty? Yes.

We come back to forgiveness as realization that people act from their level of consciousness. Let Me ask you? Do you forgive what is deemed a retarded child – do you forgive the child for having one IQ score and not another? Do you forgive an autistic child for being autistic?

Now you will say that these children had no choice, and your friend's parents did.

Then do you forgive someone because he is near-sighted or far-sighted or astigmatic? Perhaps he can change his vision, but right now that is his vision.

In every case, beloved, it is not for you to condemn, and therefore, not for you to forgive.

You can have compassion for the child and not feel vindictive toward the parents. Forget forgiveness for a moment. Just look at not being vindictive toward the father and mother. Just look at not being self-righteous. Distance yourself from them. They are not before you. They are not on Earth. You cannot report them to the police now. You can't go in with a gun and shoot them. You cannot go in and take the child away from them. There is nothing to fight, beloved. The action is over.

See her parents walking into the distance where your eyes cannot follow and your heart can return to its Source.

Can you bless her parents? You do not feel like giving them a blessing. Can you give them over to Me? Can you say: "God, I relinquish them to You." Can you forego judgment for a little while? Because you love this child, does that mean you must hate the parents?

In your heart, rescue the child. Run away with her, and leave the parents. Would you give up accusing the parents in order to save the child? You would, I know you would, and so do it now. Give up the parents. Let them escape your wrath. That is forgiveness.

Think about the courage and beauty of this child. Think about the good she does. Think about the miracle of a rose growing from a dung heap, for she is a rose. Look at the beautiful rose. Never mind from where she came. She is a beautiful rose now.

Saying you forgive someone is presumptuous. Who are you to forgive? What made you so almighty that you can forgive another? Do you really stand on such a high throne?

There is a reason to let go of all your anger and protests. The reason is that you must. Anything else is a poor choice. In the cool light of day, you have no choice but to let go. The world calls this forgiveness. So you forgive for no other reason but that you have to.

You cannot drop the parents on their head, but you can drop the subject. You can drop the subject from your mind and heart. You can let go of the child's anguish. You can let go of it for her. It is not hers to keep. It is no one's to keep. Anguish is not to be kept.

In your mind now, take those two parents. Walk with them up to the gates of Heaven. Leave them there. That is all there is for you to do, for, in truth, this is none of your business. All is between them and Me. Leave them with Me. I will not be affected. With Me, perhaps they will leave their cruelty behind.

Do you think I am saying they are not responsible? They are responsible. They are responsible for their level of consciousness. I am talking to you now, beloved. As you condemn them, you reduce yourself to their consciousness. You know it is for you to rise above. And that is what you always must do. Ring a higher bell. Make the kind of music of which you are capable. Play My song and no one else's. Am I asking too much of you?

53. Everett L. Worthington, Jr., Ph.D.

Dr. Everett L. Worthington is one of the leading scholars of forgiveness research. Professor of Psychology at Virginia Commonwealth University and a licensed Clinical Psychologist, he has published twenty books and over 200 articles on forgiveness, marriage, and family topics. He also directs "A Campaign for Forgiveness Research," a non-profit organization that supports research into forgiving and works to build a field of studying forgiveness scientifically. He considers it his mission "to bring forgiveness into every willing heart, home, and homeland."

* * * * * * *

As I read Lois Einhorn's tragic story, I couldn't stop a sense of sadness and horror – horror because humans are indeed desperately evil at times, and we all seem to have that capacity for evil. And I felt sadness—and with it, empathy, sympathy, and compassion—for her suffering.

When my mother was murdered, I found myself at one point so enraged that I probably would have bashed the murderer's head with a baseball bat had I been offered the opportunity. So Einhorn's question, "What would YOU do?" cuts me to the quick. As a child in her place, I would almost certainly have done what she did – survive. Survival involved doing despicable acts to avoid pain, further humiliation, and death. But it also likely involved mental disengagement from her acts and part of herself. It involved not thinking about what she was doing, disengaging from herself so she would not hate herself so much that suicide was her main option, perhaps thinking about getting even at some time in the future, exposing the criminal and evil acts of her parents. It is possible for me to imagine people being as evil as her parents were. It is difficult to imagine her emerging as psychologically intact as she is.

Obviously, none of the people she has invited to respond has gone through the same horrific degradation that Lois Einhorn has, so we can't really know how we would have behaved had we been coerced to commit such acts. We would have been different than we are at present. We don't know how that would affect us.

Yet, we all have our experiences of being victims (as when my mother was murdered) or feeling guilty and experiencing self-condemnation (as when my brother committed suicide). Perhaps, some of those experiences might give just a small a bit of empathy for her experiences, and inform our response with empathic tears. In the end, though, we each will respond out of who we are.

I am a fifty-eight year old man raised in a family with an alcoholic father, who humiliated his wife and children, and a unipolar depressed mother, who had to hospitalized twice and receive electro-convulsive therapy to snap her from her self-condemnation. Professionally, I am a Clinical Psychologist and a researcher who has studied forgiveness. Personally, I am a committed Christian.

The fundamental questions that must be addressed are fourfold:

(1) Can one forgive such horrendous evil in perpetrators?

 (2) If so, how?

(3) *Should* one forgive such evil?

(4) Can one forgive oneself not resisting to the point of provoking murder or committing suicide, and for thus inflicting pain and evil even under coercion.

Can One Forgive?

Jesus, of course, was persecuted, tortured, humiliated, and killed. But Jesus, Christians believe, was simultaneously fully human and fully God, so his case was special. He had a special capacity to forgive, yet part of that special case required him to carry the weight of the sins of the whole world to the cross. So his suffering was greater as well as his capacity to forgive.

I have wondered what Jesus might say to Hitler or to the other evil sinners. As outrageous and provocative as it sounds, I think it would be this: "I died for your sins." And if they repented, "I say to you today, you will be with me in Paradise." It is the same thing he says to me and to all.

But others have been tortured throughout the ages and have forgiven, and they were not Divine. Today, we call them saints, or hold them up—as Einhorn did Mandela and Gandhi—as paragons of forgiveness and other virtues. "But I am not Jesus, Gandhi, or Mandela," said Einhorn. She implies that they somehow were all possessed with a special capacity to forgive. That is more reasonable looking back. Gandhi, at the time of his forgiveness of his assassin, did not know he would be considered a paragon of forgiveness. He did not realize he would be able to forgive. He just did the hard work. Mandela, when he walked out of captivity, did not know he would be later praised as a forgiver. For all he knew, the response of South Africans could easily have been the same as Einhorn's—"And although I greatly admire all three men, I do not admire their acts of forgiveness. I think our society's encouragement of forgiveness relates to people's need to avoid dealing with pain, to deny the extent of human cruelty, and to distance themselves from collective guilt." Had South Africa responded in this way, Mandela would have been a short-term President, certainly not a hero.

I can name many ordinary people who have forgiven evil crimes against them. Chris Carrier was abducted as a 10-year old boy, stabbed repeatedly, finally shot in the head. He lived, though the bullet took his eye. As an adult, he forgave his attacker and cared for him as his attacker was on his deathbed. Chris was just an ordinary person. But he could and did forgive. So could Lois Einhorn, if she wanted to.

If So, How Could Forgiveness Occur?

I believe that any act is forgivable. That does not mean forgiveness is easy. I said Einhorn could forgive if she wanted to, but it isn't as simple as merely wanting to. There is a certain amount of transcendent mercy required to supplement our greatest straining to forgive. Where does this mercy come from? I'd say from God. Others might say from the human spirit, from nature, or from other sources.

Forgiving an act also does not mean that forgiveness thwarts justice—as Einhorn suggested (in the above quote). In fact, personal forgiveness has little to do with societal justice. I was able to forgive my mother's murderer, but I also did not want to see him released to kill again. Societal justice is an interpersonal act. Forgiveness is in intrapersonal act. They should not be confused.

Forgiveness does not act in opposition to justice. In fact, when justice is most thoroughly achieved, forgiveness becomes least difficult. Victims perceive an *injustice gap*, which I have defined as the gap between the way a victim would like a transgression resolved and the way it currently is perceived. Einhorn's injustice gap for the crimes done to her is huge. Justice can never be done to balance out those crimes. Certainly justice could not be done now that her parents are deceased. But even if they were still alive, I cannot see how justice could truly balance the scales. Even the justice she can bring about by exposing her parents' crimes in a widely distributed book will hardly scratch the surface at closing the injustice gap.

The smaller the injustice gap, the easier the transgression is to forgive. Everyone knows that it is much easier to forgive a minor insult than a major public humiliation. Justice—such as having a person apologize or make restitution or seeing a person encounter misfortune—fills the injustice gap.

But Einhorn is left with little recourse to justice. So, can she ever forgive the enormous accumulation of injustices? It boggles the mind to see how a person could do so without Divine intervention. Yet, God might have been at work already in Einhorn's case. She has emerged from these horrific events seemingly psychologically well integrated. I could not see how a person could do that on his or her own. Perhaps God has been at work in her life even when God seemed the furthest from her, and perhaps God will work in surprising ways again.

There are ways Einhorn could lessen her lack of forgiveness if she were interested in doing so (which she seems not interested in doing). She could choose a particular act and work through systematically forgiving that act. While she cannot forgive all the accumulation of years of abuse and humiliation in any one act of forgiveness, she could perhaps make some headway in the way one is said to eat an elephant: one bite at a time.

Should She Forgive?

This is an entirely different question. I believe that people should not be forced or pressured to forgive. Forgiveness is a choice. My mission in life is to promote forgiveness in every *willing* heart, home, and homeland. The key word in that mission statement is "willing."

I respect her right not to forgive. There are often many ways to regain a sense of peace that do not entail forgiving.

There are, of course, physical and mental health costs, relationship costs, and spiritual costs to holding onto bitterness. But she seems to have found peace in her adopted and loving surrogate family. Forgiveness is a way of dealing effectively with transgressions, not the only way, and not necessarily the best way for everyone.

How Does One Forgive the Self?

Apparently, though, she would like to forgive herself for her coerced complicity in evil. Yet, she cannot see how that could ever happen. She senses that she is unable to fill her injustice gap arising from her self-condemnation. She says, "I feel like I could be Mother Teresa for the rest of my life. It will not make up for all the horrible things I complied in doing." She can imagine no righteous acts—in quantity or quality—that she thinks would completely close the injustice gap. Nevertheless, in the case of her forgiveness of self, righteous acts could help.

Forgiveness of self is, I believe, often much more difficult than forgiving another person. This is true for several reasons. The person must act as forgiver and as transgressor, and it is hard to keep the two perspectives straight. In forgiving another person, one doesn't have to confront him or her all day, but self-condemnation is always in our head, always popping up unbidden as little reminders, always confronting us. In forgiveness of self, one isn't a pure victim (if we ever are). Instead, usually we are seeking self-forgiveness because we have done acts to harm others and to offend God. We need to seek to bring some balance of justice into that equation. In addition, and importantly, we have damaged our sense of self by our act of offence, and it takes time to accept our new self that meaningfully incorporates our evil acts.

Therefore, forgiving the self requires five steps. First, try to make it right with the person or person harmed (or surrogate) as much as it is up to oneself. The person one harmed might not want anything to do with one. In that case, making things right might entail doing good in general, or focusing socially beneficial actions toward virtuous ends. Einhorn is trying to confess her misdeeds to others through the writing of the book. She might contribute to animal protection causes to "make it up" to the animals she harmed. She must realize that one can never totally put the books even, but one is reducing the size of the injustice gap.

Second, one must make it right with God, or in the event of someone who does not embrace theism, one must make it right with the universe, nature, or the spiritual the way one understands that. If Einhorn were a Christian, making things right involves confession to God and receiving in faith the assurance that Jesus did die for people's sins. In Judaism, making things right involves *teshuva*—return to the path of God, which involves sincere repentance, restitution, and other steps to fully repent.

Third, having narrowed the injustice gap as much as possible, Einhorn could attempt to forgive herself. This might involve granting *decisional forgiveness*, which is an intention not to seek revenge or continue self-condemnation toward oneself. Having done innumerable acts of wrongdoing, Einhorn could never recall each one and seek to grant decisional forgiveness for every incident. Rather, she would have to take acts as proxies for the whole set of evil acts she did. She can grant decisional forgiveness for those.

Granting decisional forgiveness does not stop all emotional negative feelings, which culminate in self-condemnation. Rather, and finally, she would need to experience emotional forgiveness for the emotions of self-condemnation to lessen and perhaps eventually to subside. Emotional forgiveness occurs when one replaces unforgiving and resentful and hateful feelings toward the self by more positive emotions toward the self. Ordinarily, these positive replacement emotions could involve empathy for the self, sympathy, compassion, and love.

Reading the story Einhorn told, I certainly felt a huge amount of empathy for someone coerced to do such evil and tortured into submission. Sympathy competed with the empathy, as did compassion and an unselfish love. These positive emotions would seem particularly difficult for Einhorn to experience—especially at first when the levels of self-condemnation are particularly high, but as things are made right with those harmed, with God, and decisional forgiveness is granted, the injustice gap progressively shrinks, and it becomes easier to experience the positive emotions. The trajectory is an accelerating curve. At first, lots of effort yields almost an imperceptible amount of emotional replacement. As self-condemnation lessens, the same effort produces more results.

Difficult as it is, decision-wise and emotionally, forgiving the self is not the most difficult part of dealing with self-condemnation. The fifth step—accepting oneself as a person capable of doing evil—is the hardest part. When a person does great evil, the person might forgive, but has to face the knowledge that he or she is capable of so much evil. One realizes that having fallen once, twice, or a hundred times, it is possible to fall again.

Self-acceptance is not coming to believe that one has reformed the self—through forgiveness or otherwise—to such a degree that one is incapable of ever falling again. Instead, it is coming to see that—to use a metaphor that I hope doesn't sound trite—we are like Darth Vader. In the third of the first Star Wars trilogy, Darth Vader is unmasked. He is a simple human struggling to breathe. In fact, all evil is done by simple humans, who seem so invincible in their Darth Vader costumes, but underneath are frail, fallible humans. People are both good and evil. Aleksandr Solzhenitsyn once said,

> *"If only there were evil people somewhere insidiously committing evil deeds, and it were necessary only to separate them from the rest of us and destroy them. But the line dividing good and evil cuts through the heart of every human being. And who is willing to destroy a piece of his own heart?"*

That is a hard thing to accept and often proves to be the stumbling block to self-forgiveness.

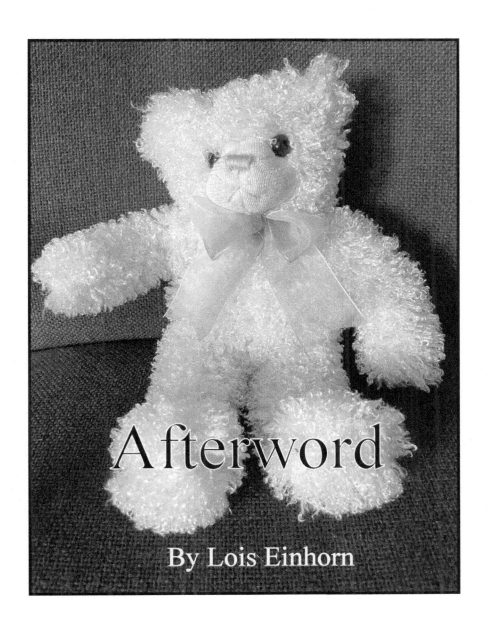

Afterword

By Lois Einhorn

AFTERWORD

In the *Sunflower*, I wish Wiesenthal had provided an Afterword, indicating how the process of writing the book affected him. Would he have given different answers after reading the thoughtful but varied responses?

My life has changed profoundly as a result of this book. In this section I share some of my thinking. And yes, I give new answers to the original questions I raised: "As an adult now, do I forgive my parents? HOW do I forgive myself?"

While writing the book, my everyday life continued with life's typical ups and downs. Of course, my heart will always feel a deep sense of grief for the lives I tortured and killed. But my life has changed in significant ways including making peace with my past. Healing is a journey that, as all journeys, will go on for as long as I live. I am still a work in progress. But significant events occurred on the journey.

About six weeks after September 11, 2001, I gave the following speech at my national professional association convention:

Responding to Tragedy with Firmness, Grace, and Compassion

Of the 6000 languages spoken in the world today, only a few are universal: the languages of tears, laughter, and love. And these are what we speak this morning.

How can we deal with the events of September 11 with all its agony and anguish? How can we feel safe in a world that allows such horrors to happen? What can we hold onto when so many of our touchstones have become tombstones?

Like everyone, I was and still am riveted to my TV, watching in disbelief the events of and since September 11. I teach at Binghamton University, four hours from New York City, but where two-thirds of the students come from there. I've mourned with my students who've lost family and friends.

This morning I want to speak first about my beliefs, then discuss what I've learned since September 11, and finally outline my personal commitments to change.

As the smoke clears, I'm more convinced than ever that we're not going to end terrorism until we end all violence. The events of September 11 have made me even more aware of the amount of hidden violence in this country. There's a relationship between the personal and the planetary: personal suffering and healing touch the collective wound and heart of humanity.

On October 18, in her syndicated newspaper column, Kathleen Parker demonstrates the arrogance that instigates much of the hate some people around the globe feel towards the US. She writes, "There is such a thing as moral and cultural superiority, and we are it."

Sure, there are many wonderful things about the US, but we are far from perfect. We began by stealing this land from Native People. We built much of the country with slave labor. And we have the largest gap between rich and poor of any industrialized nation.

In fact, the actions of our government are part of what cause terrorism. We've funded, armed, and trained terrorists. A half a million Iraqi children have died because of our government's economic sanctions. We seem to be against terrorism unless we're the ones doing the terrorizing. We should be working against terror in general and not just terror against America.

People are not born terrorists. People are not born to hate. All individuals are children of the universe, including terrorists. Everyone and everything are interrelated. We must recognize, as Native Americans teach us, that we are all relatives—whether they be two-legged, four-legged, or no legged creatures that walk, fly, swim, or crawl. The Earth itself is a visible, audible living presence. When one living being suffers, everyone suffers. When we poison the Earth, we poison ourselves.

I firmly believe that the only way to overcome evil is to step out of the ego and realize that evil is a human creation. The ego denies the sacredness of each moment. The ego says we're separate and in competition. The ego doesn't see that we all belong to one universal family.

This new war is called "Operation Enduring Freedom." Does enduring freedom for some have to mean enduring oppression for others? As Mahatma Gandhi eloquently said, "An eye for an eye makes the whole world blind."

We need also to separate individuals from governments. I lived in Israel during the Yom Kippur War. I literally got bombed for my 21st birthday! The morning after the war began, I saw families saying

276

goodbye to their sons, husbands, and fathers. The woman standing next to me said goodbye to her son, not knowing if she would see him again. Immediately after, she turned to me and said, "Egyptian soldiers have wives and mothers also." At a moment when I did not expect compassion, this woman understood the difference between a government and its people.

With the haunting images of September 11 forever burned into our minds, we don't have the ability to forget. But we do have the chance to change. We must take what has happened as an opportunity to set new priorities for our lives. I've asked myself: What have I learned from the events of September 11? And what am I going to do about it?

These Are Some of the Things I've Learned

* I've learned that I should always leave people with loving words because it may be the last time I see them.

* I've learned that I have the right to be angry, but that doesn't give me the right to be cruel.

* I've learned that it's okay to turn off the news and watch something fun; it doesn't mean I don't care about the world.

* I've learned that I am a part of the Earth, not apart from the Earth.

* I've learned to look for comfort in the whistling of wind, the swaying of sumac, the fluttering of fireflies, and the singing of stones.

* I've learned to smile and look people in the eye more often.

* I've learned that it's okay to hug my students and tell them I love them.

* I've learned to speak my truth as clearly and humbly as possible and to listen to others, for they too have a story to tell.

* I've learned that it's okay and necessary to feel passionately and to laugh and cry freely.

* I've learned that I want to go through life with a baseball mitt on my hands so I can give something back.

* Finally, no matter how uncertain I am about the path ahead, I've learned that love is the ultimate healer of all things.

277

Now, What Am I Going to Do?

* No matter whether we believe that people live 1 or 100 times, we need to make each life as joyful and meaningful as possible. I plan to squeeze the most bliss out of each day.

* A Congolese proverb asks, "The teeth are smiling but is the heart?" I choose to live more authentically so both my teeth and heart will smile.

* Beauty exists in everything, everywhere. I will absorb and savor the beauty that surrounds me.

* In the words of cartoonist Bill Keane, "Yesterday is history, tomorrow is mystery, and today is a gift; that's why they call it the present." I will strive to live life in the perpetual present.

* I dedicate myself to trying to understand the roots of hatred and to learning (and teaching) more about other cultures so I can celebrate and cherish people who differ from me.

* I will not shield myself from suffering or hide myself from homelessness. I will try never again to dismiss other people's pain as being too remote to warrant my compassion.

* I promise to do my part to help end "nursery crimes" and "scary tales" (my words for child abuse).

* I will fight for fair wages for all people to support the soles of their feet as well as the souls of their hearts.

* I will embrace the Earth, viewing it as my home, habitat, and heaven, and pledge to do my part to protect and preserve it.

* I pledge to take seriously the precept found in one form or another in every religion: to love our enemies. We must help fill all people's bellies with food and hearts with love. We need to invite all living beings to eat at the same table. I vow to do my part to help make these things happen.

In sum, the events of September 11 make me believe that we cannot truly live and know genuine freedom until we face our innermost demons. Only by seeing the Earth and all people as sacred can we shift from swords to speech, from conflict to compromise, from hostility to harmony, and from hatred to healing. Let each and every one of us in this room become a messenger of peace for All Our Relations now and for generations to come.

I firmly believe what I said that November morning, especially about how everyone and everything are interconnected at the deepest level. But I felt stuck: How could I reconcile these beliefs with embracing my birth parents? How could I embrace people who are capable of behaving in such sadistic ways?

I realized the answer came from my statement, "People are not born terrorists." My parents were not born abusers or sadists. As all people, they were born pure, innocent, and divine. It is here where my parents and I connect.

Fortunately, my parents never got my soul. No part of me ever identified with them. At age five, I looked into my father's eyes and saw Hitler. I have stopped trying to answer the question, "How did I prevent my parents from seizing my soul?" Instead, I feel blessed that they did not succeed in doing so.

I believe we all must work at understanding further the cycle of abuse. We seem to know more about why people continue the cycle (not only of abuse, but also of alcoholism and other types of addictive behavior) than we do about why some people break the cycle. If we understand further what makes pure beings become evil, we can help to prevent history from repeating itself. We need to provide more forums for victims to be heard and believed, AND we need to provide support for abusers. In the 1950s, little help existed for my parents.

As you, the reader, know, when I began this book, I had major problems with the word "forgiveness." To me it was an "F" word, in part because I believed the word implied condoning, and many people use the word without changing their actions. I had the same problem with the word "remorse." In *The Sunflower*, Karl expressed remorse but did not act remorsefully. If he really felt remorse, he would have told his Nazi superiors what he told Wiesenthal.

Few people would condone the behavior of hurting children purposefully and sadistically. I cannot condone the behavior, but I can and do forgive my parents. I realize that responding to violence with violence (and I consider lack of forgiveness to be a form of violence) only perpetuates the cycle. The only appropriate way to respond, in my opinion, is with love and compassion because as Elie Wiesel, another Holocaust survivor, said, "Hatred devours the hater as well as the hated. Hatred is a cancer; it grows from cell to cell, from limb to limb."

At my best, I forgive Hitler and today's terrorists. I know that no one is born holding a gun or figuring out ways to hurt others. Even when

I'm out of these states and do not forgive Hitler and others, I know this possibility exists in me.

I feel compassion towards my parents, praying that in the spirit world, they receive the love and nurturing they did not receive in this world. Because they lived tormented and torturous lives, people such as my parents who intentionally abuse others have hurt themselves more than we can ever hurt them. They also can never know true love, joy, and peace.

The ACT of forgiveness is a process, not a quick one-time event. For me part of the process involved releasing resentments and giving up hopes for a better or different past. Russell Friedman at the Grief Recovery Institute (see his response) sent me *The Grief Recovery Handbook*. I used it to write the following letter of completion to my birth father. The letter constituted a significant step in my process of forgiveness:

Dear Dad,

I write this letter as a way of completing my relationship with you. I have discovered some things that I want to share with you in order to free myself of the self-constructed prison I have made around memories of you.

* Dad, I apologize for not being thankful for your giving me life. I feel sad that you talked about yourself as "an accident." I am glad you lived because without your living, I would not be here today.

* Dad, I apologize for not telling you that I admired you when you went bankrupt when I was 8 years old. I did not see you as a "failure" (as you described yourself). Instead, I admired you for having the heart NOT to fire men who needed their jobs.

* Dad, I apologize for not telling you how much I appreciated your taking me to Washington D.C. when I was five. I especially remember talking to the parrots in the lobby. I want you to know that today I connect my interest in speech communication to that incident.

* Dad, I apologize for not telling you how much I appreciated your getting me swimming lessons when we moved to Virginia when I was eight (and all the kids knew how to swim except me).

* Dad, I apologize for not telling you how much I appreciated your asking my cousin to tutor me over the summer in multiplication and division tables and cursive writing so I would not be held back in third grade.

* Dad, I apologize for not telling you how much I enjoyed the two weeks you (and Mom) spent in Israel with me (and my then husband). Going to the Wailing Wall was a beautiful and humbling spiritual experience.

* Dad, I apologize for (especially in your last years) not appreciating all the positive and caring things you did for me as a child and an adult. You taught me to appreciate reading, language, and laughter. Dr. Seuss is still my favorite author. Dad, thank you for the pin, "It all starts with Dr. Seuss." I have built a pin collection around it.

* Dad, I apologize for not telling you how much I admired and appreciated your sense of humor. I apologize for not telling you that I thought it was normal and nice when you made jokes at Grandpa's funeral. I attribute my sense of humor today to you.

* Dad, I apologize for not telling you how much I appreciated humorous events such as helping you to plan a birthday party for Mom when she was planning one at the same time for you.

* Dad, I apologize for not telling you how proud I was of your intellect. I know you considered yourself "stupid" because you did not have a college education. But to this day I consider you among the most intelligent people I've ever met. I always admired your ability to have a conversation or tell a joke about any subject. I always admired (and was astounded) at how fast you read. I proudly remember wanting to put you on the game show "Jeopardy." I still think you would have made a great contestant.

* Dad, I apologize for not appreciating that you gave me the tools and skills to help heal from a tortured past—valuing a good education; a sense of humor; the ability to appreciate beauty; and especially the ability to be loving, compassionate, and demonstrative.

* Dad, I want you to know that I consider myself responsible for what I do as an adult and don't blame my childhood for current problems. I've given up all hopes for a better or different yesterday.

* Dad, I want you to know that I consider you responsible for what you did to me. But I am not going to let these memories continue to haunt me.

* Dad, I want you to know that I take responsibility only for things that I can control. For example, I had no control over the weather, food becoming moldy, traffic jams, and so forth. I refuse to accept blame for things I did not do.

* Dad, I also consider you responsible for the actions you did and did not do. I know now that I could not have caused you to have a stroke or heart attack or Mom to commit suicide (as she threatened), and I will not accept blame for what I did not do.

* Dad, I can never condone all the horrible things you did to me and forced me to do to my sister and live and stuffed animals. I truly do not understand how you could have been capable of such brutality. I do not need to understand. I am not going to let my memories of these things continue to hurt me or control my life.

* Dad, I acknowledge that you did not take me to the doctor when I complained of pain when having bowel movements, and I probably would not have needed seven abdominal surgeries had you done so. But I am not going to let my memories of this hurt me any longer.

* Dad, I acknowledge that you made me "choose" which live or stuffed animal to hurt and destroy or made me "choose" between beating my sister and having her beat me. I say goodbye to the guilt and shame I've carried. I will not let these memories hurt me any longer.

* Dad, I acknowledge that you were upset and abusive when I gave my Patty Play Pal doll to local children who were poor. I am proud of having done this and will not let my memories of this hurt me any longer.

* Dad, I acknowledge that you frequently told me I was "a little piece of shit" ("not good enough to be a big piece"), "the world would be better off without your existence," "your best isn't good enough," and similar things. I say goodbye to the shame and will not let these memories hurt me any longer.

* Dad, I acknowledge the hundreds of memories I have of things you did to hurt me, and I'm not going to let my memories of these things hurt me anymore. In addition to the above, these memories include scores of sadistic and ritualistic ways you made me torture my sister (and her me) and torture and kill live and stuffed animals.

* Dad, I want you to know that I say goodbye to the guilt, shame, anger, and hate, and I will not let these memories hurt me anymore.

* Dad, I acknowledge the many wrong/harmful messages you gave me. These include: "Don't make a peep or we'll kill you." "My problems are worse than yours." "You're ruining my day, week, life, etc." "Other people have it worse." "You must have done something horrible or you wouldn't have this pain." I am not going to let these (and other similar) messages hurt me any longer.

Dad, I want you to know that when I have flashbacks, triggers, and/or nightmares, I will remind myself that these things really did happen, but they happened in the past. Now I am safe and surrounded by loving people. I will not let my memories of the things you said and did (or did not say and do) hurt me any longer.

Dad, I want you to know that I'm going to expose your abuse not to hurt you but to try to help others. I want to help people realize the prevalence of child abuse. I want tortured souls like you (and Mom) to be able to get help and comfort so more people can break the cycle of abuse. And I want people to understand that a relationship exists among ALL pain and suffering.

Dad, I want you to know that I am thankful for the strengths I've gained the hard way, but gained nonetheless—courage, endurance, and especially the ability to love, laugh, and really live (not just exist).

Dad, I want you to know that I have made a good life for myself, both personally and professionally. I think you would be proud of how I turned out. I want you to know that I am proud.

Dad, I want you to know that I have experienced unconditional love (both giving and receiving it), intense joy, and profound oneness with everyone and everything (including you at the time of your birth).

Dad, I have dealt with the pain you caused me—this time experiencing the intense feelings I suppressed as a child—and I have healed and moved on with my life.

Dad, I want you to know that I value myself today just for being and am proud of the person I am.

I am writing this letter, Dad, to say goodbye to the pain I associate with you in all its manifestations. Dad, I say goodbye to the pain and anger that I associate with you. I release myself of guilt and shame, and I return to you WITH BLESSINGS that which is rightfully yours.

Goodbye, Dad.

Most people who advocated forgiveness in their responses for this book told me in private communications that they think this letter constitutes forgiveness. I acknowledge positive memories of my father, discuss how we are connected, do not mince words about my father's actions, and release myself of guilt and shame with blessings rather than with vengeful feelings. To me this letter constituted important steps in the process of forgiveness, but it did not complete the process.

Strangely, I did not complete the process until I accepted that I have a place in the world. Up until this point, I had given up blame and shame and felt compassion towards my parents. Yet, I still needed to reclaim my soul and reconnect to the universe.

Answering my second question, "HOW do I forgive myself?" was more complicated than forgiving my birth parents. Everyone (including me) agreed that I needed to forgive myself. The issue here was HOW. April Flores, a former student, said, "You never blamed your sister. You and she were mirror images of the other." Yes, she was right. My sister and I were not allowed to be close as children; thus, sad as it is, it's not surprising that we've never been close as adults. In fact, I've lost complete touch with her, not seeing or speaking with her in over thirteen years. Yet, I have never blamed my sister nor even considered it possible for her to be at fault. How then could I stop blaming myself? Several factors have helped me including family, love, nature, beauty, spirituality, and teaching.

I am honored and blessed that my daughters Vaneza and Ana were a part of my life. I still consider them my daughters, the angels of my soul. They have left footprints on my heart that no one can erase or replace. I truly believe that our souls were meant to be together forever. Just thinking about them enlivens my ecstasy, lights my life, softens my spirit, and hallows my heart. Our love is divine and sublime, magical and mystical.

I also have indivisible bonds of love with Eric whom I have considered my adoptive Daddy for years, and who several years ago officially adopted me in a Native American ceremony. In addition, Debby and Jean, two incredibly special friends, and I consider each other as sisters.

My new family has helped me to heal, grow, flourish, and live. They believe me even when I don't believe myself. They believe in me, even when I don't believe in myself. They treat me with respect and dignity. I keep thinking I love my daughters, Dad, and sister more than one human being can possibly love another, and yet my love for them continually grows, seemingly with no end. They have opened their hearts as well as their heads to me. With them I am free to feel, free to cry, free to be angry, free to grow, free to be myself.

Ironically, my birth parents often commented about how many people truly loved me. I have always had and continue to have close friends in my life who I love just the way they are and who love me for me – with no strings attached. Carroll C. Arnold, a mentor and friend, used to call me his "granddaughter." His death felt so different than the death of my birth parents. I miss him more than words can express.

Although I teach and write about words, no words exist to express how each member of my new family makes me feel or how much I love them. Just thinking about them makes me smile and feel warm and fuzzy inside. They speak to me of rainbows and beauty, and bring me love, peace, and joy. Like Helen Keller and Annie Sullivan, they "and I are comrades journeying hand in hand to the end. When the way is dark, and the shadows fall, we draw closer."

In addition to my human family, I have a large family of animals – both live and stuffed. My pets include eight cats, all with their own PURRsonality and one dog. Most were strays, abused and picked up by the police. I suspect we identify with each other in ways that even we do not fully understand. Each of my animals has been a gift – not a gift to open, but a gift that has helped to open me.

My nature friends also make up part of my new family and have helped me enormously. I have always received enormous comfort from nature, especially trees and water. I marvel at the vibrant palette of colors in the Creator's handiwork. I feel embraced by the Earth, cradled in her strong arms. I often feel hugged by trees—enveloped snugly and securely in their branches. I'm a proud tree hugger!

I connected to earth-based spiritual traditions. I read widely, trying to find meaning and comfort wherever I could find them. At the time, as I was writing a scholarly book on the Native American oral tradition, I found myself moving towards Native American spirituality. For me, these new ideas naturally flowed from the spiritual ideas of Judaism. All of nature and life are sacred because God is the Creator: "The earth is the Lord's and all that it holds" (Psalms 24:1). Praying on the Earth (in sweat-lodge ceremonies) is incredibly moving. Accepting the Earth as sacred was necessary before I could accept myself as sacred.

I have meditated for over twenty years, first as a way to deal with living in constant physical pain. Now I meditate almost daily. As with most skills, the ability to experience deep meditations increases with practice. I have the good fortune of having several animal totems that visit me during meditation. When my Monkey leaps onto me and together we jump from tree to tree, his playfulness fills me with joy. When I swoop and soar with my Eagle friend, I look at situations from a broad perspective, surveying the world below me, seeing the essences and shadows and awakening my inner and outer visions. My Peacock has taught me how he loses his feathers without losing his core self, suggesting that I too can give to others without losing myself in the process. My Dove teaches me how I can be an important *piece* in helping to create *peace* in the world.

Out of the depths of my pain, I have emerged to experience true joy. I have always believed that joy and sorrow go together: People cannot experience ecstasy, love, wonder, and joy unless they also have experienced pain, suffering, anguish, and sorrow. One cannot exist without the other, and the deeper the one, the deeper the potential for the other. Evil spelled backwards is not good but live. Truly living is not just existing. It is living vibrantly and vivaciously, joyously and palpably; it is being alert, alive, fearless, and unfettered by society's norms.

For me, getting to this point required a psychic purging, going through the pain – not above it, not below it, not around it. Rather than moving away from the pain, I needed to move towards it, confronting my shadows and fears. I allowed myself to feel the intense suffering I had squashed. I now view pain as a prerequisite to feeling truly alive and to knowing genuine freedom, joy, and love. I see a relationship between the senseless suffering of the Earth and all her blissful beauty. Only by facing my strongest demons, deepest darkness, and innermost terrors have my pangs of conscience and crushing shame ended. Risk always precedes relief. Like James Joyce's *Ulysses*, I have said, "And yes. I said yes. I will. Yes." I endure and maintain hope. I stop asking why the past happened, trying to find meaning in senseless acts. I accept that I can grow from the experience without understanding its purpose. I cross an invisible barrier and have said, "I want to heal. I want to live."

I surrender myself again and again, giving up attempts to control and trusting that divine love will surround me and sustain me. I try to submit completely to the Great Mystery – majestic and miraculous. I work at making my defenses such as denial and numbness ineffective. Surrendering involves letting go of the need to understand the Earth, instead accepting her and living by her, with her, on her, and in her.

I try to see the extraordinary in the ordinary. This has required letting my mind go blank at times, melting away all the multitudinous thoughts and tensions of my life, and maintaining a focused state of awareness. By attending to acute, astute, and antiphonal awareness, I have been able to get to the core of issues and the core of my being. Making peace with my past has softened my heart and freed me to relax into the bounties of the universe where peace, love, and beauty envelop me.

Meditation, visualization, and modern dance have taught me how to concentrate on my breathing, which has helped me to reconnect to my body, to feel comfortable within my own skin. I have reclaimed my body, scars and all. I have accepted and embraced my inner child. I now look in the mirror and see a sensitive woman with a loving heart. I'm beginning to like her!

A keen cultivation of the senses has been essential. I focus on being aware of what I see, hear, smell, taste, and touch and to use my eyes, ears, nostrils, tongue, and fingertips. I trust my sensory perceptions even when no verifiable facts exist to corroborate them. I allow the exquisite sounds of silence to cascade over me. I watch the sun peek out from behind the hills. Making more sense out of my senses has helped me to move beyond survival, beyond merely existing, to living, thriving, and rejoicing in life.

The rhythm of the heartbeat is a critical sound for me. In Native American sweat-lodge ceremonies, I feel and hear the heartbeat of the Earth. I feel as if a gravitational force runs vertically through my center, aligning me, balancing me. The heartbeat of people and the Earth are incredibly comforting rhythms that have a transcendent effect, inspiring and moving me in unexpected ways. I give thanks, pause, and reflect. I explore new worlds. Worlds within. Worlds without.

Perhaps more than anything else, feeling connected to all of life has helped me. I recognize the need for self-esteem, not other-esteem. I value truth more than approval. I want to be happy more than right. Obviously I need to think what I am doing is right, but I do not need others to agree with me. Being true to myself on a soul level gives meaning to my life.

I have learned to be spiritually open. I often feel a sense of spiritual ecstasy, an inner peace that feels so natural. This involves feeling blessed to be alive, blessed to be me, and blessed to be able to feel. At my best, I come away with a renewed sense of wonder, awe, marvel, humility, reverence, and respect for the Creator's handiwork.

My prayers today consist largely of expressions of gratitude. I feel enamored by creation and impassioned by life. Everything in life and in the cosmos is a contemplative jewel, a treasure. I continue to pray for strength and courage, but I focus more now also on love and peace. My process of praying differs from when I was a child. Instead of saying, "God, please help me and the world find peace," I now first pray *for* peace, then become *like* peace, and then *am* peace.

From the beginning of my healing, I was bothered by the metaphor in much of the literature. People who had been abused were characterized as fragmented with the goal of becoming whole. I believed then (and still believe) that people who have suffered go beyond wholeness, beyond ending up where all other people begin. As Ernest Hemingway wrote, "Life breaks us all sometimes, but some grow strong at the broken places." I think I have moved beyond wholeness. I would not wish my past on anyone, but through it, I think I have become a more compassionate, sensitive, and caring individual, more human and humane. I have become more patient, although this is still very much a work in progress! I empathize more easily with all people who have suffered. I realize that people can hurt our bodies and rob us of many things, but they cannot take our spark, our spirit, our soul. At times I feel an intoxicating joy of being alive, a spiritual ecstasy, feelings many people may never experience.

Leaving the safety and protection of the cocoon, I have found the courage to emerge from the chrysalis, stretching my wings, becoming my true self. I carve out my own unique path of beauty. I try to treat each day with reverence, appreciating each joyous moment as a gift to savor and cherish. As I become free, I share my joy and bliss with others.

My joy and beliefs about the universe have greatly affected what and how I teach. I now view teachers as lovers. Specifically, I seek to help students accept, value, appreciate, and celebrate ways in which they are different; to feel worthwhile as unique and special human beings; and to become more aware, accepting, and appreciative of differences in others.

I've developed the phrase, "Your presence is the greatest present," and I discuss how this phrase works for me. The processes of healing and forgiving, at least for me, will never be completely over. But during the worst of the pain and now when I experience flashbacks, I want someone just to be with me without thinking they need to fix things. I let others know how just how much their presence helps me.

I have created courses on "Compassionate, Nonviolent Communication" and "Communication, Ethics, and Social Action." I don't know if we can create a world using only compassionate, nonviolent communication, but I know we can create a better world if we become more compassionate and less violent in our communication with others and ourselves. This course helps us to speak and listen to others and ourselves with more respect, dignity, love, compassion, and forgiveness.

Loving others begins with loving ourselves. Thus, I want not just to touch the souls of my students, but also, to teach them how to touch their own souls. I ask students to practice the Golden Rule in reverse: treat yourself with the same compassion and kindness as you treat others. When we love ourselves, we inevitably love others. We spend significant time in my Compassionate Communication course on how to give ourselves empathy.

A bumper sticker on my office door summarizes what I now see as the purpose of my course on Communication, Ethics, and Social Action –"to comfort the disturbed and disturb the comfortable." We deal with several sensitive issues, such as racism, stereotyping, censorship, and free speech, and with sensitive questions such as: "Has political correctness gone too far?" We also discuss in detail HOW to turn anger and apathy into advocacy and action.

My teaching in ALL courses focuses on how ONE person CAN make a difference. I try to model what I share, creating a safe and supportive atmosphere, rife with trust and caring where students feel free to disagree with me and with each other, knowing they won't be judged. All my courses now deal with sensitive topics with students expressing their ideas and feelings openly, honestly, and authentically. In ALL courses, I teach students to deal with their hearts as well as their heads, and I try to connect with students at the heart level. Frequently I hug students and say, "I love you;" and in turn, they hug me and tell me how much I'm loved. Many students have described my classes as "like a family," even in classes of forty-five students.

In varying courses and in varying ways, I come back to the assumptions that we live in abundance (not scarcity) and are all inherently interconnected. John Dear, a Jesuit peace activist, says, "Violence occurs when we forget and deny our basic identity as God's children, when we treat one another as if we were worthless instead of precious." Mother Teresa makes a similar point, "If we have no peace, it is because we have forgotten that we belong to each other."

The only drawback to the Teacher as Lover view is that at the end of each spring semester I suffer from "empty nest syndrome" as I say "goodbye" to over one hundred of "my children" in one day, the last day of classes before summer break. This past spring, my students made this time even more difficult as they gifted me with cards with detailed messages from each student, a t-shirt with a class photo on the front, an engraved plaque, a purple vase with a handmade white rose, a glass necklace, beautiful earrings, a book, Thing 1 and Thing 2 ornaments from The Cat and the Hat, and a $22 gift card for smoothies.

The intangible rewards have been incredible. I've seen students transform from shy or perfectionistic individuals to confident people whose love literally overflows. I've watched students stand up for themselves, often even against formidable odds; make constructive social changes; go outside their comfort zones; take risks; and practice "random acts of kindness." What more could I (or anyone) want from teaching (or life)?

I end this book with voice and vision, passion and power, wonder and wisdom, and life and love. I firmly believe the saying: "No one is free when others are oppressed." If all people do their small part in making a difference, major changes can and will occur. We can create a loving universe for our children and grandchildren. Let all of us approach life with a sense of wonder and awe, seeing the miracles and blessings that surround us.

This book serves as a tribute to the power of love, testimony that even severe pain can be transformed into a gift of love. I agree with the adage attributed to Hermes Trismyegistus: "As above, so below." What is true in the macrocosm (universe) is also true in the microcosm (human being). I also believe the opposite is true: "As below, so above." If I can conquer the monster of self-hatred that lived in my psyche for so many years, so too can society move out of bondage into freedom and peace. The suffering I experienced was not personal suffering but human suffering. The work that needs to be done in the world right now is not one person's work, but all of humanity's work. We need to pray not only for pain to end, but also for the strength and courage to act fearlessly in healing the pain of the Earth and all her inhabitants. I hope my words and the words of the respondents have found their way into your head and heart and that they will inspire you to discuss the issues raised in this book and act accordingly.

I want to close with two brief pieces I've written:

Religion as Poetry

What if religion consisted of poetry rather than theology?
What if metaphors and other images
replaced doctrines and dogmas?
Would we then realize that we are all
God and Goddess, Priest and Priestess,
and the Divine exists within us
and we exist in the Divine?

This last piece was inspired by John Lennon:

Imagine

Imagine a world
where all people treat everyone and everything
with love, compassion, and authenticity;
a world where each human being mourns
for past and present miseries;
cries for all casualties;
abhors anguish;
and renounces racism.

Imagine a world where everyone's feelings flow freely,
where all sentient beings are spontaneous and sacred,
and where everyone has
the liberty of living, loving, and laughing.

Just face the possibility that such a world can exist,
a world where everyone and everything are holy.

**Sand Art in Bandon, Oregon, collage by Cleone Lyvonne Reed
at Circles in the Sand [TM]**

Endorsements for © 2006

Forgiveness and Child Abuse: Would YOU Forgive?

This book is a unique treasure of inspiring experiences of forgiveness, the key to spiritual growth and happiness. You will reread this book often and be uplifted – and your heart will open to a world of miracles beyond imagining.

~ **Lynne D. Finney, J.D., M.S.W.**
Author of *Clear Your Past, Present, and Future; Reach for the Rainbow: Advanced Healing for Survivors of Sexual Abuse; Windows to the Light— Enriching your Spirit with Haiku Meditations*; *Connecting with the Universe* (CD)

I avoid pain at all costs, but this collection of soul-searing honest writing would not let me alone. I had to read it, and once I started, I couldn't put it down. This is an intimate brave book, unlike any other I have ever read. It took me on a journey from the depths of inhumanity to the heights of the human soul. I am left wanting a discussion group where I can share the responses that mean the most to me. I can only imagine that all readers will want to write to the author and give her their answer to the profound questions she poses.

~ **Gloria Wendroff**
Teacher, founder and author of *HeavenLetters, Love Letters from God*

FORGIVENESS and CHILD ABUSE performs a public service in reminding us that child abuse is more widespread than anyone wants to believe. The responses to the question of whether to forgive vary widely because there is no right answer. Each survivor must decide for him/herself. Society must give survivors protection, support and most importantly, we must believe them.

~ **Barry Goldstein, Esq.**
Attorney, Executive Committee Member of Family Court Reform Coalition
Author of *Scared to Leave, Afraid to Stay: Paths from Family Violence to Safety* and *The Quincy Solution: Stop Domestic Violence and Save $500 Billion*

Full of wisdom, insight and truth from a powerful assembly of scholars, writers and visionaries. Profound reading.

~ **Dr. Bernie Siegel, M.D.**
Surgeon, teacher, speaker, author of *Love, Medicine and Miracles*;
Peace, Love and Healing, 101 Exercises for the Soul, and many more

By posing common questions about forgiveness within the context of the uncommon abuse of her own childhood, Professor Einhorn challenges all of us to face the issues of child abuse in our culture, and to recognize that resolution is not beyond us.

~ **Judith Spencer**
Author of *Suffer the Child and Satan's High Priest*

Lois Einhorn seeks out and receives any trauma survivor's dream: commentary by the wise on the thorny issues of terror, guilt, forgiveness, and healing. In the process she offers us all a worthy exploration that is stunningly relevant to this sad, violent world we inhabit.

~ **Chellis Glendinning, Ph.D.**, Psychologist and Author of
My Name Is Chellis & I'm in Recovery from Western Civilization
CHIVA: A Village Takes on the Global Heroine Trade
Off the Map: An Expedition Deep into Empire and the Global Economy

Lois Einhorn has produced a fascinating book about forgiveness and child abuse, using the horrendous abuse she suffered as a child as a starting point, and garnering comments from over fifty people from disparate walks of life, many very prominent. She gets them to answer, and ultimately she answers such questions as: "At what age are children responsible for their actions? Aren't all abusers emotionally children?" In addition, her respondents raise further difficult questions for us all to wrestle with, such as: "How do you handle the acts of people with multiple personality disorder? Are the current problems in the Middle East due to the Jewish people's refusal to forgive Hitler?" This is a book that will tear your heartstrings as well as make you think long and hard about moral principles that may have seemed obvious in the past. Finally the book ends on a positive and optimistic note as Lois manages to forgive and find great meaning in her life.

~ **Eric Loeb, Ph.D.**
Psychologist

As is evident from Lois's story, forgiveness frees the giver without condoning that which it forgives. Lois makes it abundantly clear that her emerging freedom was the byproduct of forgiving those who hurt her. Let's hope that her story encourages others to reclaim their lost hearts and restart their lives.

~ **Russell Friedman**
Co-author of *The Grief Recovery Handbook*
And *When Children Grieve*

Forgiveness and Child Abuse: Would YOU Forgive? is a testament to the strength of the human spirit. In the ravages of child ritual abuse, Dr. Einhorn is able to cultivate love and kindness. How is it possible to move beyond the legacy of terror and hatred engendered by such brutality? Many of the fifty contributors share their own stories of injustice and anguish, and the compassion and wisdom that emerged from within. How does humanity at its best find its root in humanity at its worst? This mystery is revealed as Dr. Einhorn and her contributors share their journeys of healing, lighting a path for all survivors of human cruelty.

~ **Ellen P, Lacter, Ph.D.**
Expert in the treatment of ritual trauma

If your own parents systematically tortured you, and forced you to hurt others, what should you have done? A dazzling array of answers to this dire question, from half a hundred respondents, illuminates the pages of this engrossing book.

~ **Dale McCulley**
Expert in childhood trauma
Producer of more than a dozen films on child abuse
Author of *Multiple Exposure*

Lois Einhorn's work is ironically a work of optimism – it reinforces the view that by sheer will people can overcome adversity they did not bring on themselves. The author, schooled in communication, promotes the power of the individual to overcome a dastardly scenic reality visited on her in childhood.

~ **Richard Vatz, Ph.D.**
Distinguished Professor of Communication
Scholar and media analyst

"The Personal and the Planetary are one." I have heard these words but never understood them until now. Lois Einhorn tells her story and asks us difficult questions. The responses she elicits from individuals from around the world provide some answers, but not all. Lois Einhorn asks us about responsibility, about guilt, about power, about choices. How do we answer these questions in a nation where one out of every six children is sexually abused? How do we answer these questions in a nation in which murder rates are regarded as being at an "acceptable" level in any given city? How do we answer these questions in a nation whose leaders declare "A War on Terror" rather than explore concepts of international economic justice in a world where the five hundred richest individuals have the same collective income as the world's poorest 416 million? I encourage readers to approach this book with compassion and to seek for understanding in their own hearts. How best can we serve each other: personally, politically, nationally and internationally? Lois Einhorn's book raises questions that we should all consider.

~ **Susan Thornton, Ph.D**., Professor and Editor
Author of *On Broken Glass: Loving and Losing John Gardner*

Lois Einhorn's remarkable life journey is illuminated by her wit and insight as she fights to not only survive but to live life to the fullest under the most abusive of circumstances. Her book is a valuable exercise in healing, both for Lois and the reader; because despite all of her misery, Lois's incredible capacity for empathy and forgiveness emerges to literally save her life. Her struggles to find forgiveness and thus life itself are inspirationally heroic. Their telling reveals the incredible empathy, joy, and love that Lois really is.

~ **Robert W. Plath**
Founder and Director of *World Forgiveness Alliance*

Forgiveness and Child Abuse: Would YOU Forgive? is a powerful and moving tale of personal horror. Dr. Einhorn's writing is simultaneously direct and poetic; and because the many responses she elicits are varied and complex, most every reader, viewing his or her own life, will find a personal path to reconciliation and peace. We owe deep gratitude to Dr. Einhorn for her brave act of self-revelation. All healing begins with a story that is shared.

~ **Rabbi David A. Katz**
Co-editor of *Reading between the Lines: New Stories in the Bible*

AMAZON REVIEW: *5.0 out of 5 stars*
Forgiveness, Wholeness, and Beyond

This is a book about forgiveness and abuse. It is a story for and about the victims of child abuse. It is a story that asks the question: "You are a child in a family that sadistically abuses. You are forced to torture and destroy. What should you do now as an adult? Do you forgive your parents? HOW do you forgive yourself? This question calls for a thoughtful introspection by the reader to formulate an answer or response.

Fifty-three well-known personalities responded to this question. The group includes therapists, spiritual advisors, activists, children's advocates, song writers, and other leaders in the field of forgiveness and abuse. The responses of these experts make up the body of the book. Their responses provided healing for the victims of these unspeakable acts and horrendous atrocities: physical, sexual, and verbal. The answers are profound and reveal beautiful insights in personal forgiveness and the resulting freedom this can produce in the victim.

Many of the respondents share their own personal stories of abuse. Award winning writer, Derrick Jensen, observed "We become a family of amnesiacs. There's no place in the mind to sufficiently contain these experiences." These are stories of heroic battles, of overcoming; fear, anger, bitterness, and survival.

I found the book poignant, haunting, gripping and powerful, a book that calls for action. Dr. Einhorn wrote this book as a tribute to the power of love, and as a testimony that even severe pain can be transformed into a gift of love.

Dr. Einhorn was honored by the World Forgiveness Alliance as Heroine of Forgiveness, Reconciliation, and Peace. She is well qualified to author this work. This book is a must-read for child advocates, therapists, spiritual counselors, and for the victims of abuse. It is also a book for school administrators, teachers, preschool specialists, church and community leaders, and for policy formulators in government office.
~ Richard R. Blake, VINE VOICE

ABOUT THE AUTHOR

LOIS EINHORN, Ph.D.

Lois Einhorn, Ph.D. has been a Professor of Rhetoric at the State University of New York's University Center at Binghamton for over forty years. Highly accomplished, she has published nine books and many articles; and she has received many honors, awards and grants including five major teaching awards—often the youngest then and since to receive these honors.

Largely because of her new ideas and own personal forgiveness process resulting from writing *Forgiveness and Child Abuse*, Dr. Einhorn was honored as a 2004 *Heroine of Forgiveness, Reconciliation, and Peace* by *The World Forgiveness Alliance*, an award previously given to Mahatma Gandhi, Martin Luther King, Jr., Nelson Mandela, and Desmond Tutu.

Lois was also recognized by *Marquis Who's Who* for Lifetime Achievement Award in 2017, as a Distinguished Humanitarian in 2018, and as a Distinguished Professional Woman in 2021.

A prolific author and dynamic speaker, she is widely recognized as an expert on the topic of forgiveness and is involved in national discussions.

Dr. Einhorn published the following books: *Effective Employment Interviewing: Unlocking Human Potential; Abraham Lincoln the Orator: Penetrating the Lincoln Legend; Helen Keller, Public Speaker: Sightless But Seen, Deaf But Heard;* and *The Native American Oral Tradition: Voices of the Spirit and Soul.*

Robert D. Reed Publishers is the publisher of five books by Lois Einhorn: *Forgiveness and Child Abuse: Would You Forgive?* (2006), *Compassionate Fairy Tales: A Mother Einhorn Collection*, illustrated by Debby Gwaltney (2011), *Why Do We All Love Dr. Seuss? Discovering the Mystery and Magic of an Icon* (2012) and *PETE SEEGER'S PUBLIC COMMUNICATIONS: "Surrounding Hate and Forcing It to Surrender"* (2022), and this book, *Would You Forgive: From Child Abuse to Self-Love* (2022).

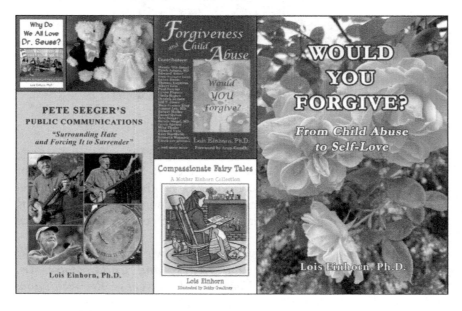

Dr. Einhorn said as we put the finishing touches on this book, "I consider my proudest accomplishment to be having a teddy bear named after me. It means much more to me than any awards!" (See the story about the Lois teddy bears in the Preface.)